Jo and

MW01566211

Relational Integrative
Psychotherapy

May 2021

Relational Integrative Psychotherapy

Engaging Process and Theory in Practice

Linda Finlay

WILEY Blackwell

This edition first published 2016
© 2016 John Wiley & Sons Ltd

Registered Office
John Wiley & Sons Ltd, The Atrium, Southern Gate, Chichester, West Sussex, PO19 8SQ, UK

Editorial Offices
350 Main Street, Malden, MA 02148-5020, USA
9600 Garsington Road, Oxford, OX4 2DQ, UK
The Atrium, Southern Gate, Chichester, West Sussex, PO19 8SQ, UK

For details of our global editorial offices, for customer services, and for information about how to apply for permission to reuse the copyright material in this book please see our website at www.wiley.com/wiley-blackwell.

The right of Linda Finlay to be identified as the author of this work has been asserted in accordance with the UK Copyright, Designs and Patents Act 1988.

All rights reserved. No part of this publication may be reproduced, stored in a retrieval system, or transmitted, in any form or by any means, electronic, mechanical, photocopying, recording or otherwise, except as permitted by the UK Copyright, Designs and Patents Act 1988, without the prior permission of the publisher.

Wiley also publishes its books in a variety of electronic formats. Some content that appears in print may not be available in electronic books.

Designations used by companies to distinguish their products are often claimed as trademarks. All brand names and product names used in this book are trade names, service marks, trademarks or registered trademarks of their respective owners. The publisher is not associated with any product or vendor mentioned in this book.

Limit of Liability/Disclaimer of Warranty: While the publisher and author have used their best efforts in preparing this book, they make no representations or warranties with respect to the accuracy or completeness of the contents of this book and specifically disclaim any implied warranties of merchantability or fitness for a particular purpose. It is sold on the understanding that the publisher is not engaged in rendering professional services and neither the publisher nor the author shall be liable for damages arising herefrom. If professional advice or other expert assistance is required, the services of a competent professional should be sought.

Library of Congress Cataloging-in-Publication Data

Finlay, Linda, 1957-
 Relational integrative psychotherapy : engaging process and theory in practice / by Linda Finlay.
     pages cm
 Includes bibliographical references and index.
  ISBN 978-1-119-08730-4 (cloth) — ISBN 978-1-119-08729-8 (pbk.)   1. Eclectic psychotherapy.   I. Title.
  RC489.E24F56 2015
  616.89′14—dc23

                                                                          2015017681

A catalogue record for this book is available from the British Library.

Cover image: © agsandrew/Shutterstock

Set in 10.5/13 ITC Galliard Std by Aptara Inc., New Delhi, India.

1   2016

To Ken Evans – he inspired a generation.

Contents

Foreword by Ken Evans	ix
Preface	xi
Acknowledgements	xiii
1 What is Relational Integrative Psychotherapy?	1
Part I Being and Doing Processes	**13**
2 Meeting and Contracting	15
3 Engaging the Therapeutic Process	30
4 Empathising and Attuning	46
5 Holding, Containing and Boundarying	59
6 Resourcing: Nurturing Skills and Mobilising Coping Strategies	76
7 Intuiting, Imagining and Interpreting	88
8 Challenging	104
9 Integrating	120
10 Ending	136
Part II Theory Applied to Practice	**149**
11 Cognitively Orientated Therapy	151
12 Existential Phenomenology: Theory and Therapy	167

13	Gestalt Theory and Therapy	183
14	Relational Psychoanalytic Theory in Practice	198
15	Systemic Theory and Therapy	212
16	Transactional Analysis	226

Postscript	241
References	243
Index	255

Foreword
Ken Evans

Relational Integrative Psychotherapy by Linda Finlay is a *tour de force*. Drawing on a wealth of knowledge from her experience of different therapies she interweaves them, engaging a coherent relational focus that is both impressive and elegant. Linda's mastery of the art of writing is evident throughout the book as she fearlessly unpacks highly complex theory with clarity and humility.

In part I Linda takes us on a journey through integrative psychotherapy from the initial engagement with the client through the highs and lows of the relational endeavour to its ending, and thus beginning.

The reader will encounter the conviction and passion Linda brings to her clinical practice as a relational integrative psychotherapist. Numerous evocative examples connect theoretical reflection with clinical vignettes. In reading the vignettes I trust you will feel, like me, openly invited into her clinical room, to think and feel alongside her about her clients, her own embodied response as the therapist and her critical reflection on the process 'between' herself and the client.

In part II Linda reaches into six modality approaches and artfully extracts those essences from them that bring fresh insight and a deeper knowledge of the relational: Gestalt Therapy, Transactional Analysis, Cognitive Behaviour Therapy, Relational Psychoanalysis, Family and Systemic psychotherapy and Existential Phenomenological psychotherapy.

Students will benefit enormously from this comprehensive survey of the key modalities impacting relational integrative psychotherapy and I confidently predict this book will be a key text for students of integrative psychotherapy for many years to come. Seasoned therapists will also appreciate this book as a truly helpful resource offering a point of access to and bridge across what other modalities offer to the continued evolution of our clinical practice.

x FOREWORD

The publication of this book coincides with the 'coming of age' of the European Association for Integrative Psychotherapy (EAIP), as it celebrates 21 years since its foundation in 1993–4. I intuit a certain synchronicity here because in several important respects Linda's book exemplifies a central tenet of the EAIP, which is that "no single form of therapy is best or even adequate in all situations" and in this regard "there is a particular ethical obligation on integrative psychotherapists to dialogue with colleagues of diverse orientations and to remain informed of developments in the field" (EAIP Statement of Philosophy, www.euroaip.eu). Linda admirably continues in the tradition established by Norcross and Goldfried and others as she invites the profession of psychotherapy to look beyond dogmatism: "I see our mission as blending competing voices that can at times express themselves stridently. We achieve our deepest theoretical integration when we are able to internalise competing voices into a transformed, coherent way of being."

I wholeheartedly commend this book as a significant step towards this mission.

Dr Ken Evans, Fellow RSA, Fellow EAIP, Hon Member EAGT
President, European Association for Integrative Psychotherapy (EAIP)
Vice President, (External Affairs) European Interdisciplinary Association for Therapy with Children & Young People
President, European Association for Psychotherapy (1994–1995)
Visiting Professor of Psychotherapy, USEE
Visiting Professor of Theoretical and Applied Psychology, Union University
Co-Director, European Centre for Psychotherapeutic Studies

Preface

Truth has no path, and that is the beauty of truth, it is living. (J. Krishnamurti, Freedom from the Known)

There are myriad ways to navigate the rich and varied terrain of *relational integrative psychotherapy*. Here, no single 'truth' prevails: many paths beckon, and models and practices evolve as we live them.

This book sets out to map the intricacies of this landscape, in order to help practitioners negotiate its many options and make their personal choices. My own favoured route involves a humanistically orientated blend of existential-phenomenological, gestalt, transactional analysis (TA) and relational psychoanalytic perspectives, but in this book I seek to present a spectrum of routes and show their interconnections. I aim to honour the richness of our field as a whole, rather than promote any particular relational integrative model. I also seek to explore key questions: how do we pull together potentially contradictory ideas and varied practices in a coherent way? How can we embody the relational qualities necessary for genuine existential healing (Hycner, 1991/1993)?

This book embodies, and is reflective of, my personal efforts to navigate this perplexing field. When I started as a person-centred occupational therapist in the 1970s, I made somewhat eclectic use of psychodynamic group work and cognitive-behavioural strategies. My interest in psychotherapy grew as I ventured into play therapy, art therapy and drama therapy, and my horizons were widened further when I became an academic and a phenomenologist. When eventually I began my integrative psychotherapy training, I had to learn how to integrate my understandings of divergent approaches, theories and techniques into a *relational way of being* that made sense to me.

xii PREFACE

Writing this book has, for me, proved an integrative healing journey. By stepping back to reflect on what it is to be a relational integrative therapist, and then setting this down in words, I have been helped to a better understanding of our field and the often argumentative voices which echo across it. My challenge has been to stay open to alternative approaches and value the contributions they offer. Perhaps this too will be your challenge as you read on.

In the pages that follow you will encounter familiar routes and be guided towards wider vistas that may inspire you to strike out in bold new directions. My hope is that this map will help you choose your own particular road ahead.

Organisation of the Book

Chapter 1 addresses the question: 'What is relational integrative psychotherapy?' I broadly define what is meant by 'relational' and 'integrative', acknowledging that these are contested terms used in varied ways.

The chapters in part I explore those 'being and doing' **processes** that apply across modalities. Regardless of theoretical orientation, we all aim to engage clients in therapy and empathically attune to their needs. We intuit, interpret, contain and hold clients' emotions; we offer challenge and enable them to resource themselves; and so forth. Eventually, when clients have internalised our nourishing relationship and are able to feel differently about themselves and more connected to others, we work towards ending therapy. Throughout the chapters of part I, I highlight the central part played by the therapeutic relationship. The aim is to provide an enriched perspective on our field rather than a 'how to' manual.

Part II introduces key ideas associated with the different **theoretical perspectives**. These chapters stand alone as resources to be dipped into rather than read in sequence. I've chosen to focus on the major fields: cognitive, existential-phenomenological, gestalt, psychoanalytic, systemic and transactional analysis. My emphasis throughout is on examining how theory might be applied in relational and integrative ways.

I rely heavily on illustrations of relational integrative work **in practice** and draw on a range of material in an effort to show its diversity and depth. Most examples have been taken from published sources. Some case studies are based loosely on my practice and experience but most are constructed fictionalised accounts. Where relevant I note those (anonymised) stories where individuals have generously given their specific consent to reproduce them. I invite you to dwell with the examples – both the ordinary ones and the extra-ordinary. Allow them to resonate; let yourself be awed by the profound, poignant and at times seemingly magical work in which we engage.

Together with **Case illustrations**, I've used **Research** and **Theory** boxes at regular intervals to highlight our evidence base and theory/techniques applied in practice. Numerous **endnotes** provide specific theoretical explanation and deeper analysis. Significantly, each chapter contains discussion of complementary and competing theoretical ideas towards the goal of integrating theory in relational ways. I selectively highlight particular perspectives in each chapter; reading across the chapters as a whole will hopefully enable a more holistic, integrated understanding.

Acknowledgements

Many people have helped with the evolution of this book. First I want to acknowledge Ken Evans, who has mentored and encouraged me over the years, and whose work continues to inspire me. I was extraordinarily touched when Ken offered to write the foreword to this book and I thank him for his generous words. Five other 'teachers' who continue to influence me through their seminal writings are Patricia DeYoung, Richard Erskine, Lynne Jacobs, Ernesto Spinelli and Irvin Yalom. I cite their work frequently in this book and I hope I have done respectful justice to their ideas. Thirdly, I would not have been able to write this book without the nourishing conversations with, and expert guidance of, many friends and colleagues, in particular George Bassett, Angela Carr, Margaret Chapman, Bob Cooke, Kate Evans, Vivian Finlay, Anne Gilbert, Jill Kay, Pete Lavender, Lydia Noor, Barbara Payman, Amanda Phillips-Wieloch and Vivien Sabel. Special thanks need to go to Mel Wilder and Sue Ram for their invaluable editing. The omissions and misunderstandings within the book are, of course, mine alone. Finally, my thanks need to be extended to Darren Reed (commissioning editor) for believing in the project, and Karen Shield (project editor), Hairiani Rashid (production editor) and the rest of the publishing team for seeing the manuscript through to publication.

Linda Finlay
December 2014

1

What is Relational Integrative Psychotherapy?

Learn your theories as well as you can, but put them aside when you touch the miracle of the living soul. Not theories but your creative individuality alone must decide. (Jung, 1953, p. 73)

There are currently many different ways of doing *relational integrative psychotherapy*, a plurality fostered by a *Zeitgeist* which celebrates both the 'relational' and the 'integrative' dimensions of psychotherapy. Rather than rely on a single-school approach, with its specific theory and methods, psychotherapists are increasingly looking beyond traditional boundaries towards more holistic practice.

The variety of practice now available to us is not surprising, given our ability to draw upon more than 400 theories and models of psychotherapy (Norcross, 2005). This array testifies to the richness and dynamism of our field. While competing and contested approaches challenge our identity and often appear idiosyncratic and unconvincing, they also signal creativity, openness and respect for divergence. No blanket view or single technique can hope to embrace the complexity of human behaviour. We need to trawl widely to find therapy approaches which encompass both the individual and their social world and that engage intrapsychic, embodied, interpersonal, cultural and transpersonal levels (Norcross & Goldfried, 2005).

It's probably true to say that much psychotherapy is relational and integrative at heart. If so, the convergence of these two movements may well rebalance an "over-fragmented field" (O'Brien & Houston, 2007, p. 4). In common with others, Markin (2014, p. 327) argues for a more "coherent and less polarizing professional identity", noting that defining ourselves as coming from a particular modality sets up false dichotomies when, in practice, we routinely straddle multiple approaches.

Relational Integrative Psychotherapy: Engaging Process and Theory in Practice, First Edition. Linda Finlay.
© 2016 John Wiley & Sons, Ltd. Published 2016 by John Wiley & Sons, Ltd.

This introductory chapter addresses the question, 'What is relational integrative psychotherapy?' The first two sections explore the concepts of **relational** and **integrative**, with the aim of providing an inclusive synthesising sketch while recognising some divergent voices. A third section discusses the **challenges of integration** we confront when practising in this relational integrative field. At the end of the chapter, a section titled 'Concluding reflections' begins a pattern for the rest of the book: I offer a conclusion of each chapter along with some personal thoughts and an implicit invitation to dialogue with me . . .

Being 'Relational'

All therapists would probably concur that we humans are shaped by our social contexts and that our sense of who we are is intimately entwined with our relationships. Research consistently shows that, for people in general, close relationships are what matter most. When those relationships fail to give us what we need, we lose confidence. If relationships constitute the core of psychological problems, they can also be harnessed in the pursuit of growth and healing. Psychotherapy can be understood as fundamentally concerned with this relational context, in terms of past, present and future (see box 1.1).

Box 1.1 Case illustration: Working relationally

Connie came into therapy to work on issues of intimacy in relationships after a string of problematic relationships with men. It emerged that Connie had been born addicted to heroin and had spent the first five years of her life living in random squats or on the streets with her neglectful mother, a substance abuser. Her mother remained toxic – both literally and figuratively – until Connie was taken into care and lost contact with her. She was eventually adopted by a solid nurturing family and had a reasonably good childhood. But damage had been done.

During therapy, every time the therapist became physically or emotionally close, Connie backed away. Together they recognised how Connie had learned to shut out others and close down her needs to avoid being abused and/or abandoned. The therapist attuned to Connie by progressing slowly, carefully, gently and in a respectful way. Over many months the therapist was consistently there for Connie, gradually decreasing the (emotional and physical) space between them. A significant moment of healing eventually occurred when Connie was able to cry while being held in the therapist's arms.

WHAT IS RELATIONAL INTEGRATIVE PSYCHOTHERAPY?   3

Within this general acceptance of the relational context of therapy, some practitioners promote the **therapeutic relationship**, rather than the individual client, as the *primary* focus of therapy.[1] This is the stance of this book. The basic argument is that as our only real access to another's experiencing is through our relationship with the Other, that relationship must be our therapeutic *vehicle*. As Yalom declares in his much-quoted professional 'rosary': "*It's the relationship that heals, the relationship that heals, the relationship that heals*" (1989, p. 91, emphasis mine).

Four key tenets are central to this committed relational approach:

- Therapy offers a **microcosm**. The therapeutic relationship lies at the centre of things, acting as a here-and-now microcosm of what clients experience in their social world. In this microcosm, the client's relational being is disclosed (Spinelli, 2015).
- The significance of *between*. The mysterious intersubjective space *between*, where we touch and are touched by the Other in multiple, often unseen ways, is of particular interest.
- The therapist is **present**. The therapist endeavours to be a safe, steady human presence that is willing to 'be-with' the client moment to moment, whatever emerges. The therapist is genuine and *congruent*,[2] aware of their inner experience and communicating it honestly to the client. "Presence involves bringing the fullness of oneself to the interaction. Therapists must be willing to allow themselves to be touched and moved by the patient" (Jacobs, 1991, p. 4).
- The relationship works as a **collaborative** partnership. Relational therapy does not involve a client talking to a powerful, distanced therapist who gives information or makes interpretations; it is a constantly evolving, negotiated, co-created dialogical process to which both therapist and client contribute (Evans & Gilbert, 2005). Here relational therapists need to ask themselves regularly, 'How am I contributing to our relationship? Is the way I am being facilitating or inhibiting the client's awareness and contact?'

Working relationally means privileging the emergent, here-and-now intersubjective relationship *between* therapist and client (see figure 1.1), for this is where we flexibly attune to each client's relational needs (DeYoung, 2003; Spinelli, 2015). It's about opening to the other while being willing to give of self. The therapist needs to have the courage to stay in 'the process': to be emotionally present to intrapsychic and interpersonal dynamics and be aware of the particular sociocultural context,while being prepared to take some risks towards the co-creation of experience, understanding and knowledge. The challenge is to embody ways of 'being' and 'being-with' (as opposed to just 'doing') naturally and effortlessly, rather than be led by some intellectual principle. It's about *being present as a human being first; as a therapist second* (Finlay & Evans, 2009).

4   WHAT IS RELATIONAL INTEGRATIVE PSYCHOTHERAPY?

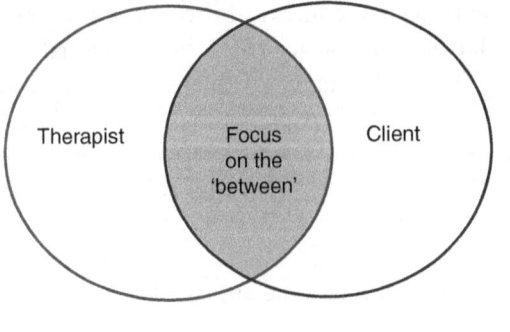

Figure 1.1   The 'between'

> Where the dialogue is fulfilled in its being, between partners who have turned to one another in truth. . .the world arises in a substantial way between men [sic] who have been seized in their depths and opened out by the dynamic of an elemental togetherness. The interhuman opens out what otherwise remains unopened. (Buber, 1965, p. 86)

How we operationalise this relational dimension and bring it into therapy varies according to perspective and context (Paul & Charura, 2015). A key debate revolves around the extent to which we privilege the here-and-now *inter*subjective relationship between therapist and client rather than the *intra*subjective one, where therapy might focus on relationships within, between parts of self (internal voices) or where past developmental relationships are accessed transferentially. This is a matter for theoretical debate and impacts on our choice of which theories to integrate.

Embracing 'Integration'

The term 'integration' derives from the Latin *integrationem* (renewal, restoration), itself from *integrare* (to make whole). It denotes a process of bringing parts together into a whole and moving forward in a (re-)new(ed) way.

Applied to therapy, our integrative project relates to at least two integrating movements: *client integration* and *theoretical integration*.[3]

First, there is integration related to clients' growth.[4] Here therapists focus on clients in holistic, integrating ways, working with them to enable them to *hold polarities* and make new connections with previously disowned parts. The New York-based Institute for Integrative Psychotherapy explains the process as

> taking disowned, unaware, or unresolved aspects of the self and making them part of a cohesive personality, reducing the use of defense mechanisms that inhibit spontaneity and limit flexibility in problem solving, health maintenance, and relating to people, and re-engaging the world with full contact. It is the process of making whole. Through integration, it becomes possible for people to face each moment openly and freshly without the protection of a pre-formed opinion, position, attitude, or expectation. (Institute for Integrative Psychotherapy, n.d.)

Chapter 9 focuses on this process of 'client integration'. In this first chapter, attention is focused on the second meaning of integration: 'theoretical integration'.

Theoretical integration involves adapting to both client needs and context by blending different theoretical frameworks and their methods. There is recognition that, given the diversity and complexity of human beings, no single specific approach can be clinically adequate for all clients and all situations. Research has repeatedly shown that no one therapy approach has superior efficacy, and therapists have embraced the idea that there are common processes that cut across traditional alliances (Norcross, 2005).

That said, theoretical integration does not mix approaches in an *eclectic*, piecemeal way. Rather there exists a continuum of practice, from a blending of approaches and techniques in pragmatic and instrumental ways at one end to wholesale integration at the other.[5]

An example of pragmatic, instrumental integration is the employment of gestalt 'empty chair technique' in a cognitive-behavioural skills training programme. Another example is the use of person-centred techniques of 'reflecting back' within a psychodynamic encounter. The use of mindfulness interventions (based in both Buddhist and cognitive traditions) constitutes another instance.

A deeper-going version of integration (the one favoured by this book) embraces a synthesised approach that is internally coherent and offers a new emergent meta-framework. Currently there are numerous **published integrative models** on offer. Palmer and Woolfe (2000) discuss various British models, while Norcross and Goldfried (2005) examine those originating in the USA (see box 1.2).

Box 1.2 Theory: Integrative models

Within the *humanistic* integrative tradition, Evans and Gilbert (2005) offer a relational-developmental model which draws on relational psychoanalysis, transactional analysis and gestalt therapy. Gilbert and Orlans (2011) offer a multidimensional relational framework that brings together physiological, affective, cognitive, contextual and behavioural systems. The "Multidimensional Integrative Framework" presented by Lapworth and Sills (2010) focuses on self-experience, relationships, and a temporal past–present–future frame.

Moursund and Erskine's (2004) 'relationship-focused integrative psychotherapy' approach encompasses an even bigger field, including transactional analysis, client-centred work and gestalt and borrowing from behaviourism, object-relations psychoanalytic self-psychology, systems theory and neo-Reichian body therapy. Wachtel (2014) promotes his 'cyclical psychodynamics' model, which blends relational psychoanalysis with systemic, cognitive-behavioural and experiential views.

(Continued)

Other published and empirically investigated integrative psychotherapy approaches draw from across the cognitive-behavioural and psychoanalytic spectrum. Well-known approaches include: Ryle's (1990) **Cognitive Analytic Therapy** (CAT) (combining psychoanalytic and cognitive approaches); Linehan's (1993) **Dialectical Behaviour Therapy** (DBT) (combining psychodynamic and cognitive-behavioural approaches); and Stricker and Gold's (2003/2005) **Assimilative Psychodynamic Approach** (which combines cognitive-behavioural experiential and family-systems techniques in psychodynamic therapy).

In the counselling–psychotherapy field, Faris and van Ooijen (2012) offer a postmodern, systemic *relational integrative model* (RIM) which blends cognitive-behavioural therapy (CBT), psychodynamic and humanistic approaches. There are also a number of practice-orientated trans-theoretical models in use, including Egan's (2010) skilled helper model and Cooper and McLeod's (2011) pluralistic approach. Prochaska and DiClemente's (2005) cycle of change has been widely applied and researched.

Beyond these formally prescribed models, every integrative practitioner finds their own path or preferred way of working (see the *British Journal of Psychotherapy Integration*, every issue of which offers students an opportunity to articulate their own evolving **personal model**). Their journey will be guided by: *personal* values and assumptions about the nature of human beings; the specific needs of each *client*; their *professional* experience and training; their work/*institutional* setting; and the cultural-political-ideological *context*.

In the US context, for instance, the evidence-based practice movement and managed care system demands empirically based treatments. Brief therapy programmes validated by outcome studies are favoured.

In the UK, fluid, intuitive approaches are acceptable in private practice. However, the NHS programme 'Improving Access to Psychological Therapies' has prompted a move towards recognising only empirically substantiated interventions approved by the National Institute of Health and Clinical Excellence (NICE).[6] This has created a split in our field, with practitioners lining up on one side or the other. Integrative approaches may one day offer a much-needed bridge across this chasm.

Challenges of Theoretical Integration

Theoretical integration confronts us with critical challenges. Different approaches cannot be blended willy-nilly. Philosophical commitments, values and assumptions can be incompatible and resulting theories and practices are not always complementary.

Speaking personally, I become uneasy when I see inexperienced therapists pulling ideas and techniques 'off the shelf' without appreciating their subtle theoretical complexities and context. An example of this is the fast-growing area of mindfulness, where certain Eastern philosophical principles (holism, non-being, compassion) appear to be getting lost in translation when attempts are made to apply them as Western cognitive-behavioural interventions. Another example is the way some practitioners refer to the practice of 'bracketing' as a means of being more objective: the opposite of the original phenomenological intention, which attends to subjectivity.

Fundamental differences in **approach** cannot be wished away. For example, humanistic therapists repudiate the concept of the 'unconscious', so central to psychoanalytic work; they prefer to regard some things as 'out of awareness'. In terms of technique, Freudian dream analysis, which assumes the existence of the unconscious, cannot simply be transplanted into gestalt dream work, which is understood differently. Similarly, the psychoanalytic focus on past experience is contrary to the humanistic stance of staying in the 'here-and-now'. Applied to the concept of transference, the psychoanalytic understanding posits a regression back to earlier relationships which are displaced onto the therapist. From a phenomenological and gestalt perspective, the past is always in the present. The client is seen to bring into therapy certain relational expectations based on their experiences of life, for instance, expecting to be swiped.

> *Integrative therapists* might straddle these positions by not fully accepting a view of the unconscious as something that is inevitably inaccessible and by attending to past–present–future as the time frames emerge in sessions.

There are also different perspectives concerning the **nature of the Self**. Person-centred notions of an authentic 'core' Self and behavioural views about fixed personality traits have been strongly critiqued by others. Psychoanalysis, transactional analysis and postmodern perspectives, for instance, emphasise how multiple, fragmented selves (or ego states) emerge in different social contexts, while existential therapy emphasises the process of being/becoming – the 'self' is a product of relational processes rather than a separate entity.

> An *integrative therapist* might compromise by acknowledging the idea of 'parts of self' or 'sub-personalities', for example. Instead of seeing the person in terms of fixed enduring characteristics, they might see the self as emerging in a process of 'self-ing'.

8   WHAT IS RELATIONAL INTEGRATIVE PSYCHOTHERAPY?

Views about the **role of the therapist** constitute another minefield. Traditional psychoanalysis insists the therapist should remain a neutral figure who interprets transferential processes. Gestalt therapists argue instead for the therapist to be less knowing and to be a fully present, non-interpreting human being. For their part, client-centred precepts concerning being non-directive contrast with the more directive interventional styles of systemic and cognitive-behavioural practitioners.

An *integrative therapist* is likely to take a responsive and collaborative stance rather than being either non-directive or authoritative. The precise style adopted will depend on which theoretical perspectives are favoured.

These examples indicate some of the dance steps required to blend competing perspectives. The key is to remember the **relational**. *It is our relational stance which bridges theoretical differences.* It's our concern for the quality of therapeutic relationship which binds our diverse orientations (Markin, 2014). This is in tune with Spinelli's (2005) plea to therapists yearning for integration to "attend to the source of that yearning and permit it to lead us back to its interrelational grounding" (p. 9).

In many ways, relational integrative therapists have more in common with each other than they do with their traditional school of origin. A relational psychoanalyst, for instance, would probably feel more at home with a relational existential-phenomenologist than with a traditional Freudian therapist. A relational therapist working cognitively would probably find more commonality with a transactional analyst than with a therapist operating in a reductionist, cognitive-behavioural way. The holistic, field-theory perspective of gestalt therapists shares common ground with the perspectives of phenomenological and systemic therapists.

To illustrate this implicit relational convergence, box 1.3 shows, firstly, a therapist using a *developmental-relational gestalt* frame to explore the client's reactions; and, secondly, a *cognitive-behaviourally* orientated integrative therapist working relationally.

Box 1.3 Case illustrations: Working relationally

A developmental-relational-gestalt approach

THERAPIST: Tell me some more about what that was like for you phillip, to witness your brother get beaten. ... [i]t must have been really tough for you ...

At this point there is a dramatic physical change in Phillip's presence, from a sad slumped body posture to an erect and rigid position and with a face contorted with rage and distain .... 'You haven't a fucking clue what it was like for me'. ...

I imagine I experience something of what it must have been like for him as a child – sarcasm, dismissal, humiliation and a deep sense of being 'wiped out'. ....

THERAPIST: Phillip, I was listening intently to you talk about your father beating up on your brother, and feeling a lot of compassion I reached out to you in your obvious distress. I then experienced you responding to me with sarcasm and angry disdain, which impacted me deeply. I experienced being dismissed by you and feel unseen, fearful and angry. I want to ask you 'Who did this to you?'

Phillip's posture instantly deflated, as did his seething anger, and with eyes filled with tears he replied sorrowfully, 'That's just how it was for me'. (Evans & Gilbert, 2005, pp. 118–119)

The cognitive behavioural analysis system of psychotherapy (CBASP)[7]

THERAPIST: How would your first husband have reacted had you told him about your experience with the repairman?

SUSAN: He would have poured himself a drink and told me I had driven him to drink. He was just like daddy. He would have called me stupid, dumb, an imbecile, and the biggest loser he had ever known. (Susan is crying softly now.)

THERAPIST: Now, I want you to describe for me what my reaction was to the way you dealt with the repairman?

SUSAN: It was okay, I guess.

THERAPIST: Think back, what did I do, how did I look throughout, what did I say? I want you to think carefully about how I behaved with you a few moments ago.

SUSAN: You certainly didn't make me feel stupid. You helped me see what I could have done better, you encouraged me, and then you were pleased when I said that the second way would have probably gotten me what I wanted.

(McCullough, 2005, p. 294)

In both the examples in box 1.3, the theoretical lens is implicit as the therapist makes space for a **relational dynamic** to emerge. Precisely how this dynamic is put into words and explained varies according to the dominant theoretical framework. For example, in *psychoanalytic* discourse we might say that the therapists have focused on the 'transference' and have challenged projections. In *gestalt* terms, the 'critical introject' is de-toxified and worked through. In *transactional analysis*, the therapists are seen as questioning and re-working

'Critical Parent' injunctions/messages, while in *cognitive* terms they are challenging proactively the impact on the client of the negative reactions of significant others. Whatever 'it' is called, the therapeutic relationship remains both the focus and the tool.

Concluding Reflections

There is a sense in which the field of integrative psychotherapy, with its multiple languages and cultures, resembles the United Nations rather than a single, unified territory. This field goes beyond single-school approaches to harness the potential of different theories and techniques in a **holistic** way. Relational integrative variants emphasise the emergent, co-created, dialogical therapeutic relationship along with both the intrapsychic and the sociocultural contexts. The aim is to integrate clients' needs and disowned parts of self towards their embracing a more comfortable, relational way of being.

A key challenge we face as relational integrative therapists is to work out *what*, *how* and *when* to integrate. A critical appreciation of theory, and some artful finesse, are needed to navigate the contradictory messages of different theories. I see our mission as blending competing voices that can at times express themselves stridently. Interestingly, there are parallels here with the integrating work we do with clients in terms of **holding polarities** (see chapter 9).

We achieve our deepest theoretical integration when we are able to internalise competing voices into a transformed, coherent way of being. This is the position I strive to embody in this book – if not always successfully. I also seek to celebrate plurality and promote dialogue between perspectives. I acknowledge the value of approaches that lie outside my personal *humanistic-integrative* model: for instance, developmentally orientated psychoanalytic and systemically based cognitive-behavioural integrative approaches.

That said, my own preferences inevitably set the tone of this book. My primary allegiance is to existential-phenomenological and gestalt theory and practices, with some interweaving of transactional analysis and relational psychoanalysis. Cognitive and systemic thinking also informs my work, which seeks to allow therapy to flow in response to the here-and-now relationship. For me, change comes about primarily through the process of working together dialogically and creatively. It is this process, rather than instrumental techniques, prefabricated protocols or theoretical dogma, that is the primary agent of change.

Relational work inspires me. It remains a privilege and an honour to witness another's experience and help them make sense of it. Relational practice touches heart and soul; the possibility of healing transformation is present for both client and therapist, in all sorts of yet to be imagined ways. In the space '*between*' anything can, and does, appear (Finlay & Evans, 2009).

Trusting the process takes courage, but its harvest of rewards is immeasurable.

Notes

1 However, Wachtel (2014) makes the interesting point that too much attention can be paid to the therapeutic relationship at the expense of outside ones, and this needs to be kept in mind.

2 Congruence is one of Carl Rogers' (1951) core conditions of person-centred work and refers to therapists' qualities of being genuuine and real (without facade). *Existential phenomenological* and *gestalt* therapists extend this notion to encompass openness and presence.

3 The Institute for Integrative Psychotherapy sees integrative therapy as offering three domains of integration: integrating the client's personality; integrating theory; and synthesising affective, cognitive, behavioural and physiological systems within a person and in relation to the social and transpersonal systemic context.

4 Daniel Siegel (2010) identifies eight domains of integration in his version of **integral neuroscience**: integration of consciousness; bilateral integration (brain); vertical integration (body); memory integration; narrative integration; state integration (parts of self); temporal integration; and interpersonal integration. A final transpirational domain has been added and constitutes the sum of connections.

5 Norcross (2005) suggests there are four routes to integration: technical eclecticism, theoretical integration, a common factors approach and assimilative integration. He notes that most practice probably falls under eclecticism rather than being truly and systematically integrative.

6 In counter-measure, the New Horizons programme from the Department of Health (2009) recommends addressing mental health in empowering, personalised, user-focused ways, and current Government policy aims to make mental health services more widely accessible (Department of Health, 2013).

7 **CBASP** (McCullough, 2005) is an empirically validated, integrative, *cognitive-behavioural* approach from the US which draws on Piagetian cognitive development theory, social learning theory and *psychoanalysis*.

Part I

Being and Doing Processes

Psychotherapy processes

2

Meeting and Contracting

One attempts to establish a relationship that is experienced by the client as being increasingly trusting and trustworthy. (Spinelli, 2007, p. 132)

The first meeting with a prospective client sets the tone for therapy. Much happens in a short space of time as we meet the client, listen to their story, make an assessment, give information, negotiate any future therapy contract *and* attempt to engage the client therapeutically. While the nature and format of early contact vary significantly according to the individuals concerned and the context (institutional, cultural, theoretical), it helps to have clarity of purpose and a sense of how to nurture the therapeutic alliance.

As therapists, we tend to develop a personal style with routines that seem to work for us. The pattern of an initial session depends on these as well as our theoretical orientation. My approach in my private practice is to have an hour-long session which the client pays for, followed (if we decide to proceed) by roughly 20 minutes of complimentary time in which I provide information and discuss contracting (some therapists offer the entire initial session for free). What we cover in this first meeting is largely led by the client, but the explicit agenda is to hear something of their story and for them to taste the relational integrative way I work.

This chapter discusses some of the issues all therapists face at this early stage, regardless of theoretical orientation, around: **first contact**, **problem formulation**, **use of diagnosis**, **treatment planning**, and **contracting**. Particular theoretical attention is paid to relational *psychoanalytic* perspectives on attachment and varied examples across *existential phenomenological, gestalt* and *cognitively* orientated fields.

Relational Integrative Psychotherapy: Engaging Process and Theory in Practice, First Edition. Linda Finlay.
© 2016 John Wiley & Sons, Ltd. Published 2016 by John Wiley & Sons, Ltd.

First Contact

In their first meeting, therapist and client check out whether or not they can work with one another. There is a lot to process in these early moments of contact, characterised by relationship building, mutual information giving and intuitive sensings. Stern uses the lively metaphor of animal-like sniffing-out through "intersubjective searching, improvising, and co-creating" (2003, p. 25) to describe this.

The first few minutes can be incredibly revealing. Therapists listen and observe intensively. We attend to *overt* clues which spring from explicit conversation and also *implicitly* through body language. We note those subtle sensings and inferences that emerge intuitively at **intersubjective** and **transferential** levels. If this is a first experience of therapy the person may be uncertain and anxious. I might find myself reassuring them, perhaps acknowledging their courage in taking a step towards therapy.

As the prospective client tells their story we are drawn in, alert to issues and vulnerabilities that seem figural and which might in time become the therapy focus (see box 2.1). In those first few moments we are invited into a relationship, an experience where one impacts on the other. As we touch the client we too are touched. We might discover ourselves reacting unexpectedly and perhaps invited to repeat the client's early script patterns, say by becoming their Critical Parent (see chapter 16). As transference and counter-transference emerge (see chapter 14), therapy begins too (Clarkson, 2003) . . .

Box 2.1 Case illustration: Being impacted by a new client

As I open the door to Sheila, it is as if a large ball of pain hits me right in the stomach. I feel shaken and need to ground myself by breathing slowly and deeply and telling myself, 'This is not my pain'. My experience is in sharp contrast to Sheila's appearance of a well-dressed and confident woman in her mid-fifties whose manner is friendly and businesslike. She says a colleague had referred her, as there are some issues she needs to work through. As Sheila talks she gives no hint of the pain and shock I am still feeling. ... My experience tells me that she may have built some defences against whatever has happened to her and that I need to go slowly and carefully at her pace. (Faris and van Ooijen, 2012, p. 84)

In *relationally orientated therapy*, the focus is on the relationship. Rather than attending exclusively to the client and their presenting 'pathology', the therapist has other concerns. Whether a client feels shy, distant, adversarial or keen to share with me is possibly of greater interest. What does contact with this person feel like? How am I reacting? As I focus on the 'between', what seems figural? What is it like for me to be with this client who is tense, scared, shy, embarrassed, angry, seductively charming, playful, silent . . .? Am I finding it difficult to concentrate? Is my response being hooked in some way?

Subsequent work homes in on what continues to be enacted in the **here-and-now relationship**. A key question to explore during the opening encounter (and always) is the extent to which the client's particular way of being-in-relationship (with me, the therapist) is similar to their relating outside the therapy room. This would be the start of seeing the therapy space as a microcosm of the person's world and habitual ways of being.

One issue that therapists across modalities are alert to in these early stages is that of **risk**. Is the client in danger of harming themselves, or contemplating suicide? Is there a history of trauma and abuse? Are any child protection issues at stake? What social supports do they have? What self-care do they engage? Some therapists ask explicit questions about lifestyle: the extent of self-harming, drug or alcohol use and dietary patterns, for example. Others will have specific risk assessment forms they are required to go through with the client such as the CORE system (Clinical Outcomes for Routine Examination).

Whatever the initial questions asked, it is important for the therapist to feel able to ask direct questions and set a tone that invites as open a **collaboration** as possible. If I feel reluctant to ask how much someone might be self-harming, for example, that is itself informative; I might wonder, for instance, about the client's level of shame or consider the possibility that some avoidant pattern is being re-created. I might even bring that into the open by saying: 'I'm aware that I'm feeling a reluctance to probe too hard about how much self-harming you're doing and yet it is important for us to be able to talk about it. I'm wondering, is this something you find hard to talk about?'

Problem Formulation and 'Storying'

Problem formulation can be understood as the client's 'story' (Gilbert & Orlans, 2011). With the client, we co-create a story which describes their current relationships, challenges and way of being. What is it the client is struggling with? What life issues are currently figural? What quality of relationship is emerging between therapist and client, and does this reflect wider social relationships? What is the client's relational history: relationships with significant others, attachment style, early socialisation experiences? How are they presenting? Are there signs of trauma, anxiety, depression or other mental health issues? In what ways is their life embedded in wider social-cultural, economic and political realities?

A client might, for instance, have sought therapy because they are struggling with a recent bereavement. In this case, therapy would probably focus on helping the client express their grief and find new meaning in life. It would then be a matter of working out the pacing and depth of work to be engaged. In cases of protracted, complicated grief, slower, developmental, attachment-focused explorations may be advised. Or perhaps the client is seeking to break out from a pattern of unsatisfying, problematic relationships. If there are issues relating to abuse and trauma in the past, our problem formulation might include a hypothesis that the client is inclined to repeat self-destructive ways of relating or has problems of intimacy or attachment. Alternatively, a client's ethnic and cultural background may require particular consideration: for example, if they are an immigrant, an asylum-seeker from a war-torn country or an individual who has suffered racist abuse, then future therapy might focus on managing the challenges arising from this interface between the personal and the political.

How therapists then set about exploring these problematic issues will differ according to theoretical orientation and context.

Developmentally orientated integrative therapists may couch initial formulations in terms of predominant *attachment styles* and *personality adaptations* and interpersonal relating.[1] For instance, gestaltist Elinor Greenberg (1999) finds that clients with disorders of the self, specifically those commonly described as Borderline, Narcissistic or Schizoid, tend to relate in therapy in certain characteristic ways. She offers the following guidelines: if the client seems to be asking mostly for love, then their primary adaptation is likely to be 'borderline'; if they are seeking admiration, then 'narcissism' is figural; if the client's preoccupation is with safety and they cannot stay emotionally present to reap the benefits of either love or admiration, then the client's 'schizoid' process is to the fore (see box 8.2). While this theory would probably not be made explicit initially, it may help suggest whether more focused short-term or relational long-term work is advisable.

Existential phenomenological therapists (see chapter 12) encourage clients to reflect on age-old philosophical questions like 'Who am I?' 'How can I live a meaningful life?' 'Who is important to me?' 'What in their life gives me meaning?' 'What choices am I making?' Therapy involves seeing the givens of our existence through different eyes. It seeks to enable a new freedom to change, or accept that which cannot be changed, along with the ability to take responsibility for future action (Deurzen, 2012).

The primary focus of the initial meeting is then to enable the client to describe something of their current struggle. I might explicitly ask clients to describe their experience: to tell their 'story' or ask them 'What is it like to be you?' Simply describing – and being witnessed – can be powerful and potentially transformational. In this initial contact I might also offer some validation, for instance, reassuring the person that they are not 'crazy' and offering hope that therapy can help and they will gain something.

Use of Diagnostic Categories

The use of 'diagnosis' is an anathema to many therapists: whether, and how, we should make diagnostic formulations is fiercely contested.

Humanistic–integrative practitioners, in particular, prefer more intuitive, phenomenological ways of seeing where the focus is on exploring clients'

MEETING AND CONTRACTING   19

relational way of being and how this might be influenced by their social context. In a dialogical, person-to-person spirit (Hycner, 1991/1993), we prefer to be unknowing and open to our client. People are infinitely more complicated and contradictory than any label suggests. We are concerned to do "justice to the way clients live their lives, rather than to eradicate specific problems or focus on particular symptoms" (Deurzen & Adams, 2011, p. 1).

So we resist diagnosis (and other ways of categorising someone), seeing it as reductionist, dehumanising and anti-therapeutic. It goes against the grain for us to objectify, judge, and make assumptions based on professional expertise. We do not want to psychopathologise and fix clients as a category when the focus of the therapy journey is on *change*. Taking diagnostic systems too seriously may "threaten the human, the spontaneous, the creative and uncertain nature of the therapeutic venture" (Yalom, 2001, p. 5). Our challenge is to find a way to "speak *about* the client without doing damage *to* the client" (Brownell, 2010, p. 190).

As part of working out where we stand in this debate, it is worth distinguishing between medical diagnoses and psychological **diagnostic formulations** such as considering personality and attachment styles.

Medical diagnosis

The DSM (*Diagnostic and Statistical Manual of Mental Disorders*) published by the American Psychiatric Association offers a common language and standard criteria for the classification of mental disorders. However, at the time of writing, the latest DSM – DSM-5, operative from May 2013 – remains the subject of vociferous debate (see box 2.2). Many voices are raised against engaging a medical model, exhorting us not to be overly reliant on official medical diagnosis.

Box 2.2 Theory: DSM-5 diagnostic categories

Neurodevelopmental disorders
Schizophrenia spectrum and other psychotic disorders
Bipolar and related disorders
Depressive disorders
Anxiety disorders
Obsessive-compulsive and related disorders
Trauma- and stressor-related disorders
Dissociative disorders
Somatic symptom and related disorders
Feeding and eating disorders
Elimination disorders

(*Continued*)

Sleep–wake disorders
Sexual dysfunctions
Gender dysphoria
Disruptive, impulse-control, and conduct disorders
Substance-related and addictive disorders
Neurocognitive disorders
Personality disorders
Paraphilic disorders
Other mental disorders

In 2011, US psychologist Brent Robbins co-authored an open national letter on behalf of the Society for Humanistic Psychology, inviting public debate on the DSM. Other organisations, including the British Psychological Society (2011), have endorsed this call. One concern is that normal human responses (including grief responses) could be labelled pathological using DSM criteria.

Debate about the DSM aside, there is no question that we need to understand the medical-psychiatric view when it is part of our work in wider mental health settings. Such understanding helps us contextualise a client's history and appreciate their experience of various treatments. For therapists working with people with severe and enduring mental health problems, it may be necessary to know if clients have a clinical diagnosis of, say, schizophrenia or bipolar disorder. Such knowledge provides information about a client's need for medication or the likely course and prognosis of their illness. In some countries, like the USA, diagnosis is also needed for insurance purposes, as a way of framing clinical need. As Roubal, Gecele and Francesetti (2013) point out, "diagnosis is not a description of the person in front of us, it is merely a tool that enables us to organize meaningfully our experience with this person and so helps us to be grounded and present for an encounter". Diagnosis becomes figural where it offers a kind of clinical **map** of possible perspectives (Roubal et al., 2013).

Relational-centred therapists understand that when medical diagnosis is to the fore, the tendency is to privilege information which endorses 'problem formulations' and to gloss over information which does not fit preconceptions. Some labels, such as 'personality disorder', or fixing someone on the basis of their envisaged personality style, are more problematic. These categories are regularly revised and even discarded, reminding us that we are dealing with culturally and **socially created phenomena**. Social behaviour can rarely be understood as fact or certainty. Further, focusing on someone as a 'borderline' personality, for example, may actually bring out those very traits in a self-fulfilling prophecy (Yalom, 2001). As Gilbert and Orlans (2011) argue, a diagnostic formulation is best understood as tentative, not a label for life. We need to corral our observations as 'hypotheses to be revised' (see box 2.3).

> **Box 2.3** Case illustration: Diagnosis as a provisional hypothesis
>
> One client puzzled me during our first meeting. Initially she presented as socially skilled, emotionally contained and professional. But then she told me she had been in therapy for ten years and she was looking for another therapist as her previous one had just retired. Suddenly she began speaking in a frightened anxious-child voice. Another person seemed to have entered the room and I wondered about her history. The possibility she could have dissociative identity disorder (DID) occurred to me. I sought to bracket this while holding my awareness of DSM criterion (300.14), which says that DID might be diagnosed when a marked discontinuity appears between two or more personality states and sense of self (with associated alterations in affect, behaviour, memory etc.). Eventually, it emerged that this client had previously been given a diagnosis of DID (though some of her 'selves' did not know of it. This was significant information and helped our discussion about how to manage therapy with her different selves.

Psychological formulations

Beyond medical diagnosis, the use of other category systems also comes in for critical scrutiny and views are contested.

In the *gestalt* tradition, symptoms or behaviour defined by others as 'pathological' or 'maladaptive' are seen as a protective *creative adjustment*[2] for the person in the face of a painful damaging situation. These are relational patterns which developed in order to survive and the behaviour is there because it had an important function. The gestalt view is that people adjust to the demands of a situation while creating a way of being which meets their own needs and, in this way, problems can be 'solved'. For instance, a client with neglectful or abusive parents may have taken some responsibility for the deficits in their environment which protects both parents and the client from facing the inadequacy of the parenting.

Diagnosis tends to be eschewed in favour of awareness of the *contact boundary* and observing here-and-now experience. That here-and-now experience includes the therapy relationship, so we might wonder, 'How am I impacting the client's experience at this moment (and vice versa)?' A client's whole embodied presentation is seen to give clues: for example, a therapist might note the person is inclined to be avoidant and tends to deflect feelings at the contact boundary (the point of contact between the client and their environment, including the relationship with the therapist).

Yontef (1988) recommends attending to client experience in terms of *time zones*. Evans and Gilbert (2005, p. 91) utilise this idea in their integrative 'diagnostic

22 MEETING AND CONTRACTING

model', which assimilates relational versions of cognitive, gestalt and psychoanalytic elements:

Time zone	Perspective	Focus of interest
Here-and-now and there-and-now	Functional	Functional and dysfunctional behaviour
Here-and-then	Relational	Contact and resistance
There-and-then	Developmental	Repetition and self-object dimensions

In *relational psychoanalysis*, greater diagnostic attention is paid to *attachment styles* where a client's (and a therapist's) predominant style is seen to be re-enacted in current relationships (see box 2.4). For instance, *securely* attached adults have a more positive, empowered, resilient sense of self and perceive others as being lovable and trustworthy, *insecure-avoidant* adults historically in receipt of unresponsive caregiving are found to keep a distance from others and be self-reliant, *insecure-resistant* (ambivalent) adults have received inconsistently responsive caregiving, and become overly dependent and needy with limited emotional regulation, while the adult with a *disorganised* attachment may be dissociated, or overly controlling (perhaps engaging excessive caregiving).

Box 2.4 Theory: Attachment research

Attachment theory arose from the theoretical work of John Bowlby (1969, 1988) on 'maternal deprivation' and the empirical research by Mary Ainsworth (Ainsworth, Blehar, Waters and Wall, 1978) and others such as Mary Main and Peter Fonagy. It focuses on how individuals handle separation, loss and reunion. Attachments to caregivers in childhood are seen to influence ways of relating in adulthood.

Ainsworth engaged in the now infamous 'strange situation' laboratory experiments (see numerous YouTube examples). These experiments set up various scenarios whereby an infant's interactions were observed over a period which included dealing with separations from, and 'reunions' with, the mother or other caregiver and a stranger. From this research Ainsworth identified three distinct responses:

- *Secure* attachment, where the infant uses the parent as a secure base; although distressed on separation the baby can be soothed. The stranger is engaged in the presence of the parent.
- *Insecure-avoidant* attachment occurs with a rejecting primary caregiver; the infant is not apparently distressed on parting (but anxious inside)

and is superficially/defensively unresponsive to the parent on their return. Responses to caregiver and stranger show little difference, and the child cuts off from contact.

- *Insecure-resistant* (ambivalent) attachment occurs with an inconsistent caregiver; infants are distressed by separation and both clingy and resistant on reunion.[3] The infant tends to be fearful of the stranger and emotionally sensitised, and scans for threats.
- A fourth category, *disorganised* attachment, was subsequently added (Main & Solomon, 1990):, it occurs when parenting relationships are abusive: the child's behavioural responses exhibit signs of traumatic stress (the child freezes, dissociates).

The therapist is a potentially significant attachment figure so therapy offers the opportunity for re-parenting and 'corrective emotional experience': "The therapist's role is analogous to that of a mother who provides her child with a secure base from which to explore the world" (Bowlby, 1988, p. 140). Initial diagnostic formulations in therapy will thus be made with an eye towards what clients need from the therapy relationship. Generally, clients who tend towards anxious-avoidant styles of relating need longer-term 'holding' therapy while ambivalently attached clients often benefit from shorter-term therapy with clear structure/boundaries.

From this developmental-psychoanalytic perspective, key questions can be asked to explore the individual's attachment needs and patterns, including:

- Which parent did you feel closest to, and why?
- When you were upset as a child what did you do?
- How did you and your parents respond to the first major separation you remember having?

Treatment Planning

Theoretical orientation also influences the focus and manner of assessment and treatment planning. *Psychodynamic* therapists consider early life history, attachment patterns and ego strength; *cognitive* therapists focus more on current behavioural patterns and cognitive schemas. *Systems-orientated* therapists consider the family members as a unit and identify key interactional patterns.

Beyond modality, clients' motivation and needs should determine the course of any initial planning. Clients need to be active agents in creating and living their lives (Cooper & McLeod, 2011). Some good questions to ask are:

> 'So what has brought you here today?'
> 'Have you a sense of what you'd like to get out of our work together?'
> 'What are you wanting to change or be different in your life?'

Some therapists prefer to use more structured, form-based goal-setting techniques which can be utilised later in evaluating outcomes of therapy. See, for instance, the *Simplified Personal Questionnaire Procedure* by Elliot, Mack and Shapiro (1999) or *PSYCHLOPS* by Ashworth et al. (2004).

Six main (often overlapping) areas of therapy aims/goals are commonly identified:

1. **Support** The individual may be struggling to cope, for instance post-bereavement, and seeking some extra (often time-limited) support.
2. **Psycho-educational**. The individual may ask for help with coping with specific issues, such as their anger, or anxiety and panic attacks.
3. **Crisis intervention**. After a traumatic incident (such as a car accident or sexual assault), the person might benefit from debriefing, support and practical advice as well as from longer-term work with the trauma and post-traumatic stress.
4. **Existential decision-making** Some individuals enter therapy to explore and examine life decisions or dilemmas, such as whether to leave their marriage or to have optional surgery.
5. **Insight, understanding and self-acceptance** Some individuals seek a more open exploration of their self-identity, needs, thoughts and feelings.
6. **Relational dynamics and developmental needs** Some individuals start with the recognition that they feel 'stuck' and would like long-term psychotherapy, for instance to work with their chronic insecurity, a crippling phobia or problematic patterns of relating to others.

Sometimes clients arrive with specific 'problems' to be solved. Perhaps they are experiencing panic attacks or marital conflict; they are feeling depressed and unmotivated; or they are concerned about their anger getting out of hand. Often potential clients approach me with an explicit request for cognitive-behavioural therapy (CBT). A provisional therapy plan can be negotiated accordingly: for instance, one that includes a few sessions focused specifically on anxiety management techniques.

A different example was an individual who arrived acknowledging her overuse of substances (particularly cannabis) to soothe away emotions. She was beginning to realise that she had very little idea who she was and what she felt, without substances. She was seeking therapy, she said, to learn how to handle her emotions and get to know herself better. We evolved no specific therapy plan but kept our work open-ended, agreeing simply to 'go exploring together'.

Alternatively, clients might present with a range of problematic issues. The task then is to agree the most suitable focus. Sometimes, it takes time to find the therapeutic path and the therapist might need to actively seek out those damaging processes currently out of awareness rather than wait for the client to volunteer them (box 2.5).

> **Box 2.5** Case illustrations: Establishing the priority issue

Example 1

Martina came to the initial session concerned for her husband who had Asperger's Syndrome and whose recent retirement had left him feeling useless and irritable. Initially the therapist suggested seeing them as a couple, but he refused, so Martina and the therapist agreed to a *brief therapy* contract to explore ways Martina could *mobilise her resources*.

The contract seemed straightforward initially but after the first session the therapist felt a deep, inexplicable sadness which lingered long after Martina left. His intuition suggested Martina was carrying some profound grief, perhaps out of her awareness.

In the fourth session Martina let her therapist in to see the source of this grief. Her parents had inexplicably disappeared one day when she was about four, so her older sister had taken care of her and brought her up. Martina had grown up and left to go to college and to travel. Then she learned how her beloved sister had ensured their survival through dealing drugs and prostitution. Years later her sister died from a drug overdose and Martina was devastated. She acknowledged that she had never recovered from this loss and still felt guilty somehow about being the cause.

While the therapist was not surprised to find some underlying grief, neither of them had expected to work through layers of unprocessed guilt and trauma. They re-contracted for long-term work.

Example 2

Susie came into therapy with big smiles and assertions that she was a 'sunny, positive person'. While she had 'recently been through a difficult time', she was now 'feeling on the level'. When asked what she needed from therapy she could only reply 'I don't know'. It took three more hard-working sessions before they touched deeper feelings and Susie acknowledged what she called the 'volcano' inside her. Another session was needed to identify the healing she wanted and discern a path for therapy. Contracting therefore occurred in stages.

Contracting

Each therapist engages the contracting process in ways that fit the context and people concerned; there are no blanket rules. However, there are things to consider, and also the process of negotiating the contract can be revealing. The contract has practical and *ethical* functions and can be seen as a concrete symbol of the intention to **hold** and **contain** the therapy process safely and professionally (see chapter 5).

As the contracting discussion progresses, it is important to reach some agreement about the nature of the work ahead and, even if exact aims/goals are not specified, to get some sense of what the person would like to achieve through therapy. This begins the process of actively involving the person in their own therapy.

One key question is the person's **motivation** for seeking therapy. Is it their own decision or has a partner or family member told, or encouraged, them to come? Are they willing to commit to regular sessions: six sessions, say, with the possibility of future negotiation for longer-term work?

A useful question in initial sessions is 'Why now?' Why has the client decided to come to therapy at this particular time? Often the issue of concern (for instance, problematic relationships) will have been present for some time. The response can be revealing. One client might say his wife will leave him unless he sorts himself out. Another might acknowledge that a problem has begun to interfere with their life and must now be faced.

Decisions are needed about **boundaries** and **limits**. It is useful to see this exercise as about 'safety' and 'mutual respect' rather than imposing 'rules of engagement'. The terms of contract for the payment of fees and what to do about non-attendance need to be specified, for example. Of course therapists differ in their requirements, often depending on the context of their practice (be it private practice, public health care or the voluntary sector).[4]

The boundaries we set and maintain go to the heart of the safe space we are trying to create for our clients. Boundaries are not just rules or 'defensive practice' to avoid vulnerability to professional misconduct action. Rather, they need to be applied in the given context and relationally negotiated.

> For a therapist to hold careful boundaries because they believe they must, or because they are afraid of the uncontrollability of closeness, cripples the potential for relatedness. But for a therapist to hold such boundaries as an honouring of the client's woundedness is itself relational. (Totton, 2010)

For client relationships where there are **safety** and **risk** issues, extra care may be needed when contracting. For instance, a therapist might negotiate a contract with a self-harming or suicidal client that s/he agrees not to attempt suicide for a specified duration; or clients with a problematic alcohol habit may be informed that they need to be sober when they attend therapy, and if they are under the influence, the therapist reserves the right not to see them.

A **written contract** specifying matters relating to attendance, confidentiality, risk/safety and ethics (i.e. that the client consents to the conditions of therapy) can be useful, not least because it demonstrates to the client that the therapist aims to be ethical and professional. When drawing up such a contract, I always ask clients if they have something they'd like to include: for instance, they may request that they be contacted only via their mobile phone, and not via work or home landlines. I might also add something in about texting that allows for brief communications about appointments but would discourage extended exchanges, not least because these can be misunderstood and boundaries around what constitutes the formal therapy become confused. Discussions like these not only respect the client's needs but also emphasise the collaborative nature of therapy. Then, if a client is reluctant to sign the contract or is trying to evade having weekly sessions, might there be a commitment issue which needs further attention? This person might value having another session to explore what therapy involves before signing a contract.

As part of this written contract, I also clarify *limits to confidentiality*. In an emergency, for example, I may contact the client's GP or referring agencies for health concerns; if child protection is an issue social services may need contacting; and a Course Leader may need to be informed in cases of a trainee's habitual non-attendance.

Opening space which invites the client to ask questions and clarify the nature of psychotherapy is vital. Some therapists offer a *written leaflet* giving information to supplement verbal information. I might take a few minutes to talk about the importance of the therapy relationship and how the therapy space can prove an interesting microcosm of life 'outside'. I might mention the findings of *current research* which point to the efficacy of psychotherapy and the healing powers of the therapeutic relationship itself, which offers opportunities to share, be witnessed, work through things, be supported and listened to. I might also at this point, acknowledge how therapy can be emotionally unsettling and challenging to engage.

Sometimes, a more informal approach is needed. I occasionally draw on the story related by Evans and Gilbert:

> You will recall the story of Christopher Columbus who with a small flotilla of ships set out on a voyage of discovery? . . . Well there were times during his adventures at sea when the wind blew strong and fair and the small ships made good progress. But there were times when the wind fell away completely . . . and the ships [were] stuck in the doldrums for weeks on end. And there were times when the thunder roared and the lighting flashed . . . huge waves threatened to overwhelm the ships . . . . The experience of therapy can reflect all three descriptions of this epic voyage. (2005, p. 103)

At the end of the story I might well say, 'Columbus wasn't sure where he would end up. That's a bit like therapy, where we go on an exploration and voyage together.' Therapy as a whole, like the first session, is a step into the unknown.

Concluding Reflections

This chapter has discussed issues arising during the initial meeting with a client including problem formulation, use of diagnosis, treatment planning, and contracting. While there are a number of practical, instrumental considerations to attend to, the key processes at stake involve tuning into the person's world and relationship building.

Diagnostic categories, set procedures and explicit treatment plans offer a safe structure but we need to move beyond recipes and open ourselves to the relational process. We need ritual *and* spontaneity. Excessive ritual becomes controlling and deadens creativity; excessive spontaneity leads to a lack of containment and security (Hoffman, 1998).

Ultimately, it is important that the client feels they have gained something from the first session (hope, insight, nourishment) and that it might be worth coming back. Perhaps they found it helpful to tell their story and have it witnessed. Perhaps they appreciated their experience being normalised or being told they are not 'mad'.

The relational task in this first meeting is primarily to provide a prospective client with a sense of **boundaries**, **trust** and **hope**: they need to begin to experience the relationship as a safe, trusting and trustworthy space, and hope is what brings the person back for further sessions and makes investing in therapy worthwhile.

> Hope is born of the kind of contact that happens between therapist and client . . . Before the client leaves, the therapist needs to establish herself as someone who is present, respectful, and willing to be involved; as someone who understands what this client wants and has an idea of how to accomplish it; and as someone who knows how to build and maintain an effective therapeutic relationship. (Moursund & Erskine, 2004, p. 125)

Towards the end of the initial session, I will usually seek to re-emphasise the **relational connection** by asking the client how they have experienced the session and talking with me. I might ask 'You've said how hard it is to talk about your feelings, and yet you've talked a lot about your feelings here with me today. What has that been like for you?' Such relational reflections are an invaluable exercise in what I call 'relational-emotional literacy' and set the tone for therapy to come.

In that first meeting, the art of therapy lies beyond checklists, protocols and assessment criteria; it involves mutual trust, connection and engaging the client in therapy – the focus of the next chapter.

Notes

1 Attachment theory was originally the province of *psychoanalysis* but today it's more integrative (Wallin, 2007). *Humanistic* therapists also draw on attachment theory to speak of old unmet relational needs which are replayed in current relationships.

2 'Creative adjustment' can be equated with psychoanalytic notions of 'defence mechanism' or the cognitive idea of 'coping strategy'.

3 Using a *humanistic-integrative* frame, Erskine (2011) describes four styles of insecure attachment: (1) inconsistently responsive caregiving,

which results in a highly adaptive, clingy relational style where there is an implicit fear of loss of relationship; (2) predictably unresponsive caregiving, which leads to emotional detachment and an implicit fear of vulnerability; (3) predictably punishing caregiving, which is seen to result in traumatic confusion and an implicit fear of violation; and (4) invasive and controlling caregiving resulting in diminished affect and withdrawal and an implicit fear of invasion. Erskine stresses that these are just four possible styles of many, and that usually we have a *combination of styles* (arising from having had many different attachments).

4 In my own private practice, I ask for a minimum 24 hours' notice if a client is going to cancel; without this they *may* be charged in full. It also works both ways. If I miss a session without adequate notice, I am likely to give the next session for free.

3

Engaging the Therapeutic Process

In the first moments of the very first session I knew that I was done for. She (the therapist) met my eyes and did not leave them. I wouldn't be able to fool this person... If I took this person as my therapist she would get beneath all that crap. I did not want that – but I did want it. (Mearns & Cooper, 2005, p. 52)

Some of the most important moments in therapy occur in those fragile first few weeks when we invite the client – perhaps distressed or disturbed – to engage in the therapeutic process. During this period, we ask clients to take up the challenge of working actively with us, on themselves, in their own therapy. Despite feeling vulnerable and exposed, clients need to be prepared to open themselves and risk us penetrating their dark, painful, secret spaces. In turn, we as therapists need to listen attentively to them to ascertain where they are in their process at any particular moment. Our questions and responses must invite trust and inspire hope, often in the face of considerable hopelessness. Step by delicate step, client and therapist build their working alliance so that – together – they can explore the client's private world. Always this is a joint journey into the unknown.

The client is likely to be full of questions: What is expected of me? Will I be judged? Who is this therapist? Can I trust this individual to conduct me safely out of the familiar and through unknown territory? Such questions lurk during this initial phase when clients contemplate their own readiness to commit to therapy and therapists wonder if clients will turn up again.

In this phase, the relational integrative therapist seeks to build on the relationship established in the first meeting. The primary goal is to **nurture the**

Relational Integrative Psychotherapy: Engaging Process and Theory in Practice, First Edition. Linda Finlay.
© 2016 John Wiley & Sons, Ltd. Published 2016 by John Wiley & Sons, Ltd.

ENGAGING THE THERAPEUTIC PROCESS   31

therapeutic alliance and fully engage the client in therapy. The first section of this chapter focuses here. Like the foundation of a building, the alliance is invisible but underpins and supports all that grows above. It must provide sufficient safety to allow clients to drop defences and 'let go', and so to begin feeling and exploring unknown internal worlds.

Four further interlinked processes converge in the early stages of therapy: **ensuring safety**; **listening, sensing and making sense**; **enabling change**; and **being present to relational processes**. *Gestalt* and *transactional analysis* (see chapters 13 and 16) approaches are foregrounded with alternative approaches interspersed, including a specific trans-theoretical model.

Nurturing the Therapeutic Alliance

A cooperative therapeutic alliance underpins all effective helping (Clarkson, 2003). This alliance involves three main components: agreement about **goals**; consensus on **tasks** and processes of therapy; and a positive affective **bond** or attachment (Bordin, 1979). In short, it is necessary to have at least some mutual understanding about the nature of therapy, as well as a shared desire to nurture a relationship built on trust, communication and acceptance.

Research findings (see box 3.1) stress the value of clear contracting, agreed goals and processes, and key information-giving for ensuring mutual responsibility for the therapy. The client needs to have a sense of what they are aiming for, and a solid therapeutic alliance forms a platform that enables therapist and client to work together through those more challenging moments of therapy when one or other wants to withdraw.

Box 3.1 Research: The importance of the therapeutic alliance

Impressive numbers of research studies support the claim that, irrespective of modality, theoretical orientation or technique, relational factors are central to the effectiveness of therapy (Cooper, 2008; Gelso, 2011; Markin, 2014).

Orlinsky, Grawe and Parks (1994) suggest that the power of the alliance emerges in more than 1,000 studies. Horvath and Bedi (2002) see the development of such an alliance as the "highest priority" in the early stages of therapy.

The working alliance predicts therapy outcomes (Norcross, 2011); some studies even suggest that an authentic **therapeutic alliance** is

(Continued)

the *most important* factor in predicting clinical outcome (Lambert, 1992). Other research indicates a moderate level of correlation between a good alliance and positive therapy outcomes (Horvath and Symonds, 1991; Horvath and Bedi, 2002). In a meta-analysis of 201 studies, Horvath, Delre, Flückinger and Symonds (2011) found that positive outcomes are down to having a strong therapeutic alliance above methods/techniques (i.e. change is attributed to the alliance 7.5 times more than to specific methods). Other studies show that clients with positive alliances with therapists are less likely to drop out of therapy (Piper et al., 1999).

Lambert (1992) estimates that around 30% of client improvement is due to variables inherent in a good relationship, such as empathy and warmth. Research also suggests that a lack of progress or improvement after the first few appointments should act as a warning to therapists, encouraging them to open or widen discussion with the client about the goals and processes of therapy (Miller, Duncan & Hubble, 2005).

Exactly how therapists engage clients in therapy varies according to various factors, including their personal style, theoretical approach and context.

Person-centred therapists following Rogers (1951) create safety through being non-judgemental, empathic, authentic and congruent. Working relationally, these therapists draw on their own intuition of how to be-in-relation with the client while remaining reflexive[1] (i.e. critically self-aware) about what may be happening in the relationship.

Psychodynamic therapists are concerned to provide a safe space to enable the expression and interpretation of significant unconscious, relational themes from the past and in the present. New ways can then be found as the therapist represents aspects of the client's internal relational world (Greenberg & Mitchell, 1983). Specifically, therapists practising from the tradition of *self-psychology* (Kohut, 1984; see box 4.2), underline how essential it is for the therapist to be able to enter into the subjective world of the Other in a concerned and empathic manner. Here the client is invited to use the therapist as a 'self-object' (e.g. offering affirming mirroring) to heal past deficits.[2]

Therapists differ on what they see as the most effective way of facilitating growth but all acknowledge the importance of the relationship. The challenge for integrative therapists is to find a way of responding to clients' needs in attuned flexible ways, rather than simply sticking to some theoretical formulae. Box 3.2 shows *existential*, *gestalt* and *cognitively orientated* approaches being combined in action in an organic, responsive way.

ENGAGING THE THERAPEUTIC PROCESS 33

Box 3.2 Case illustration: Building a therapeutic alliance

Marco entered therapy following a traumatic 18 months during which he had undergone surgery and chemotherapy after being diagnosed with prostate cancer. He had been given the all-clear and his prognosis was moderately good, but he was left feeling vulnerable and anxious about his health. He experienced regular nightmares in which violent deaths figured prominently; he would frequently wake with palpitations and in a cold sweat.

Phase 1: Establishing a therapeutic alliance and treating the anxiety symptoms

The therapist's first intervention was to offer compassion for Marco's traumatic journey and respect for his finding a way to cope. She reassured him it was unsurprising for his anxiety to show in this way now the pressure was off. She hoped that by 'normalising' Marco's responses she would help him to feel enabled to express his existential terrors and explore the impact of his recent traumatic experiences. Marco, however, found his behaviour 'unmanly' and tended to deflect[3] away from any emotional focus.

Recognising his scientific background as a chemical engineer, the therapist shifted tack slightly and described some recent research findings about the effectiveness of CBT. Taking a psycho-educational approach, she guided Marco through basic relaxation techniques. As he began to accept her as an ally, they became able to work explicitly on reducing his anxiety responses. Marco was now better motivated to engage short-term therapy geared to learning anxiety management techniques while expressing his fears within a safe, trusting relationship with his (empathic, compassionate) therapist.

Phase 2: Healing deeper relational wounds

After eight sessions, Marco's sleep disturbance was largely under control and he was invited to consider whether he wished to embark on a longer-term exploration of the roots of his anxiety. Marco understood that if he did so, his work would shift from a teaching–learning approach focused on his behaviour to a more open exploration of his current and past relational experiences. Through the therapist's gentle challenging, he recognised how he had found it hard to accept the therapist's care and deflected away from contact with her. He recognised this as a familiar pattern in other relationships and felt ready to undertake a more far-reaching journey of self-exploration.

34   ENGAGING THE THERAPEUTIC PROCESS

Beyond questions of theoretical orientation, relational integrative therapists are primarily focused on how the therapeutic relationship is opening up, and what is emerging. Perhaps the most important ingredient in relational work is the therapist being "present as a person meeting the person of the other" (Yontef, 1993, p. 24), from the "depths of one vital center to another" (Hycner & Jacobs, 1995, p. 219). It takes particular *grace* – beyond knowledge, protocols and skill – to make contact at the threshold of human relating, to be open to the gift of the other (Hycner, 1991/1993).

Ensuring Safety

When a client first enters our therapy room, we both have lots of questions. Why should the client trust us? What will enable them to open up and face their internal demons? Why have they risked exposing themselves to a relative stranger? What do they need before they will go exploring with us? What might block them from committing to therapy?

Answers to these questions come back to the basic concern to create a safe, comfortable, trustworthy, *boundaried*, permission-giving space. The client needs to know that their therapist is competent and has their best interests at heart. There needs to be a balance between spontaneous openness and containing control (Totton, 2010).

Certain general practices can help us create a safe space (a contract of confidentiality for example). But safety cannot be asserted or produced at will. It involves attuning to the client and responding appropriately to them, demonstrating *over a period of time* that the therapy space is safe. Importantly, what is safe for one client may not be for another: for example, some clients may perceive a reassuring touch as kind, safe 'holding', but others may find it invasive and disturbing. The skill and art of the therapist lies in attuning to the specific needs of the individual as they progress through therapy.

When thinking about how I might make a space safe, I find it useful to draw on *transactional analysis* theory regarding the use the 3 Ps: Permission, Potency and Protection (Crossman, 1966).

- **Permission** involves the therapist giving clients space to: feel their feelings, speak their truths, and be themselves. The therapist provides the client with new messages about themselves and the world: 'you can do this' or, 'you have the power to think your way out of this' or, 'you can change'. Appropriate action by the therapist, including modelling, conveys permission to the client.

  A useful example of permission-granting comes from my teaching experiences over the years when students are panicking about how to start writing up a case study or other academic work. In the grip of fear and shame they are overwhelmed and lose their ability to think. Rather than jumping in with a lecture on an aspect of theory or procedure I invite the students to tell me what they do understand about the task. This enables me to work out where each student is and gives me an opportunity to validate their contribution. I try to convey a message, 'you know this theory' or 'you are capable of thinking clearly', while I try to model clear thinking (see box 3.3).

- **Potency** refers to our (benign) power as therapists. Our interventions enable clients to feel that we know what we are doing, and why. Such potency works in part through inspiring *hope*. New clients will frequently ask that key question, 'Can you help?' A positive (or at least considered) reply is of crucial importance to the ambivalent client who is wondering whether or not to invest in therapy.

  Potency is also about becoming more powerful than the client's inhibiting, damaging introjects (i.e. internalised messages stemming from family or society). For example, a client may feel that they are unable to speak openly because if they honestly express their anger they will be rejected or abandoned. Our role is to show we can survive their anger, that we will not reject them, that we will give all necessary support against being abandoned. And for that to carry conviction, we must be perceived as having the power to grant that protection.

- **Protection** involves creating a safe, boundaried, confidential space which keeps the client safe from harm. For instance, if the client needs to do some cathartic anger work, we protect them by setting up the room so that nobody (client or therapist) can get hurt. If the client fears a negative judgement on revealing a shameful secret, we need to communicate *non-judgemental*[4] acceptance and compassion, and might set out to explore the relational history feeding the fears. If a client starts to project messages such as 'You'll think I'm awful', we need to challenge the projection and then explore the source of such introjected messages (in this case, that the client is 'awful' in some way). By so doing, we encourage our client to travel beyond such damaging introjects.

Box 3.3 Case illustration: Challenging through permission giving

Phillip's discomfort and barely concealed embarrassment at coming to see me at all render the prospect of his continuing in therapy very unlikely. I strongly suspect that unless we can establish some deeper level of contact today that will provide hope sufficient to overcome his acute embarrassment, then he will not return for a second session. So even though the therapeutic alliance is fragile and tentative I nevertheless decide to trust the unconscious invitation to contact that I intuit is coming from Phillip and take a risk. . . .

(Continued)

36   ENGAGING THE THERAPEUTIC PROCESS

'Phillip, I experience you talking to me in an apparently unconcerned and indifferent manner, but at the same time you look very sad, is that right?'

Phillip looks surprised, alarmed even, and tears up. Choking on his words he apologizes while attempting to sound unaffected, 'Sorry, I didn't realise I was appearing so emotional.'

Phillip's resistance to his feelings touches me and I remark that it must be difficult to be in contact with his feelings and at the same time try and hold everything together?

Phillip replies, tearfully attempting and failing to appear unaffected, 'Sorry I am not used to showing myself like this, I'm . . . sorry . . . I'll be ok in a minute.'

I reply as a challenge to obvious introjects, 'Why do you think you have to apologise?' 'Isn't it ok to feel what you feel, Phillip?'

Phillip looks at me with what appears a range of conflicting emotions, anger, bewilderment, vulnerability and hope, and remarks rather confusedly, 'Not in my family . . . a man doesn't show his feelings . . . It's not ok . . . is it[?]' (Evans & Gilbert, 2005, pp. 87–88)

One of the key ways we keep clients safe is by being respectful and keyed in to their needs. This is where listening deeply becomes necessary.

Listening, Sensing and Making Sense

Listen
When I ask you to listen to me
and you start giving me advice,
you have not done what I asked.

When I ask you to listen to me
and you begin to tell me why
I shouldn't feel that way,
you are trampling on my feelings.

When I ask you to listen to me
and you think you have to do something
to solve my problem
you have failed me,
strange as that may seem. . .

[. . .]

When you do something for me
that I can do for myself,

you contribute to my fear
and inadequacy.

But when you accept as a simple fact
that I do feel what I feel,
no matter how irrational,
then I can quit trying to convince you
and can get about the business of understanding
what's behind this irrational feeling. . .

[. . .]

So please listen and just hear me. . .

[. . .]

Anonymous

The term 'therapy' comes from the Greek *therapeia* meaning 'attendance'. A further development in the meaning of the word 'attend' is to listen, and so to *attend closely* to what is being revealed.

The skill of listening involves staying with the client rather than jumping in readily with knowing advice and problem-solving. Being more unknowing ourselves, we give respect and space for the client's knowing. This kind of listening is different from everyday listening. Transactional analyst Eric Berne (1972) coined the phrase 'thinking like a Martian': it's having the ability to observe human interaction without expectation and prior assumptions about what the communications of others *should* be. We might call this focus on what the communications mean here and now 'clean listening'. It's a skill that children possess naturally but subsequently lose (Stewart, 2014).

Clients need to know that we're listening, that we're hearing them, that we're there for them. Without this, they are unlikely to engage in therapy. The experience of being listened to in a very concentrated and focused way, of being heard, seen, and witnessed, perhaps for the very first time, can be transformative. Clients who can take in our holistic, 'unifying gaze' in that contact-full place may begin to feel they have something interesting and important to say.

When listening, the therapist tunes in, conveying warmth and acceptance through steady eye contact, nods and perhaps a benign facial expression. The listening is engaged with the whole body, which aims to hear, see and sense as much of the Other as possible. The therapist learns to attend closely to the client's choice of words, and to non-verbal clues such as bodily expressions and tensions, changes of breathing and posture. It's about listening to the client in a sustained way, attempting to enter the client's world. More than listening to words, we respond to the metamessages and what is being communicated both in and out of awareness.[5] 'What might your sigh be saying?', we wonder.

It is not simply the therapist who listens. Our enterprise is **co-created** and we must remain alert to signs that our own messages are heard. Even if clients struggle to hear our message, their difficulty may be a legitimate focus of therapy, and shows their preparedness to face problematic relational processes. However, if our words fall on deaf ears then perhaps our client is not engaged with the therapy process and our contract needs reconsideration. Alternatively, we may be wrong somehow and need to use this opportunity to check out how the relationship is working and what might be causing the 'deaf ears'.

The process of tuning into, and making sense of, an individual's world starts with asking them to tell their 'story'. As the narrative unfolds, relational integrative therapists strive to be as present as possible, both to the client and to what is happening within the therapeutic relationship; we listen carefully to clients' current and past experience while working within the here-and-now relationship. Together, therapist and client journey in search of sense and meaning, and perhaps contemplate life changes.

One key focus of sense-making is to explore what purpose or **function** the person's feelings or behaviour serves. For instance, does excessive alcohol consumption have a self-soothing, reparative function? If clients are full of shame and negative self-talk, does this have a self-stabilising function – are these the messages they've always heard and is that how they see themselves? Or, might a client's neck tensions be a *retroflection* (a holding in) of the need to protest, its function being to self-stabilise an overwhelming fear (Erskine, 2014)?

The tuning-in involves resonating with the client: that is, engaging an **emotional, bodily sensing** that goes beyond cognitive understanding and empathy (see chapter 4). In this attuned space, we seek to raise awareness and make links between present and past, simultaneously challenging unhelpful or inconsistent relational patterns. At the same time we attempt to respect the client's way of being and appreciate the creative adjustments[6] they have made in order to survive. For instance, rather than seeing dissociation as pathological, it could be seen as having a creative, stabilising (if archaic) function: the child 'leaves' to keep safe.

We can never fully understand what it is like to be an Other. We know only what they say about their world (explicitly or implicitly) and what we are experiencing in the emerging relationship between. In my own practice, for example, I rely quite substantially on the ability of my bodily felt-sense to give me clues about what may be happening with my client.

Enabling Change

Having the opportunity to explore thoughts, feelings, fantasies, fears and desires, and the space to make sense of subjective experience with an attuned Other, can bring about awareness which eventually leads to change (see box 3.4).

> **Box 3.4** Case illustration: Making sense of a client's world
>
> **Vince** entered long-term therapy to explore his obsessive-compulsive tendencies and his feelings of guilt about walking out on his wife and baby daughter. Years before, and acting on the belief that his family were 'better off' without him, he had followed a job opportunity in another country. While he believed it had been a good move for him, he was also racked with guilt and shame about being a 'useless' father and human being. In the first few therapy sessions, he was full of self-critical bile, and in a torture of doubt as to whether he had made the right decision.
>
> Vince's therapist noted how themes of **abandonment**, in various guises, surfaced regularly in Vince's personal history. As a child, Vince had spent many months in various relatives' homes while his mother was in rehab. She in turn had been brought up by grandparents, rather than her own mother and father. Vince's father had been brought up in an orphanage and had been largely absent during Vince's childhood. Vince's sister gave her child up for adoption when she was 15, while his brother had had several children with different mothers. Listening to these stories of relational breakdown and abandonment, the therapist asked Vince to consider whether, through his self-flagellation, he might in a sense be abandoning himself.
>
> While aware that considerable shame, guilt and grief were lurking in the atmosphere, the therapist noticed that she herself didn't *feel* anything; somewhat to her surprise, her normally considerable store of compassion and empathy seemed to have run dry. In the face of Vince's self-denigration, she felt deadened. The therapist shared this curious bodily experience with Vince. She asked him if he too sometimes felt so overwhelmed with emotions that he ended up feeling deadened.
>
> Vince's response was electric. He came alive suddenly, astonished that she could recognise how it was for him. It was at this point that he became more fully engaged with therapy and committed himself to confronting and exploring the emotions underlying his 'desensitisation'.[7]

The actual process that is engaged to bring about 'change' depends partly on the theoretical perspective. *Psychoanalytic* therapists would primarily look for insight into unconscious processes and focus on intrapersonal conflicts; *gestalt* therapists would seek increased awareness towards self-integration; *systemic* and *cognitive-behavioural* therapists would focus on maladaptive cognitions and behavioural change.

40   ENGAGING THE THERAPEUTIC PROCESS

In relational integrative terms, the therapist engages clients' processes. For instance, it is not sufficient to just note a client's so-called 'resistance'; therapist and client together work to identify the intersubjective danger that makes/made the resistance necessary.

> It is only when the analyst shows that he or she knows the patient's fear and anguish and thereby becomes established to some degree as a calming, containing, idealized other, that the patient begins to feel safe enough to . . . allow his or her subjective life to emerge more freely. (Atwood & Stolorow, 2014, p. 50)

Taking an integrative *trans-theoretical approach to change*, Prochaska and DiClemente (1982, 2005) suggest 10 distinct change processes: (1) consciousness raising; (2) self-liberation; (3) social liberation; (4) counterconditioning; (5) stimulus control; (6) self-re-evaluation; (7) environmental re-evaluation; (8) contingency management; (9) helping relationships; and (10) dramatic relief. They propose a 'stages of change' model which can serve as a guide for both therapists and clients to identify client's motivation in terms of what processes need to be engaged (see figure 3.1).

This cycle of change model has been used (and researched) extensively and has been employed most commonly to work with specific behavioural change: for instance, dealing with substance abuse or promoting healthy behaviour.[8] The model offers a way to match the processes of change to the stage reached (see box 3.5).

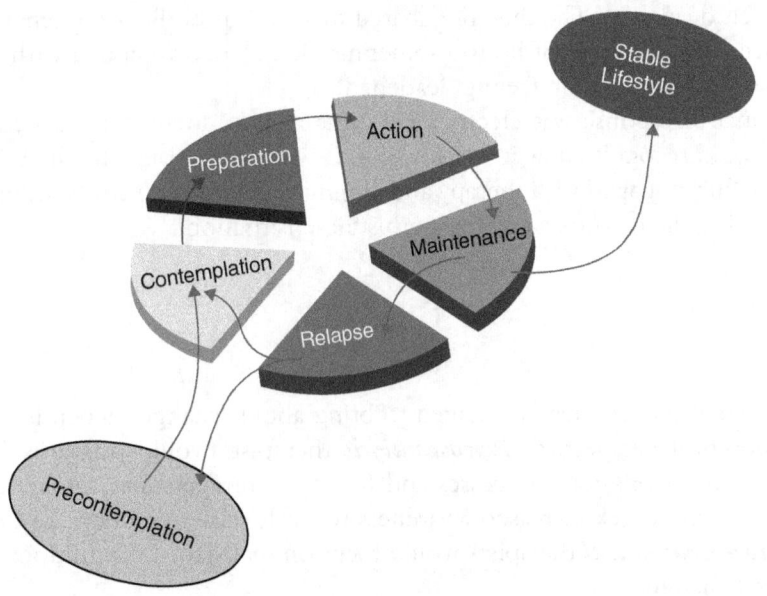

Figure 3.1   Prochaska and DiClemente's (1982) Cycle of Change.

Box 3.5 Theory: Bringing about change

In the initial **precontemplation** stage clients do not see themselves as having a problem or needing to change: in fact, they tend to resist change. (They are not seen as being uncooperative or as resisting the therapist in this model.) Clients in this group may have been forced to come to therapy by outside agencies (for example the mother who is forced by Court Order to attend therapy having had a child taken into care; or the child who is brought to therapy by a parent). Working with this stage, the therapist needs to be more of an empathetic, non-judgemental ally. Rather than attempting to coerce the client to change, it can be helpful simply to increase awareness about the problem and surrounding issues.

When the client is ready to **contemplate** change, the therapist is both supportive and challenging while taking care to be patient and avoid guilt, blame or premature impulsive action. Together therapist and client focus on making the client's fears explicit while acknowledging that change will be in the client's best interest. Clients are often in this phase early in therapy when engaging the therapeutic relationship. They probably recognise they have a problem and are contemplating change, but still sit on the fence; they don't yet want to commit to changing (for example, the client might have checked out treatment options but hasn't yet signed up).

In the **action** phase, the client is fully engaged in therapy and committed to change (for instance, they have decided to give up alcohol or leave an abusive partner). At this point, the therapist might assume a more formal teaching role and the client can lean on the confidence of the therapist about how to move forward. Over time, the client becomes more independent and less idealising of the 'therapist as expert'.

In the **maintenance** phase the therapist acts more like a consultant, letting go in order to enable the client to assume full ownership of the change. If the client relapses in their problematic behaviour, then the full cycle may be engaged once more.

Being Present to Relational Processes

Perhaps the biggest lesson learned by students training to be relational therapists is to move beyond wondering 'What can I do to help my client feel better?' to '*What kind of relationship does my client need?*' (Markin, 2014). Then it's a matter of evolving that relationship.

The therapeutic relationship needs constant care and vigilant attention. Yalom recommends attending to it explicitly, at least once an hour:

42   ENGAGING THE THERAPEUTIC PROCESS

Does the patient seem distant today? Competitive? Inattentive to my comments? Does he make use of what I say in private but refuse to acknowledge my help openly? Is she overly respectful? Obsequious? Too rarely voicing any objection or disagreements? Detached or suspicious? Do I enter his dreams or daydreams? . . . All these things I want to know, and more. I never let an hour go by without checking into our relationship, sometimes with a simple statement like: 'How are you and I doing today?' (Yalom, 2001, pp. 11–12)

The likely focus of work in the early stages is raising awareness of clients' experiences and relationships in the outside world; however, this exploration occurs in the context of the therapeutic alliance. The alliance itself offers a blank canvas for potential relational themes, including those relating to positive/negative feelings, acceptance/rejection, safety/risk, attachment/separation, confluence/conflicts, similarities/difference in social identities, and asymmetry of power. Working through and integrating these complex human themes presents challenges for both client and therapist. "The challenge will be whether the participants can work through the relational barriers and inhibitions and genuinely meet each other in a way that is functional to therapeutic change" (Paul & Pelham, 2000, p. 116). The relational dance begins.

As the dance proceeds, the therapist strives to remain attuned, open and responsive to the client's relational field. This can only happen if the therapist starts from a relatively 'unknowing' position characterised by active curiosity and genuine compassion. The therapist needs to approach each session without the desire to cure or influence and without the illusion of understanding based on theoretical certainties (Bion, 2005). We should not be in a hurry to soothe, rescue or reframe clients' hurts and angers. If a client is angry they are calling attention to injustice and they may be seeking the right just to be angry. We need to be prepared to allow things to spontaneously emerge in the intersubjective space between therapist and client – and to have faith that it will (Finlay & Evans, forthcoming).

Our work is to be flexibly attuned to what each individual is needing relationally. A client who has been overwhelmed by a smothering parent or an aggressive, demanding partner might require a therapist who is quietly non-intrusive and calm, allowing the client to be. A client who has been sexually or physically abused is likely to need a therapist who uses touch and/or anger cautiously. A client whose significant others have been more passive, flat or non-responsive might need a therapist who offers a more lively way of being. There are no rule books; we must rely on our sensitive attunement together with intuitions and awareness of our counter-transferential responses.

Then we can be "co-opted and prompted to incarnate themes and roles from the client's drama" (Paul & Pelham, 2000, p. 118), perhaps by working with transferences and projective identifications (see chapter 14). But it is important that we *do not simply replay and repeat* the client's life drama. Instead, therapy offers an opportunity to experience different outcomes and a *new way of being*. It is in this space of exploratory challenge, creativity and acceptance that healing can emerge.

ENGAGING THE THERAPEUTIC PROCESS 43

Box 3.6 shows how therapy with a relational *transactional analytic* orientation attempts to move beyond both the replaying of *scripts* (that is, 'life plans' that include introjections about how we 'should' be) and the repetition of patterns towards creative reparation. We also see the impact of a temporary relational rupture. But ruptures in the therapeutic alliance, in the form of a break in trust or where negative transference intrudes, also offer important therapeutic opportunities for repair.[9]

Box 3.6 Case illustration: Being present to relational processes

Nicole, a 26-year-old single mother, seemed locked in a persecutory *drama triangle* with her ex-partner, whom she perceived as routinely undermining her. Yet in their arguments she often ended up shouting abuse at him; she seemed to lurch precariously between being 'victim' and 'persecutor'.

Listening to Nicole's stories of escalating conflict with her ex, the therapist sought to bring Nicole's emotional (if not physical) safety into the frame by inviting her to step back and attend to her own needs. But Nicole appeared locked into her toxic relational patterns, developed from her early relationship with a violent father. She seemed unwilling – or unable – to try out different responses.

With Nicole continuing to describe arguments which resulted in her feeling hurt and aggrieved, the therapist decided to offer a gentle confrontation. Might Nicole be choosing to accept the abuse in some way and, if so, what was the pay-off for her?

Nicole admitted her fear of being alone and that contact with the ex was better than nothing, particularly as he offered help with child-care. When the therapist expressed her concern for Nicole's *self*-care, her client turned on her. She shouted, 'F*** off! You have no right to attack me like this and make me into the "victim". I'm not a f***ing victim. You're talking therapist shit! Who do you think you are to tell me how I should be?'

The therapist was deeply impacted by this attack and felt 'wiped out'. Momentarily losing her thinking, she became a hurt, anxious child. Despite this she recognised that her counter-transferential feelings may represent something of what life must have been like for Nicole with her violent, disparaging father. The analysis helped ground her and she was able to focus on Nicole once more. She held Nicole's gaze. 'Is this the way your father shouted at you when you were a kid? I'm feeling massively swiped by you. Is this what it was like for you growing up?'

Nicole immediately crumpled in tears. 'Yes, exactly like. And with my ex.'

Resisting the pull to replay *drama triangle* dynamics (see chapter 16), the therapist attempted to model a process of stepping back and establishing boundaries. 'Nicole, I am fine with you expressing your anger but I don't want your swipes,' she told her. 'I think it's important to try to work out where your anger is coming from and who it needs to be aimed at.'

Concluding Reflections

The focus of this chapter has been on the early weeks of therapy, when we seek to motivate clients to engage themselves as fully as possible in therapy and the therapeutic relationship. Initially our role is to be a witness and help to raise awareness of the client's experience. Later it can be contextualised, normalised or worked through.

For those of us with personal experience of being a client, the difficulty of therapy is well understood: to be brought face to face with our pain can be excruciating. As therapists, we have a crucial role to play in gently nudging clients to move beyond habitual safe ways of being and enter uncharted, open waters. To achieve this, we must listen attentively, tuning into the needs, emotions, and complex inner world of every client (this process is examined further in the next chapter).

None of this is possible, however, without the foundation of an effective **therapeutic alliance**, one that offers clients safety, a trustworthy refuge, and the opportunity to drop their defences. If a client is going to 'let go', they need to know they will be respected and kept safe. The therapist's skill comes in recognising what it means for the client to 'be safe'. Is it not shaming, or not dismissing, or not ignoring, or not abandoning? Or is it an actively positive, loving, admiring, reflective and kindly presence, perhaps offering straight, honest and respectful challenge?

The therapist particularly engages a client's readiness to change and their commitment to therapy. As Yalom (2001, p. 139) notes, "It is the engagement that counts, and we therapists do most good by identifying and helping to remove the obstacles to engagement." Thus engaged, therapist and client can set sail, a limitless horizon stretching ahead.

Notes

1   Reflection and reflexivity can be seen on a continuum. At one end, reflection can be understood as 'thinking about something'. At the other end, reflexivity is a more dynamic, continuing, non-judgementally critical self-awareness (Finlay & Gough, 2003).

2   Evans and Gilbert (2005) assert that Kohut's self-psychology and other 'one-person' psychologies (like psychoanalytic and client-centred therapy), where the focus is on the client's intrapsychic growth, don't go far enough to focus on the *relational* ground between client and therapist. They argue that *dialogical gestalt psychotherapy* (Hycner, 1991/1993) and *relational psychoanalysis* (Mitchell and Aron, 1999) both

helpfully extend practice to encompass a 'two-person' relational perspective. In addition, they call for therapists to attend more to the broader cultural-ecological context.

3   'Deflection' is a term used particularly in *gestalt* therapy to describe a process of turning aside from direct contact with another so as to reduce awareness of and the impact of the environment or self. It can take many forms: for instance, cracking a joke to reduce intensity, not looking at the other, being verbose, being vague, beating about the bush, or intellectualising.

4   The idea of being non-judgemental originally arose from the *person-centred* work of Rogers and is sometimes applied in simplistic, blanket

ways whereby the therapist's unconditional positive regard can result in the therapist not being fully present. Many **relational-integrative** therapists prefer a non-judging version which still includes them authentically disclosing their own values. Instead of saying, 'I think you *should* have . . .', the therapist might say, 'If that had been my decision, I think I might have . . .' or 'My religious beliefs would lead me to xxx but I can respect your different cultural values.'

5   In neuroscience terms, the process of tracking the emotional world of the client is captured by the idea of 'right brain'-to-'right brain' communications (Schore, 2012).

6   Erskine distinguishes between *creative adjustment* and *accommodation* in recognising that the person will sometimes adjust to their situation; with accommodation there is a change of self in order to survive: for instance, becoming a 'quiet, good girl' instead of a 'naughty chatterbox'.

7   'Desensitisation' refers to dysfunction in the *sensation* phase of the Gestalt cycle (though it can occur in other phases too) and commonly occurs when sensations from the body (e.g. discomfort) are ignored or when information from the environment is blocked out. The 'neurotic' person avoids experiencing themselves or the environment; sensations and feelings are diluted or neglected (Clarkson, 1989); see chapter 13.

8   Prochaska and DiClemente recognise that their model of change focuses on 'intentional change' as distinct from any developmental or environmental change that may cause people to alter their lives. They acknowledge that for more complicated issues and sustained change, it may be necessary to work more deeply at interpersonal and intrapersonal conflict beyond an immediate focus on changing behaviour.

9   Put in neuroscience terms, affectively charged moments of therapy such as these *rupture–repair processes* present an opportunity for the therapist to offer affect-regulating relationship where new internal working models are encoded in the client's brain (Schore, 2012).

4

Empathising and Attuning

I do not ask the wounded person how he feels, I myself become the wounded person, My hurts turn livid upon me as I lean on a cane and observe. (Walt Whitman, 'Song of Myself')

Empathy and attunement are the foundation of therapy. When we empathically attune to another we gently tune into, sense, and resonate with their experience. It is like the two violins in a room: when the strings on one are plucked, the other vibrates too if it is tuned to the same frequency (Rowan & Jacobs, 2002, p. 80).

While much evidence shows that empathy and attunement are among the most demonstrably effective elements of the therapeutic relationship (Cooper, 2008), as processes they remain elusive. Their multi-dimensional nature, involving cognition, emotion, body and developmental-relational elements, makes them hard to describe. The fact that different theorists define them in varied ways adds to their complexity: while some use the terms fluidly and interchangeably, others distinguish between them sharply. As ever, much depends upon the theoretical lens applied. In this chapter I contrast *person-centred* and *relational psychoanalytic* perspectives. Loosely speaking, person-centred therapists focus on 'empathy' while relational psychoanalytic therapists favour 'attunement'.[1]

To avoid becoming mired in semantics and theoretical debate, I adopt a heuristic device to visualise the two concepts as separate but overlapping circles, with the overlap representing 'empathic attunement' (see figure 4.1). In line with this idea, I begin this chapter by discussing **empathy** and **attunement** separately. Then, in a

---

Relational Integrative Psychotherapy: Engaging Process and Theory in Practice, First Edition. Linda Finlay.
© 2016 John Wiley & Sons, Ltd. Published 2016 by John Wiley & Sons, Ltd.

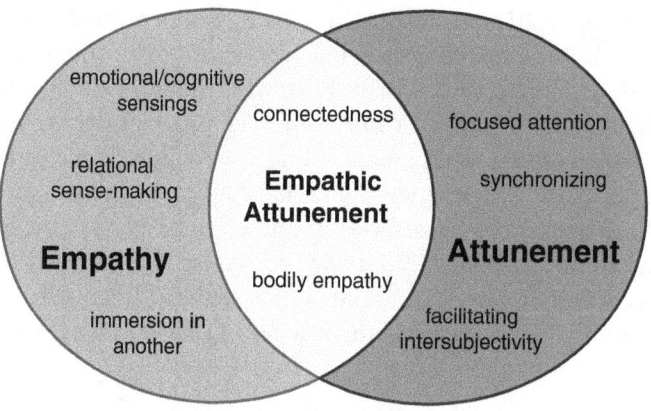

Figure 4.1   Empathy and attunement

section on **empathic attunement**, I try to capture how, in practice, therapists move between levels of contact and involvement in a kind of relational rhythmic dance.

Empathy

The term 'empathy'[2] – the English translation of the German *Einfühlung* – means 'feeling into', gently sensing another person in order to better appreciate their experience. In popular parlance it is known as 'stepping into another's shoes'. Carl Rogers (1980, p. 142) described it as the condition of being sensitive to "felt meanings which flow in the other person". For him, empathy is a *process* rather than a state; as such it is relational and embodied rather than simply cognitive/affective:

> It means entering the private perceptual world of the other and becoming thoroughly at home in it. It involves being sensitive, moment to moment, to the changing felt meanings which flow in this other person . . . .. It means temporarily living in his/her life, moving about in it delicately without making judgments . . . as you look with fresh and unfrightened eyes. (Rogers, 1975, p. 3)

The description above links to Rogerian *person-centred* counselling techniques of reflecting back clients' meanings through summarising and use of matching non-verbal back-channel responses (head nods, uh-huhs). Done well, such techniques involve much more than simply repeating clients' words. Instead, implicit meanings are engaged.

Beyond technique, empathy is a *relational* process. When clients go into therapy, usually they struggle to articulate their troubles; more is felt and sensed. Here, we check out their meanings. 'Behind your words I'm hearing you say you've lost hope. Am I picking that up right?' Or 'That's some burden you've been carrying. I'm guessing you feel robbed?'

48 EMPATHISING AND ATTUNING

In moments of **relational depth** (Mearns & Cooper, 2005), we empathically attune to the whole of the client's being (resonating with them) and experience a profound immersion in their world. However, empathy involves neither fusion with the client nor projection of our own perspective. Instead, we strive to be *open to the client's Otherness*. It's not, 'I know your experience of raging against your mother because I experience the same.' Rather, it's about getting in touch with something unexpected and allowing oneself to be awed in the face of the unfamiliar. Murphy and Dillon (1998, p. 88) recognise that empathy requires a shift in perspective to listen within the other's perspective: "It's not what I would experience *as me* in your shoes; empathy is what I experience *as you* in your shoes."

Bodily Empathy

Numerous humanistically orientated therapists have built on Rogers's recognition that empathy is not just a cognitive or affective process. Kepner (2003), taking a *gestalt* perspective, makes the body figural by seeing therapy as enabling clients to reclaim a fully embodied self. He offers an impassioned plea for therapists to attend to their own embodied souls as well as those of their clients. Cooper's (2001) *existential person-centred* approach allows a space for embodied awareness and 'somatic empathy'. This enables an "experiencing of how another person is in their world that reaches down to the very depths of our toes, that infuses our body, and that gives us a lived, vital awareness of how it is for them as a cognitive-affective-somatic whole" (Mearns & Cooper, 2005, p. 130).

At its best, the process of experiencing clients' meanings transcends an intellectual exercise to become a kind of receiving which is an embodied lived experience in itself. When I am with a client, I am over 'there' with them, sensing, moving, empathising, responding and resonating with my whole body-self.

At the same time, we need to be sufficiently self-aware to hold on to our own **presence**. For instance, when attending to my own bodily sensations, I might experience the sense of having a clenched, tight ball in my abdomen. Is that me? Or does it belong to my client? Might my sensation be linked in some mysterious way to the client's experience? Could it be that my body is vibrating to something occurring *between*? In this mode of embodied empathy, Cooper (2001, p. 223) explains, the therapist is "not resonating with specific thoughts, emotions or bodily sensations, but with the complex, gestalt-like mosaic of her client's embodied being, that initial primal thrust of the client's experiencing as it emerges into the world".

In my practice I try to be empathically present with my clients while simultaneously engaging *reflexive embodied empathy* (Finlay, 2005, 2014). I believe it helps to have a critical, embodied self-awareness, a capacity to reflect on our own (inter-) subjectivity, processes, assumptions and interests. Box 4.1 shows how, in an effort to try to understand Kath's experience, I momentarily 'transposed' myself into Kath's body and imagined what it would be like to live within it: within a body in reality much bigger than my own. The example illustrates how, in empathy, we may partially re-experience/re-enact something of the Other's experience.[3]

EMPATHISING AND ATTUNING　49

> ## Box 4.1 Case illustration: Bodily empathy
>
> **Kath** was describing the experience of being mistrusted by her colleagues and as a result feeling attacked by them. She was finding herself becoming a different person – a 'ghost' of herself.
>
> KATH:　　I felt the person who left that college was not me. Or was a paler shade of me . . . I had to kind of slow down in a sense, not in speed sense but in a kinda closure sense . . . in a protective sense . . . I became a different kind of me, a lesser me.
>
> I was struck by the way she seemed to have lost the embodied way of being she had previously relied upon. Instead of being vivacious, bright, open, dynamic and humorous, she was describing the experience of 'pulling herself in' and becoming quiet and wary. Where once she had felt herself to be a 'big' person – in terms of both her presence and her personality – she was now being made to feel 'reduced' . . .
>
> In the course of our dialogue, she . . . somehow started to 'fade' in front of my very eyes. I could feel a strange sensation within myself, a sense of closing down, closing in, shrinking, trying to become smaller, trying to become a 'paler' version of myself.
>
> An empathic reflection. *Slowly I was disappearing. Then I realised that, strangely enough, this new reality actually felt safer. If I couldn't be seen, I wouldn't be hurt . . . I dwelt there some more . . . I could understand and accept Kath's need to 'reduce' and close down. At the same time, I began to feel something else. Losing myself also felt slightly scary. Who would I be and who would I become if I was to disappear to be replaced by a paler-shaded me? I became aware that I felt somehow sad at the loss of my customary embodied way of being. I looked at Kath and she, too, seemed to me to be sad and a little lost – indeed, vulnerable in her loss.* (King, Finlay, Ashworth, Smith, Langdridge and Butt, 2008)

Levels of Empathy

In addition to distinguishing between cognitive/affective and bodily empathy, some writers have attempted to describe different levels of empathic contact. Hart (1999), for example, suggests that nine different facets of empathic knowing occur in therapy. He contrasts 'external empathy' with **deep empathy**. In the former, the therapist is observer, perceiving another's experience *as if* they were them. With deep empathy, there is a more direct intersubjective knowing which transcends subject–object.

Similarly, Rowan and Jacobs (2002) describes three levels of 'therapist being': instrumental, authentic and transpersonal.[4] At the **instrumental** level, therapists can learn sets of skills, including a basic, safe (defended) level of empathic listening skills. With the **authentic** self, akin to Hart's 'deep empathy', we enter the

50 EMPATHISING AND ATTUNING

client's world; there is a loosening of self–other boundaries. Applied to psycho-analytic practice, projective identification would be involved along with other transferential dynamics (as in Kohut's self-psychology transferences; see box 4.2). At the **transpersonal** level, boundaries between therapist and client fall away, re-sulting in a transcendental, even soulful or spiritual 'linking' – what Buber (1965) would call 'the Interhuman'.[5]

Box 4.2 Theory: Empathy and transference in Kohut's Self-psychology

The *relational psychoanalyst* Heinz Kohut (1984) argued that the therapist's task is to provide the client with a 'corrective emotional experience' through empathy involving a sustained committed listen-ing. Here, the therapist needs to be able to see the client's point of view or, at least, let them know that the therapist is trying their best to understand.

Through empathy, the therapist can be used (as an object) to gratify the early developmental needs relating to narcissism, which Kohut sees as a healthy stage in child development. Empathy permits the natural un-folding of various narcissistic transferences from the client, which Kohut clarifies as the *mirroring* transference, the *idealising* transference and the *twinship* transference. If these needs are not adequately met, the child will not develop a healthy sense of self. It follows that it's through the therapist's empathic response ('transmuting internalization') that the client can grow. Through the transference relationship the client attempts to get certain relational desires met towards supporting their self-esteem. The process is one of moving from having the therapist as an internal self-object to the more autonomous state of having an 'inner good parent'.

Mirroring transference

In child development terms, Kohut argued that growing infants need to be shown by significant caregivers that they are special and wanted. Infants need to have their mini-achievements celebrated and their natural egocentric grandiosity valued by their caregivers in order to gain a healthy self-esteem and a sense that they will be loved for who they are, irrespec-tive of what they do. In therapeutic terms, the therapist works through this transference by mirroring: praising, applauding, acknowledging and valuing clients' feelings of pride in their achievements.

Idealising transference

As infants grow, they look up to their parent/s as strong, powerful and confident. As they explore the world, they learn to count on their parent/s to provide a sense of safety, security and freedom. The child idealises and admires this all-powerful caregiver, thereby absorbing the admired qualities of the caregiver into their own values and ambitions. In therapy, the client may initially idealise the therapist. Therapists can find this uncomfortable though the idealising becomes more bearable when we recognise its self-object function. As the therapist reveals some fallibility during the course of therapy, however, clients come to develop a more realistic picture of the therapist's limitations. If this process involves 'optimal frustrations' (such as the therapist being late for an appointment) rather than dramatic, unmanageable disillusionment (forgetting the client's name and history), the client's narcissism should follow a healthy pattern of development.

Twinship transference

Children also need to know that they share important characteristics with their parent/s: this helps them develop a sense of belonging and be welcomed into the world of human beings. As they grow, they long for and develop other affirming relationships. This stage needs to occur for the child to develop social skills with family, friends and the wider community. In therapy, twinship might be expressed by the client having a friendly interest in the therapist's experience and noting shared interests (that is, therapists show more of themselves), or by instances when therapist and client chuckle together.

As we move into another's world, we may lose our own identity momentarily. But it is likely to be unhelpful to the client for us to join them in their pain; we need to hold onto ourselves and maintain a therapy perspective simultaneously. This is the key to Buber's notion of 'inclusion': "You can see it, feel it, experience it from two sides. From your side, seeing him, observing him, knowing him, helping him – from your side and from his side" (Buber, 1965, p. 171).

In practice, then, we tend to move between levels of empathy and reflexively stepping back. Simultaneously being-with 'inside' and being 'outside', looking in, is not easily achieved.

This section has explored how empathy equates to a compassionate sensing of another person's experience. Importantly, this empathy involves an embodied-relational process and is not just focused on an individual's thinking/feeling.

Given that different levels of empathy are possible, we need to be reflexively self-aware. How deep should we go, and when? Are we becoming too confluent with our clients' experience? Do we need to apply the brakes?

Some clients may need more compassionate emotional-bodily mirroring than others. Those inclined to be highly sensitive, suspicious, or reactive against authority may appreciate a therapist's *cognitive* understanding more than emotional empathy. Hargaden (2013) amongst others suggests that the over-use of empathy can smother clients or give them a false sense of value and esteem, hindering the development of resilience and independence. Attuning more closely to our clients helps us to avoid these traps. In fact it can be argued that empathy works best in a context of attunement.

Attunement

To attune means to adjust to another in sympathetic, synchronous relationship, to bring into harmony. Musical metaphors like resonance, rhythm, duet and chorus come to mind when describing an attuned relationship (perhaps unsurprisingly given the 'tune' in at-*tune*).

Applied to therapy, attunement is the term used to describe our **reactiveness** to clients and our harmonic fit with them. The well-attuned therapist tunes in and responds to the emotional tone of the client.

The process is one of being 'in sync' with the client, tracking subtle shifts and movements in their experience and then focusing selectively on what seems most alive, significant or poignant for them. Attunement involves mediating emotion; it is akin to the way an attuned parent, noticing a child's distress, will take steps to offer comfort. It's about giving appropriate responses, not just crying because the client is crying.

Pearmain (2001) defines attunement as a sense of connectedness and **focused awareness**. She points to the subtly responsive rhythmic pattern of dialogue which emerges as attunement moves beyond empathic words (see box 4.3):

> Often in the moments between words, it is as if a kind of invisible echo continues to resonate both in the therapist and client. A deeper sound from the words continues to affect both at an experiential level. . . . The therapist's response represents the degree to which he or she is fitting with the communication of the client, or matching or recasting it to resonate with other related or deeper issues. . . . [A] new chord . . . has been created between them. (p. 103)

Box 4.3 Case illustration: Therapeutic attunement

Patrick Casement describes a patient who is speaking so quietly that he can hardly hear her. Rather than asking her to speak more loudly he begins to sense that in the softness of her asking there might be a significant communication.

> I think there is something important about the way in which you are talking to me – talking so that I can hardly hear. I could again have asked you to speak louder. Instead I have realized that I will only pick up what you are trying to get across to me if I listen very carefully, as a mother might with her infant who does not have any words. And what I am sensing is that you are feeling that I am not in touch with you. I believe that this is what you need me to understand, that I am not at this moment understanding you. (1990, p. 166)
>
> "At this point, the patient began to cry. When she could speak again she replied: 'But you understood that you did not understand. That is what makes the difference'" (Casement, 1990, p. 166). Casement goes on to recognize the possibility that this patient's parents may have often assumed they had understood her when they had not.

Many *relational psychoanalytic* commentators choose to focus on attunement rather than empathy, which they see as tending towards cognitively based roleplay. For example, Daniel Stern (1985) views attunement as a fundamentally *intersubjective* process, concerned with emotional resonance to inner states rather than with empathising with what is observed. Attunement occurs implicitly and largely out of awareness, without cognitive mediation: "Attunement takes the experience of resonance and automatically recasts that experience into another form of expression" (1985, p. 145). It is the "performance of behaviors that express the quality of feeling of a shared affect state without imitating the exact behavioral expression of the inner state" (p. 142).

Relational psychoanalysts[6] like Stern embrace the concept of attunement in **child development** terms. Attunement is seen in the infant–caregiver relationship, with its rhythmic, non-verbal 'proto-conversations' that move in and out of contact and synchronicity, repair and rupture. Successful attunement is seen in the way a parent mirrors and enables as s/he resonates to and joins with the baby. S/he matches the child, for example, when the infant is expressing joy, distress or need.[7] Infants are seen to gain a positive sense of self and to feel understood by having an attuned caregiver who mirrors and mediates emotions (Sabel, 2012). In addition, attachment theory suggests that the capacity to reflect on one's emotional experience and on the mind of the other (called 'mentalising') grow through caregivers' sensitive attunement (Fonagy & Bateman, 2006).

Of course there are also many everyday moments of *misattunement*: moments when caregivers are unavailable or for some reason fail to pick up on a child's distress. The *good-enough parent* – one who is capable of attuning most of the time – will be able to repair any inevitable mini-ruptures, helping the infant return to a state of internal emotional equilibrium. However, individuals who have had more traumatic experiences involving consistent misattunement or lack of attunement (as in the example of Connie; see box 1.1) may well grow up without a healthy sense of self and will struggle to manage their shame and regulate their emotions.

> Coming to terms with a little bit of frustration does not destroy the baby's essential trust in others and might actually strengthen trust in his or her own sense of agency. But when infants are neglected and not responded to over prolonged periods of time, they sense that their own intentionality cannot find a complement in the world. Ultimately, they will give up trying to bring about change. (Simms, 2008, p. 16)

Numerous examples of mother–baby empathically attuned and misattuned interactions are available online. A particularly powerful YouTube video is the 'still face experiment' where the mother momentarily stops attuning to her child – with rapid and dramatic behavioural consequences (Tronick, 2009).

These theories from child development have been supplemented by an explosion of research in the field of *neuroscience*, which explores the interplay between neurobiology and emotional life. Humans are seen to be biologically predisposed towards intersubjectivity and empathic attunement. Emotions and life experiences, in turn, impact on the developing brain. The relationship and attunement between infant and caregiver involves neurons 'firing and wiring' together to create the architectural structures of the interacting brains. Thus biological systems intertwine with social ones: neurobiological variables influence emotions and behaviour, and vice versa (Schore, 2012).[8]

'Empathic Attunement': A Rhythmic Dance

While empathy and attunement can be contrasted, they also intertwine. Applying the above ideas from child development theory, for instance, Greenberg, Rice and Elliott (1993, p. 104) provide a definition of attunement which implicitly embraces empathy:

> In empathic attunement, one tries to respond to the client's perception of reality at that moment, as opposed to one's own or some 'objective' or external view of what is real. . . The therapist takes in and tastes the client's intentions, feelings, and perceptions, developing a feel of what it is like to be the client at that moment. At the same time, he or she retains a sense of self, as opposed to being swamped by or 'fusing' with the client's experience.

In more recent work referring to *emotion-focused therapy*, Greenberg (2014) suggests that empathic attunement leads to clients developing a capacity for self-empathy and affect regulation.

Erskine, Moursund and Trautmann (1999) similarly argue that effective therapy depends on qualities of attunement, with empathy acting as a foundation. For them, inquiry, attunement and involvement are facets of the overall empathic frame within which the client's growth is nurtured. Attunement involves using both conscious and out-of-awareness *synchronizing* of the therapist and client process, so that the therapist's interventions fit the ongoing, moment-to-moment needs and processes of the client. Beyond empathic feeling, it's about kinaesthetically sensing and moving with the client in a contact-enhancing way.

Further, they offer a comprehensive description of how the multi-layered ways in which therapists use attunement (see box 4.4), including:

- *Affective* attunement. This involves a three-level response: noticing and empathising with the client's affect; vicariously feeling and responding to the emotion; and communicating a response.
- *Cognitive* attunement. Here the therapist attempts to understand the client's thinking and perspective, including their world view and meanings.
- *Developmental* attunement. This involves thinking developmentally and seeing and enabling the client's regression and attending to that 'child's' needs.
- *Rhythmic* attunement. The therapist is responsive to the client's own rhythmic patterns. For example, if the client is a slow thinker, the therapist goes more slowly or speaks more simply and gently when the client is regressed.

Box 4.4 Case illustration: Attuning to grief

Ruth was a mother of a 19-year-old boy who died in a car accident. . . . [I]t seemed premature for her to talk to a fantasized image of her son in an 'empty chair'. I was not certain that she possessed the internal resources to say 'hello' through imagination; I sensed that it was too soon after her son's death. Instead . . . I had Ruth look me in the eye. I asked her to tell me all about her son. I wanted Ruth to experience my full emotional resonance with her feelings and experiences of being a mother of a child who had just died. . . .

She told me that he had been driving the car. He and three other boys had been drunk and they crashed into a store front. As I inquired about her feelings she expressed her anger at his frequent drinking of alcohol and his reckless driving. . . . I . . . expressed how disturbing it is for a parent when children act irresponsibly. . . .

She told me about his brilliant school accomplishments, about the delightful things they did together in his early teenage years, and how loving he had been to her during her divorce. I rejoiced with her . . .

She wept as she talked about his birth . . . and the many instances of loving contact that they shared together. She told me how she admired her son for his many sport and academic accomplishments. Along with her I felt an appreciation of his many qualities. She could see the tears in my eyes as she recalled many special experiences that she and her son had together.

The therapy of Ruth's grief was in our interpersonal contact. . . .

The intersubjective contact – Ruth's expression of each affect and my attuned responses – was essential in Ruth's finding some relief from her grief. (Erskine, 2015, p. 302)

We inevitably move into, out of and through different intensities of closeness and distance, between synergistic merger, rupture and repair. One moment, we can feel a little distant and not well tuned in. The next, the distance dissolves as we open to the client, or perhaps following the discovery of some shared experience. We might then find ourselves drawn into an identification so intense that there may be a sensation of merging or confluence with the client. A rhythmic pulse can also be detected in the reflexive shifts that occur as we move from being focused on the client to focusing on ourselves and the emerging relationship.

Todres (1990), an *existential therapist*, offers a useful model of the experiential feel of this interactional rhythm. Drawing on the broad tradition of depth psychology and existential phenomenology, he describes the process of being empathically attuned in terms of *modes of attention*:

1. **Attentive** *Being-with* involves the therapist being absorbed imaginatively into the phenomenological world of the other – what it's like to be the client. The therapist attempts to mirror and participate in the client's world like a nurturing mother. However, the client needs to feel the therapist can 'survive' the emotional impact and can safely hold them so the therapist maintains their own presence rather than being confluent.

2. With **focusing** *Being-with,* the therapist attends reflexively to their own on-going and evolving understandings in the presence of the client's world. The therapist brings both intuitive capacity and a body of understanding to provide an integrative direction for exploration. The therapist is more active than in the previous mode, alert to images, themes and feelings towards helping the client express, name and make sense of their experience.

3. With **interactive** *Being-with,* the therapist focuses on the relationship *between* and on what is being played out in the moment. The therapist becomes aware of who they are in the other's eyes, responding to feeling idealised or violated, for example. There is a rhythm of moving in and out; being closely involved with the immediacy of the situation and also more distant, via interested curiosity. The therapist brings any confusion to their supervisor[9] and together they attempt the work of distancing towards empowering the therapist to re-enter the stream of ambiguity of the therapy. "This is a land of many colors, of rage and hope, and the therapist is asked to be resilient, often to wait and to grant the gifts of both aloneness and sharing" (p. 40).

4. With **invitational** *Being-with,* the therapist's attention is drawn to a sense of becoming, a future direction – the client's 'growing edge'. While attending to the client's experiential themes, the therapist also attempts to recognise authentic strivings which have only dimly been expressed. For example, here the therapist might see something of what a client looked for when they felt abandoned and then try "to find a voice that can say it in a way that has a future" (p. 41). In listening for the *healthy potential* the therapist offers a healing, integrative vision.

Concluding Reflections

The twinned practices of empathy and attunement involve deeply felt, tuned-in, intuitive, resonant compassion, and a readiness to be moved by that compassion. Spontaneous upsurges of intersubjective identification are combined with intense, focused reflective-reflexive concentration.

While throughout this chapter I have sought to show a range of theoretical understandings of empathy and attunement, I find the debates about whether or not our way of being constitutes empathy or attunement somewhat sterile. As a relational integrative therapist, the concept of **empathic attunement** works for me. Whatever we call 'it', the important thing is that we allow ourselves to be responsively open to the Other and can place ourselves within their subjective or intersubjective perspective.

The attainment of deeper, embodied empathic attunement requires us to let ourselves go into the process, to release our own *Being* in order to *Be-with* in the moment, to relinquish certainty. It means allowing embodied feelings, thoughts, impressions and intuitions to appear. It involves permitting oneself to be open and to be touched. It invites us to respond to the other and move to their rhythm. It means welcoming whatever becomes figural in the moment. But this is a process of embodied intertwining, not a merging: we hold on to ourselves in order to respect the otherness of the Other.

As it unfolds in the space between empathic attunement and reflection, the relational duet of the therapy encounter is a growth-enhancing experience for both therapist and client. As the music of contact plays deftly and harmoniously, there is the potential for past ruptures to heal, ancient traumas to loosen their grip.

Tuning in to the Other and to me, I also tune in to the between. It is as if I am listening intently and with all of me for a tune that is all of us (me, other and us). I listen to the tune being sung by the Other. I try and connect with the deeper song – the song of contact, meeting, connectedness, longing. Even when hidden beneath the negative or closed and cut off, I strain gently to listen to the quiet hum of faith buried beneath the weight of the life of the Other. The weight that I also know and have known – that we all know – of joy and sorrow and hope and despair. . . It feels like being grounded in a repose of lightness that is yet full and deep and open and present with myself and the Other in a spirit of acceptance and compassion. (Finlay & Evans, 2009, p. 125)

Notes

1 Kohut's (1984) focus on empathy in the relational psychoanalytic tradition acts as a bridge, offering a useful underpinning framework for integrative therapists.

2 Much of the literature on empathy/attunement in therapy takes a Western cultural perspective so a broader cultural perspective is needed. The concept of **cultural empathy** prompts us to reach beyond the comfort zone of our individualistic perspectives and engage a relationship-centred and cultural context. For instance, research by Ng and James (2013) suggests that

Chinese clients may not consider therapist empathy a priority and do not necessarily know how to react to feeling-based empathic statements. Other relational factors, such as being non-judgemental and 'having a heart to help' in terms of engaging tasks beyond professional duty, may be more salient.

3 This dialogue comes from a group phenomenological study (King et al., 2008) where we explored, via an in-depth interview, the phenomenon of 'mistrust' as perceived by one participant, Kath.

4 Rowan and Jacobs apply these three modes of therapist being and empathy across the theoretical spectrum. Instrumental empathy is potentially engaged by all practitioners (although possibly not Jungians). *Humanistic* and *psychoanalytic* therapists utilise the deeper forms, which *cognitive-behavioural* and *systemic* therapists wouldn't routinely engage.

5 Buber was an Austrian-born Jewish theologian, educator and existential-phenomenological philosopher. For Buber inclusion and empathy are not the same. He regarded empathy as a 'feeling' among many. Inclusion he saw as an attempt to experience the wholeness of what another is experiencing while holding on to the centre of one's own existence. Buber and Rogers engaged what is now seen as a classic encounter when they debated the nature of *I-Thou* (see box 9.2) and the challenges of applying it in therapy. While Rogers questioned Buber's idea of 'mutuality', arguing that therapist and client were not equal, Buber challenged Rogers's view that self-actualisation was the goal rather than a product of dialogue (Friedman, 1985).

6 Both Stern (1985) and Schore (1994) integrate theories across numerous fields. Stern draws on phenomenological intersubjectivity theory as well as psychoanalytic theory; Schore is a neuro-psychoanalyst who focuses on biological neuroscience, psychological and social interconnections.

7 Stern (1985) talks about **vitality affects**: Attuned to the rising distress of a baby's cries, the parent matches the baby's urgency by quickly picking up the child. Having checked that nothing is seriously wrong, the parent offers some calming, soothing vitality affects, to which the baby attunes, resulting in the crying fading away.

8 Accumulating evidence suggests that the right hemisphere of an infant's brain is involved in attachment and the mother's right hemisphere in comforting functions. The two **right brain** systems are seen to be mutually engaged in affective synchrony, creating a context of attuned resonance that results in a kind of right brain-to-right brain communion (Schore, 1994). Other neuroscience research has focused on the idea of **mirror neurons** (ones that might explain behaviour such as flinching when we see someone wince in pain). These have been hypothesised as underlying our ability to understand others and as forming the basis of empathy and other social skills. However, this research is as yet largely unsubstantiated in terms of human behaviour and remains controversial.

9 Like Cooper (2001), I argue that therapists need to be aware of and take care of their own bodies outside therapy so as not to interrupt any emergent embodied empathy emerging as part of therapy. There is an important role here for **supervision** (Gilbert & Evans, 2000).

5

Holding, Containing and Boundarying

A child's experience becomes a sense of coherent self only within the consistent, affirming, holding presence of responsive others . . . Without important, close others to help contain and soothe a child's hurt and fear, traumatic experience is just too overwhelming for a child to integrate. (DeYoung, 2003, p. 125)

The holding-containing of difficult emotions occurs in various ways, including through the use of medication, meditation, creative activities, deflection, and even avoidance. Therapy offers the possibility of holding-containing boundaries comparable to those a caregiver offers a child.

Holding-containing-boundarying processes are both literal and metaphorical; they involve the therapist striving to offer an emotionally protective, enabling space which metaphorically holds the client and contains their emergent feelings. The safety of the therapy frame allows clients to express feelings and experiences which may be damaging, overwhelming, or potentially explosive and often too shameful or painful to be shared with others. At the same time, the therapist contains their own issues and manages wider professional boundaries.

This chapter approaches the topic from five different angles. The first section focuses on practical and ethical **boundaries** (I use the term 'boundary*ing*' to emphasise the active processes involved). In the second section, the nature of **holding and containing** is discussed in terms of their *psychoanalytic* foundations, while the third considers the **intrapsychic, emotional** and **intersubjective** processes in more depth. It is important to emphasise at the outset that holding-containing-boundarying is not something we 'do' *to* clients: it involves a collaborative, *dialogical* process that occurs within a therapeutic relationship rooted in sharing and witnessing.

Relational Integrative Psychotherapy: Engaging Process and Theory in Practice, First Edition. Linda Finlay.
© 2016 John Wiley & Sons, Ltd. Published 2016 by John Wiley & Sons, Ltd.

In the last two sections I set out some **arguments against** the concept of holding-containing and then focus on what may be needed by therapists themselves in order to cope with being the **contained containers** of emotionally intense material.

Boundarying to Hold and Contain

At the core of therapeutic holding-containing is the (implicit and explicit) work we do to maintain clear, safe boundaries. A boundary, by definition, is something that marks a limit or line that we do not cross. The boundaries we hold in psychotherapy are layered and multiple; for example, we have:

- **legal** boundaries: refusing to break the law or practising to avoid official complaints and malpractice liability;
- **moral** boundaries: refusing to betray moral values, standards and beliefs;
- **emotional** boundaries: refusing to allow another to intrude or get overly close (physically or emotionally) when it is not wanted, and containing emotions that threaten to leak out in harmful ways;
- **relational** boundaries: providing a private space to be-with another, or maintaining the client–therapist relationship as a professional rather than personal one and minimising the confusion of *dual* relationships;
- **professional** boundaries: recognising responsibilities and maintaining professional integrity.

In practice there is nothing simple about boundary holding. We have to learn to hold many boundaries with clients and colleagues in order to keep our client safe, ourselves safe and our profession safe. But the process can be problematic. Confidentiality, for example, is crucial yet it can spawn challenging dilemmas regarding when or how it might be broken.

Boundaries establish a structure for a professional therapeutic relationship and provide a consistent, reliable, **predictable frame** for a process that otherwise remains fluid and mysterious. Boundaries guard the relationship and respect the rights and responsibilities of therapist and client and the separateness between them.

In the clinical context, boundaries prevent unhealthy levels of acting out and keep both client and therapist safe in what is often a charged, intimate encounter. They also acknowledge the power imbalance that is unavoidably part of the therapeutic relationship and set limits for the therapist's expression of power. As Krüger (2007, p. 21) says, "To live with this inherent power is to enter the realm of ethics. The only way of surviving as a true professional is to. . . live with the paradox: to behave ethically and exert power – simultaneously."

Some of our work with boundaries also concerns helping clients discover and own **healthy boundaries** (e.g. ones that ensure they are not cutting off from others while still taking care of themselves). It is not uncommon in therapy to find clients who struggle with boundaries. A client with loose or non-existent boundaries, for instance, may have learned this way of being in childhood as a way of coping with abuse. Not having boundaries in childhood may have served to keep them safe because resisting abuse could mean more hurt.

Beyond ethical codes and **professional guidelines**,[1] there are myriad situations where the delineation of our professional boundaries is problematic. Challenges arise in the field which make our heads spin and our hearts ache (Ellis, 2007). Should a therapist who runs into a client at a party engage in social chitchat? To what extent should a therapist reveal his or her religious beliefs or sexual orientation? Should the therapist accept a personal gift from a client? Should a therapist avoid going to the same church or night class as a client? Should client and therapist both serve on the same institutional committee? Should a therapist treat a client's friend? Should a marital therapist treat one person in the couple after having initially seen the couple together?

The answers to such questions vary according to the cultural, institutional and relational context of the work, the therapist's theoretical persuasion, and the therapist's personal values. Boundarying is a process rather than any form of fixed line, and often we have to work out our position case by case.

For therapists – and clients – who are struggling with boundaries, the paramount question has to be: 'Is this in the client's interests?' If we cannot answer a clear 'yes', then the boundarying is probably suspect.

Two areas of particular concern – practical and ethical/professional – are discussed below.[2]

Practical boundarying

Practical boundaries are the ones we establish in the early, contracting stage of therapy. Fees, the range and limits of confidentiality, and general arrangements regarding the timing and cancelling of appointments all need to be established, along with various implicit and explicit procedures relevant to the context (see chapter 2).

Two particular situations can test our ability to hold the boundary (and thereby contain the therapy). The first is when clients seek to carry on a session beyond the appointment time, and the second is when they ask for contact between sessions. Our time-related boundaries have a specific containing function, so it is worth thinking about these 'tests' further.

It can be tempting sometimes to let go of time boundaries and extend a session when a client is in full emotional flow or on the cusp of a critical insight. A frequently observed phenomenon is the *door handle comment*, where a client saves up something new, significant or shocking for the last few minutes of the session. 'I am about to be fired from my job . . .' However, it would normally be wrong to extend the session at this point. Clients are usually aware of the time passing and it is probably no accident that they have brought up critical material at the last moment. Consciously or unconsciously, the client may well be relying on the time boundary to guard their psychological safety: in other words, to save themselves from going more deeply into emotionally charged material.

Some clients test the limits of the professional relationship by seeking *extra contact* outside appointments: for instance, by texting/emailing messages throughout the week or by making 'crisis calls' in moments of emotional melt-down. The well-meaning but unwary therapist may fall into the trap of offer-ing extra mini-sessions but this is likely to prove counterproductive as, in these uncontracted times, the normal safe frame is not available and contact is rushed. It may be that the client is replaying (out of awareness) parts of their history in which they set up situations where they are not properly seen, thus ensuring their needs cannot be met.

Gutheil and Gabbard (1993) note the particular challenge of working with clients who might be seen as having a borderline personality disorder. Some therapists view out-of-hours phone calls as necessary and expected in light of these clients' inability to evoke a holding, soothing introject; this causes anxiety of catastrophic proportions related to the fear that the therapist will abandon them. Phone calls are then a way to re-establish contact with the therapist and be soothed out of ill-advised self-destructive behaviour. Other therapists view such calls as counter-therapeutic and hold a firmer boundary to emphasise that phone calls are reserved for emergency situations.

Deciding whether or how to respond to calls for extra contact needs careful judge-ment. Clearly some situations are sufficiently urgent to justify an immediate holding-containing response. But often the better-advised therapeutic response is to hold-contain the client within set appointment times by briefly acknowledging the client's need to make a connection but delaying detailed discussion until the next meeting.

> What your client begins to realize is that the kind of being-with that she counts on and longs for is best available to her in session. But as she settles into that rhythm, she also realizes how much more available you are to her in session than she ever imagined could be possible. (DeYoung, 2003, pp. 47–48)

Having stressed the importance of boundarying session time, it can also be use-ful to reflect on times when such boundaries might be loosened. Boundaries are not absolutes and need to be negotiated in specific contexts. I'm interested in the *gestalt* work of Lamprecht (2013) who recommends the spontaneous, contact-full writing of letters to clients, outside of (paid, contracted) sessions. Here a letter may offer valuable feedback to clients that they are important and thought about out-side sessions. They also offer a symbolic psychic/physical link to the therapist which may prove powerful for those clients who are insecurely or ambivalently attached to the therapist. Such 'relationally responsive' letter-writing can provide a valuable therapeutic function, though it needs to be handled sensitively and selectively.

Ethical and professional boundarying

Therapists clearly have a moral, ethical and professional-legal **duty of care** to ensure the safety, both emotional and physical, of their clients. Boundaries ensure that safety. That therapy explicitly taps sensitive material and can be emotionally intense is obvious. It's harder to recognise the extent to which therapy can make clients feel exposed, shamed and vulnerable, and how the experience of retelling their stories has the potential to re-traumatise them. We must honour the profound gift of trust that clients give us and be prepared to handle whatever emerges within the containing boundaries of our practice. The ethical boundaries involved in relational work ultimately require therapists to "acknowledge [their] interpersonal bonds to others, and take responsibility for actions and their consequences" (Ellis, 2007, p. 3).

One particular ethical/professional boundary much debated by therapists from different perspectives is the extent to which **touch** can or should be used in therapy (Smith, Clance & Imes, 1996). While some therapists routinely use touch and see it as being an actively therapeutic mode of being-with, for others touch is taboo. In general, therapists who subscribe to *humanistic* and *body-orientated* therapies are more likely to have physical contact with their clients. However, Deurzen-Smith (1997, p. 257), writing from an *existential perspective*, is clear that "Existential work is done through conversation and silent being together. It does not involve physical contact", and that metaphorical hugs may be the better option. In contrast, Moursund and Erskine (2004), with their *gestalt/ TA-orientated framework*, argue that touch is likely to be actively helpful in a truly contact-full relationship when painful experiences are being explored.

Decisions about the use of touch also demand reflection on the type of touch that is proposed and how that touch is likely to be received by the client (polite-ritual, compassionate or friendly touch as distinct from sexual touch which is *always* unacceptable and off-limits). The client's history and developmental level need careful consideration: a psychotherapist's touch may re-traumatise a person who has been sexually assaulted while absence of touch may replay experiences of parental coldness or neglect (Clarkson, 2003). If the client is regressed, in a young place, the touch may feel like parental comfort (see box 5.1). For a client in a more adult place, that same touch could feel sexually loaded and invasive.

Box 5.1 Case illustration: The use of 'holding' touch

While engaged in some deep reparative, relational-developmental work, a client became tearful. In a paternal counter-transferential response, the therapist felt urged to hold his client like a baby and he checked out with her if he might follow his intuition. She agreed. As she went into his arms she immediately started to sob.

Later the client disclosed that she had almost never been held by her father. When she had been a baby, he had held her and sneezed violently which resulted in her being dropped (where she sustained a neck injury that had resulted in a small but lifelong deformity). Thereafter the father refused to hold his daughter again – something that for over 40 years she had (out of her awareness) yearned for.

Sensitivity and care, combined with respectful, permission-seeking questions such as 'May I give you a hug?' are in order here. The client needs to be in charge of when and how touch is given. Sometimes, particularly early in your relationship, it might be best simply to invite the client to put their own hand on their 'aching heart' or to hold themselves soothingly.

Defining the Nature of 'Holding' and 'Containing'

The therapeutic concepts of holding and containing evoke a maternal metaphor:[3]

> What is needed is a form of holding, such as a mother gives to her distressed child. There are various ways in which one adult can offer to another this holding (or containment). (Casement, 1985, p.133)

Holding refers to the actual and symbolic image of a baby held tenderly and protectively in a mother's arms (and even before birth being held in comfort in the mother's womb). In therapy, this concept is extended to include the broader emotional and physical environment, including the provision of a safe setting and a regular routine. It is because of the relationship with our clients that they feel held and safe. The client's anxiety, alarm, confusion, distress, and pain are all held safe by the therapist.

The concept of *containing* is based on Jung's (1968) idea that the therapy process can be likened to an alchemical container in which the chemicals are the thoughts and feelings of both patient and analyst which have to be held safely. All of us have experienced times when we lose our capacity to cope with feelings. Perhaps our usual coping mechanisms, whether of avoidance or suppression, are simply not up to the task. Our uncontrolled, unmanageable feelings may then spill out, perhaps as part of an unconscious 'I feel out of control' attempt at communication.

Beyond this more everyday sense of containment, *psychoanalytic* theory (see box 5.2) uses the idea of containment to refer to the way an infant may project onto its mother painful, frightening, angry, unbearable feelings. The mother experiences these feelings and then returns them to the infant in a modified, containable way. Mirroring this process, the therapist enables the cathartic expression of emotion while containing clients' projections. By working through these emotions with a reflective, 'Adult' therapist, clients learn to think through their experience and contain their own feelings.

Such processes can be understood in the light of **attachment theory** (see box 2.4), where a caregiver's sensitive responsiveness towards an infant is hypothesised to be key in determining the individual's security in future relationships. While securely attached children learn healthy relational patterns, *avoidant* attachment histories have been linked to obsessional, narcissistic and schizoid problems, *ambivalent* attachment has been correlated with histrionic difficulties, and *disorganised* attachment seems to result in borderline styles (Wallin, 2007).[4]

Box 5.2 Theory: Psychoanalytic foundations of holding and containing

Donald Winnicott's concept of 'holding' and Wilfred Bion's concept of 'containing' are sometimes used in an interchangeable way in the psychoanalytic literature. The two concepts are in fact different.

Winnicott's 'holding'

Winnicott (1953, 1971) coined the term 'holding environment' to describe the optimal environment for good-enough parenting. He believed that emotional problems developed when a person had been deprived of adequate holding environments in childhood and so this holding was critical to the therapeutic environment.

A key function of the mother's or carer's early holding is to insulate her baby from the impact of external demands. At this stage she prioritises the needs of the baby over her own need to sleep, be nourished by others, and be separate from her baby (Ogden, 2004). In this way the mother adapts to her baby's needs and rhythms, and chooses the moments when the real world can be allowed slowly into the child's experience.

> The good-enough mother . . . starts off with an almost complete adaptation to her infant's needs, and as time proceeds she adapts less and less completely, gradually, according to the infant's growing ability to deal with her failure. (Winnicott, 1953, p. 94)

For Winnicott, a good-enough parent gradually increases the amount of time between the emotion and expression of a childhood need (e.g. crying) and the meeting of that need (feeding, comforting). Through this process, infants recognise themselves to be separate and different from their parents; they come to understand that they can survive scary moments and feelings of being overwhelmed by emotions and needs, until the parent eventually comes and provides. In contrast, the overly vigilant, so-called 'perfect' parent doesn't allow the child to experience threats or discomfort. As a result the child never learns to deal with anxiety and never develops a sense of itself as independent and capable of surviving in the world.

Bion's 'containing'

Bion (1967, 1962) is probably best known for his ideas about containment involving the 'alpha function' of the mother (or caregiver). Here,

(*Continued*)

the mother receives unwanted or overwhelming projections from an infant, processes them and then returns the experience to the infant in a modified, palatable form. In similar fashion, the therapist-container takes in thoughts or feelings from the client, and then represents them in a modified form so as to make them more understandable and less destructive.

According to Bion, infants may become overwhelmed by their experience because they lack sufficient internal controls. The mother listens to, and empathically tunes into, the child's communications, and gives them meaning before returning them in a modified, more manageable form. Containment thus develops the infant's capacity for self-regulation and plays a part in giving meaning to experience. This occurs as the infant takes in (internalises) a sense of being contained and experiences the mother's emotional availability. Eventually the child develops their own capacity for containment.

Bion wrote around the theme of containment in different, sometimes rather mysterious ways. He pointed to the *container–contained* dynamic, highlighting how largely unconscious processes (the contained) interact with the capacity for reverie, dreaming and thinking (the container). Bion (1961) extended his theorising to describe social groups in terms of their maternal holding environment.

Just as the good-enough mother knows how to listen and adapt to her baby, so the therapist listens and adapts to the client. In the creative holding-containing space, the client can maintain a closeness with the therapist while having their own separate space and separateness respected.[5] This holding-containing process goes beyond technique to become a fundamentally relational *being-with*.

Casement links holding and containing with empathy (see chapter 4) in his concept of *analytic holding*: the capacity to tolerate complete attunement with the client's feelings yet remain a functioning therapist (see box 5.3).

Patients have taught me that when I allow myself to feel (even be invaded by) the patient's own unbearable feelings, and if I can experience this (paradoxically) as both unbearable and yet bearable, so that I am still able to find some way of going on, I can begin to 'defuse' the dread in a patient's most difficult feelings.

. . . Passive containment is not enough, as it feeds a phantasy of the therapist being made unable to continue functioning as a therapist. (Casement, 1985, pp. 154–155)

HOLDING, CONTAINING AND BOUNDARYING

> ## Box 5.3 Case illustration: Analytic holding-containing
>
> In the course of telling me about how he had been referred for therapy, he began to shout and to bang the arm of his chair with a barely contained violence. . . I could feel myself becoming increasingly anxious. I realized that I was on the receiving end of a powerful projective identification;. . . my feelings were not violent – *I felt afraid*. . .
>
> THERAPIST: You are thinking and speaking for me, based on what you have experienced with other people. I would like to say for myself what I am thinking. You expect me to send you away; but I am not going to send you away. I am going to offer to take you into therapy. However, I make one condition. I know you have a lot of violent feelings, which you may need to bring into your therapy. You can bring as much violence here as you need to, as long as it is confined to words. If this becomes physical violence, I cannot promise that I will then be able to continue treating you.
>
> PATIENT: So you are afraid! (Pause)
>
> THERAPIST: Yes, you are able to make me afraid of your violence; but I believe it may be precisely that which you need me to be in touch with – without having to send you away. I think it is your own fear of your violent feelings that you are needing me to help you with.
>
> [The patient] began to calm down. . . . He had not (quite) given up hope that his fear of his own violence might somewhere begin to be contained by another person and found to be manageable. (Casement, 1985, pp. 145–147)

Intrapsychic, Emotional and Intersubjective Holding-Containing

The holding and containing of intrapsychic/intersubjective processes involves engaging with clients in nourishing, cherishing, attuned ways that respect their personhood. This enables clients to express, relive and work through current and past traumas (Stolorow, Atwood & Branchaft, 1997). At times in the empathic intersubjective relationship, boundaries between self and other (and body and world) can merge in ambiguous or confluent ways. It can be hard to distinguish sometimes if a bodily feeling or emotion belongs to client or therapist.

The example in box 5.3 offers a good example of *psychoanalytic* holding-containing-boundarying. In such work, clients' unwanted or negative emotions are expressed, projected and then ideally transformed interpretively by the therapist. It is this more acceptable, modified form which is integrated back into the client. Eventually the client becomes their own container, better able to own responsibility for their conflict and anguish (Gravell, 2010).

68   HOLDING, CONTAINING AND BOUNDARYING

Holding-containing-boundarying is also relevant to *group therapy* settings. Here, a psychoanalytic group can be thought of as a container whose boundaries distinguish the members inside from those outside the group and where bad feelings can be got rid of by projecting them onto the 'out group'. But the boundaries also hold the group members together and allow them to project within the group, with individuals representing or enacting parts of self. For instance, a group member may be found who provides a scapegoating function of holding projections of bad feelings on behalf of the group. Or the group leader can be idealised, or pressurised into providing solutions, by a passive, dependent group. As conflict and anxiety within the group rises, the group's holding-containing-boundarying function becomes even more important (Hinshelwood, 1987).

In box 5.4, a group member describes how his therapist contained both his 'victim' stance and his anger while offering a developmentally reparative intervention.

Box 5.4 Case illustration: Containing anger in a group

In a psychotherapy group one member asks about how I got paralysed when I was fourteen. Pleased to have the opportunity to tell my story again, I commence with tears in my eyes. The psychotherapist intervenes by stopping this. I protest: 'I am only telling what happened.' The psychotherapist reiterates that I should not continue with this tale of drudgery and misery, which had been told many times before. I scream at the psychotherapist, 'I hate you!' glaring at her with all the rage I can muster. . . . The psychotherapist says, 'What would your mother do now?' I reply, 'What a stupid question! My mother would hit me and then send me to my room. She would never let me speak to her like this.' The psychotherapist continues looking steadily at me with what I can only describe as compassionate concern. Then she reached out her hands to me, palms upwards, without touching me, and I dissolved into tears as I realized that I can show my anger at her without being punished or rejected. . . . (Clarkson, 2003, p. 135)

In *humanistic* versions of intersubjective[6] holding-containing, the process involves engaging deep empathy to convey nourishing love, concern, interest and acceptance. The goal is to provide sufficient boundarying that a sense of safety and security is provided which will allow the client to reclaim that which has been closed off, or integrate that which has been fragmented (Moursund & Erskine, 2004).

Interesting creative possibilities emerge in the therapeutic space when therapists are dynamically working with parts of self (see the case study of Jayne in chapter 9). For example, when carrying out a *gestalt/TA* 'Parent interview'[7] (i.e.,

HOLDING, CONTAINING AND BOUNDARYING   69

giving therapy to the internalised Parent) in a group, the therapist needs to en-sure the client feels safe and supported while the 'Parent' is being treated. The therapist might invite another group member to gently hold a cushion which symbolically represents the client. This holding helps the client's 'Child' not to feel abandoned, while offering a symbolic way to contain their anxieties.

The illustration in box 5.5 illustrates a *client-centred* approach (Axline, 1989) using sand-tray play during a therapy session. This expressive-projective mode of therapy reveals something of the child's inner world in a playful, non-verbal way as feelings are projected outwards onto the sand. The value of sand-tray play (whether with children or adults) lies in its symbolic function as well as its ability to circumvent verbal defences (such as deflection and intellectualising). Power-ful emotions can be captured and contained within the confines of the sand-tray (Homeyer & Sweeney, 2010).

Box 5.5 Case illustration: Sand-tray play therapy

Jamail was an 8-year-old boy whose soldier father was killed while serving abroad. He had been referred for therapy following behavioural problems at school and home. The therapist invited Jamail to play with the sand-tray, offering him a choice of toys and figurines. Drawn immediately to the box of toy soldiers, he started to lay out a battle scene. Jamail soon became lost in his play, at times becoming quite vocal and animated as he lined up the soldiers to be shot or blown up. The battle scene eventually ended with everyone dying and being buried in the sand. At this point, Jamail turned away to look at other toys in the playroom. The therapist decided to take a non-intrusive, non-directive approach by just reflecting back[8] occasionally what Jamail was doing.

A similar sand-play battle was re-created and enacted in the next two sessions. In the fourth session, Jamail's play became more focused on burying the dead soldiers. Significantly, one soldier who had been buried had to be rescued after shouting, 'Help, help, let me out! I'm not dead!' At this point the therapist made some explicit links with Jamail's own father being a soldier who had died. She asked him if he sometimes won-dered and hoped that his father might still be alive. When he nodded, a new phase of play therapy began which included more talking alongside the play.

Jamail continued to play out violent scenes of war and death in the sand tray. In the eighth session, he enacted an elaborate funeral scene. The thera-pist and all the other figurines in the room were brought around the sand tray to witness the funeral.

That was the last time Jamail chose to play with the sand-tray. He was discharged after two further sessions, a happier, calmer boy.

The Shadow Side: Arguments Against Holding-Containing

Part of the art of therapy lies in finding the most useful and appropriate way (and time) to engage holding-containing-boundarying. It is all too easy to make the wrong judgement. For instance, rushing in to comfort a sobbing client by offering a gentle hug may soothe the emotions away; yet this might waste an opportunity to encourage the client to express those emotions cathartically.

If a client gives off messages of feeling deeply hopeless and admits to having suicidal thoughts, how quickly should we intervene, and to what extent? The client might benefit from an immediate holding-containing intervention, such as being offered an additional therapy session. On the other hand, might the therapist be rushing in too quickly? Might the motivation to 'rescue' stem from the therapist's own anxiety and need? Offering another session may simply cover over emotions or undermine the client's own capacity and choices. It might be more helpful for the therapist to simply allow the expression of suicidal ideas (i.e., not move to contain) without panicking.

At times, our **boundary setting** with clients can be counter-intuitive. For instance, loosening or crossing boundaries may be what is required; at other times, the setting of a firm withholding boundary may demonstrate care. Refusing to engage therapeutically when a client rings up using the pretext of an emergency, but just wants to talk, is a case in point. Instead of engaging in soothing talk (which effectively says, you need me to deal with this), it might be more therapeutic and caring to model boundary setting. The therapist might say to the client, 'This (you) are too important to be dealt with in a rushed way; we need a proper session.' Containing the material within the contracted session keeps both client and therapist safe.

For some, the whole notion of therapists engaging in holding-containing is questionable given its potential for fostering unhealthy dependence. Might we inadvertently be using another's vulnerability to fulfil our own needs? Clarkson (2003) highlights the dangers of *infantilising* clients, thereby perpetuating unequal abusive power relationships which are inherently manipulative or pathologising. She argues against the unremitting use of developmental models focused on mother and child, suggesting that this involves a power-based patriarchal social division where the therapist's expertise subtly demands compliance.

Such strong words merit critical reflection. Might a therapist who mostly operates from a Nurturing Parent[9] position actually contribute to the client-Child's problems by smothering them and preventing them from growing up? Such 'help' might simply replay the client's toxic history while doing more to satisfy the therapist's own needs. What exactly are we saying when we talk in terms of the therapist having the power to hold and contain a client? Should we be so powerful? Doesn't this risk becoming a 'doing-to' the other, instead of a '*being-with*'?

Somehow therapists need to achieve a negotiated balance, a position of boundarying-controlling and enabling-supporting conducted on an ongoing basis and in a relational, dialogical way. We can use our capacity to reflect to raise the client's awareness. Modesty and admissions of error can help here. In the passage below, Casement (1985) admits to a client that he might have been unhelpful when doubting the client's capacity to cope during his absence:

> I believe I was very unhelpful to you in your last session. I may have put some of my own anxiety onto you about whether you would cope during the summer break. When I was trying to be reassuring about this, I think it probably had the opposite effect on you as if I had been trying to brush aside what you were feeling. (1985, p. 152)

The judgements we make related to holding-containing-boundarying need to be negotiated in such a *relational context* rather than slavishly following 'rules' of practice. The latter approach leads us down the route of fear-based **defensive practice**, where we act with an eye to reducing exposure to official complaints and malpractice liability.

> Therapy based on authenticity may reasonably be characterised as 'undefensive practice', as opposed to the 'defensive practice' which is becoming more and more the norm of contemporary therapy. Undefensive practitioners are vulnerable to misunderstanding, and indeed, if not sufficiently self-monitoring, to misbehaviour; but defensive practitioners, in the extreme, neither like nor trust their clients – they see them as a potential threat . . ... On one level this threat is to the practitioner's standing and income, should a complaint be made; but more deeply, one feels that the real threat is to the practitioner's insecure self-image and self-esteem. Their internal critic is projected out into their clients, who are then mistrusted and feared. (Totton, 2010)

While Totton acknowledges the place for boundaries he recommends "undefensive practice" characterised by **boundlessness**, which draws on "abundance, space, attention and care". This generosity of spirit is then communicated to the client who, in turn, may feel permission to relax a bit more about life. He argues that a therapist who cannot offer clients boundaries is dangerous; a therapist who cannot offer boundlessness is "useless".

The Therapist as a 'Contained-Container'

Beyond attempting to engage and transform clients' subjectivity, part of what the therapist holds and contains is their *own* subjectivity. We need to bracket and boundary our own internal processes in a healthy, non-defensive way. We hold-contain the leakage of our own subjectivity so that it doesn't drown our client work and also to protect us from emotional harm. How alarming and unsafe would it be for the client were the therapist be unable to cope with their own feelings? How destructive and exploitative would it be for a therapist to use the client's therapy for their own healing? How are therapists to work on clients' deep trauma, avoidance and dissociation if they are cut off themselves?

As therapists, we need sufficient robustness, emotional competence and containment to avoid loading the client with distress and disturbance accumulated from our own past experience. Heron (2001, p. 12) notes that we must ensure that our disturbance does not "drive and distort" our interventions. Only when the therapist holds their own, neither 'rescuing' nor 'persecuting', neither being destroyed nor being made unduly anxious, can a place of safety and security for the client be sustained.

This does not mean the therapist remains intact, grounded and unaffected. Nor should the therapist become a fortress.[10] Careful, intuitive judgement is needed to know when to show emotion and when to hold back. Take the situation where a therapist was working with a young man who was a full-time carer for his mother, who had a severe mental illness. He was programmed to be alert to subtle emotional reactions in others and spent his time constantly scanning his environment. If the therapist showed undue emotion, the client became overly concerned with the therapist's needs. The therapist learned to hold back from revealing how impacted she was by his story. As therapy progressed, and the client learned that he didn't need to take care of his therapist, she was able to be more authentic.

In reality, the open recognition of our imperfections, limitations and openness to damage grants us the humanity that allows us to empathise with our clients and work in their service (Adams, 2014). Gibertoni (2013, p. 50) puts it well when she writes of having "thought of myself as a container, sometimes with leaks, holes or cracks in need of repair, a pot with a cover that does not do its job very well".

Given our vulnerability, we need to be reflexive about our processes and make active use of supportive opportunities (therapy, continuing professional development (CPD), supervision and the like) which offer precious moments to be held and contained ourselves. If we lack adequate supervision for the difficult work we do at the contact boundary, particularly when such work connects with unresolved issues of our own, there is a danger of our using therapy with a client to act out (or get the client to act out for us). By offering an opportunity for reflection, supervision is part of the safety net that should surround every therapist, helping them hold and contain material that is often difficult, painful and disturbing (Gilbert & Evans, 2000).

The example in box 5.6 emphasises that students and therapists alike (and supervisors) need to be held, just as they hold their clients. Professional knowledge, skills and techniques offer some scaffolding and a safe framework in which to practise and function under pressure. But probably the best, most effective holding-containing comes from having an attuned, affirming, supportive supervisor.[11]

HOLDING, CONTAINING AND BOUNDARYING   73

> ### Box 5.6 Case illustration: To contain or not to contain?
>
> In a unit for children with extreme behavioural disorders, one child, **Leo,** presented a particular challenge to the staff. In his acting out, he found exactly the right buttons to push by testing every boundary that was set. Mostly the staff offered a consistent team response designed to contain Leo's behaviour. However a new (client-centred) trainee on placement was unaware of the team strategy. When Leo started to kick her she tried to 'accept' his behaviour and show him unconditional support. However, he soon became uncontrollably violent. The supervising therapist then stepped in to intervene, gently but firmly holding Leo. The message, the student soon learned, was that Leo needed to feel safe and trust that he could be contained – something that had not happened in his early life.
>
> In a subsequent *supervision session*, the supervisor found himself actively holding and containing the trainee who was filled with shame at her 'ignorant mistake'. The trainee now felt unsafe as she couldn't trust her decision-making and her shame was threatening to leak out into her other work in the unit. The supervisor suggested that it might be useful for the trainee to take her shame back into therapy. At the same time, he was soothingly supportive, noting that she had not known the team policy and that so-called mistakes were common in daily practice. He apologised for not intervening earlier before Leo's behaviour had escalated. (In the process, the supervisor used his **internal supervisor** to contain his own feelings of guilt and shame about his 'mistake'.)

Concluding Reflections

This chapter has focused on the significance of holding-containing-boundarying as part of both the process of healing, reparation and recovery and maintaining professionalism. I have tried to explore how we might enable clients' sense of safety, while also framing relational dynamics which may be out of awareness, including working through projections and transferences. While a *relational psychoanalytic* approach has been foregrounded, humanistic *client-centred*, *gestalt* and *existential* versions of holding-containing have also been indicated.

I hope I have sufficiently emphasised the point that holding-containing-boundarying are not things that we *do to* clients; it's not about controlling the client. As critics have noted, therapists who set out to 'hold' or 'contain' by fostering dependence run the risk of being manipulative and even abusive. Instead, the process needs to be seen as dialogically negotiated. We can't just decide to 'hold' the client. The client has to accept the holding; they need at some level to take in our witnessing and containing presence and to *feel* held. Ideally, we work *with* clients on how they might *regulate themselves*.

74   HOLDING, CONTAINING AND BOUNDARYING

Exactly how and when to engage holding-containing-boundarying is one of the key artful judgements the relational therapist makes. Sometimes our professional decision-making involves pushing at, if not crossing, boundaries.[12] We need to shape therapy in a relational context rather than adhere rigidly to rules or engage in fear-based defensive practice.

Ultimately we fall back on our intuition. If something doesn't feel 'right' it probably isn't. And we can expect to get it 'wrong' for our clients occasionally. We can only try to attune to the individual's needs, intuiting the moment when a client might open to receive our embrace (be it physical or metaphorical).

And if we are to offer holding-containing boundaries to our clients, we ourselves need to be held-contained. Our therapy, supervision and CPD, along with our books, theories and techniques, offer some of the resources we need. It is to this subject of resources we turn next.

Notes

1   See, for instance, the Codes of Conduct laid down by the UK Council for Psychotherapy (UKCP; www.psychotherapy.org.uk/UKCP_Documents/ standards_and_guidance/32_UKCP_Ethical_ Principles_and_Code_of_Professional_Conduct_ approved_by_BOT_Sept_09.pdf) and the British Association of Counselling and Psychotherapy (BACP; www.bacp.co.uk/ethical_framework/good_ standard.php).

2   Brown and Stobart (2008), in a more expansive analysis, identify seven distinct boundaries or boundary zones: boundary and containment in child development; contracting; intrapsychic containing; boundaries in organisational settings; confidentiality; professional boundaries; and endings.

3   In this chapter, I present these concepts in terms of their broader, more general usage, rather than solely in specifically *psychoanalytical* terms (see box 5.2).

4   Wallin's significant developmental work in the field of attachment integrates relational psychotherapy, mindfulness, neuroscience and trauma studies.

5   Winnicott (1971, p. 231) called this space an "intermediate" area, a transitional area between inner and outer reality where creativity and play emerge. In developmental terms, the baby (between 4 months and one year old) is leaving the

state of fusion with mother and developing relationships with objects and people in the world. The use of a *transitional object*, such as a teddy bear or a blanket, keeps the baby connected to mother while also providing space for separation.

6   I deliberately focus here on the intersubjective rather than the intrapsychic functions. Some *humanistic* and phenomenological therapists regard the *psychoanalytical* concept of 'intrapsychic' as problematic in its suggestion of something being hidden *inside* an individual; their preferred emphasis is on the *between*.

7   The technique of Parent interview is discussed more fully in chapter 16, pp. 237–239.

8   The traditonal non-directive approach highlighted here in *person-centred* therapy can be contrasted with the way a therapist is a neutral vehicle to receive transferences in traditional *psychoanalytic* work and/or who offers mirroring in developmentally orientated *relational psychoanalysis*. Contemporary relational versions of person-centred reflecting back have more in common with other humanistic *gestalt* and *phenomenologically* orientated therapy. These approaches focus more relationally on being-with and they would do more to validate the 'is-ness' of experience.

9   The capital letters in Nurturing Parent and Child in this sentence arise from *transactional*

analysis theory and distinguish the ego state (or parts of self) from the usual use of these terms (see chapter 16).

10 Orbach (2014) suggests a nice technique of imagining a protective shield around oneself while still feeling whatever is going on in the therapy. The art is to hold on to clients' emotions for long enough to make sense of them before being taken over by them. If the therapist cannot hold/contain and make sense of the emotions, or they linger long after the session, it may be necessary to give them back to the client. Or if the emotions need to be held, Orbach advises doing this with curiosity and compassion, and not being afraid.

11 Therapists need to respect a mother's understandings as she knows her baby best. Similarly, a nurturing supervisor needs to respect the supervisee's capacities and judgements (Casement, 1985).

12 Gutheil and Gabbard (1993) helpfully distinguish between harmful 'boundary violations' and neutral (or beneficial) 'boundary crossing'. They note that empirical evidence indicates that boundary violations frequently accompany or precede sexual misconduct, but the 'slippery slope' violations themselves do not necessarily constitute malpractice or misconduct. They also highlight how a boundary violation from one theoretical perspective may be standard professional practice from another.

6

Resourcing:[1] Nurturing Skills and Mobilising Coping Strategies

Resources are like assets – the more you have, the better off you are. (Rothschild, 2003a, p. 19)

Clients might come to therapy one hour per week; how do they live the other 167 hours? What resources do they have – do they need – to navigate their daily life and world of relationships? What coping strategies are they using and what new ones might be helpful? How might clients actively contribute to their own self-healing?

A basic tenet of *humanistic theory* is that as human beings we have an extraordinary capacity to (re-)create ourselves as we search for ways to meet our needs.[2] Sometimes we lose sight of life-enhancing, growth-full choices that give meaning to our lives. When we are depressed, for instance, our world shrinks inwards, becomes gloomy and dark; we become stuck, lose will and hope. But deep within we retain the potential to find and use our own strengths.

Therapy, with therapists as teacher-coach collaborators, provides an empathic space to nurture the growth of clients' own resources (Bohart & Tallman, 1999). The clients decide what they want to plant in their 'emotional allotment' then therapist and client go digging together.

The focus of this chapter is on the wide range of resources – both within the client and from their environment – that can be creatively mobilised to enhance life. Rothschild (2003a, 2003b) outlines five major classes of resources which can be nurtured: functional, physical, psychological, interpersonal, and spiritual (see box 6.1). The first section of this chapter explores the **nature of**

Relational Integrative Psychotherapy: Engaging Process and Theory in Practice, First Edition. Linda Finlay.
© 2016 John Wiley & Sons, Ltd. Published 2016 by John Wiley & Sons, Ltd.

these resources while the second considers how they might be tapped towards self-help. The following two sections focus on what we might offer in the way of tools, insight and creative support to promote healing and nourish contact-full self–world connections. Two main resourcing interventions are: nurturing **insight**, **self-awareness** and **understanding**; and taking a *psycho-educational* approach to enable the development of key skills.

Box 6.1 Theory: Five classes of resources

Functional Practical aspects such as: a safe place to live; nutritional and comforting food to eat; restful spaces to recharge; rewarding work, hobbies and daily activities; health-enhancing self-care activities.

Physical Basic health; physical strength, agility, coordination; somatic awareness.

Psychological Intelligence, logic, ability to solve problems, a sense of humour, creative talents, comfort objects or images (e.g. a 'transitional object' or imagining the therapist's face); also, coping strategies and defence mechanisms (including survival resources such as running away, dissociating, fighting).

Interpersonal Supportive social network including spouse/partner, friends, family, colleagues and even pets, in the present or remembered from the past.

Spiritual Religious and non-religious practice including prayer, meditation, mindfulness, communing with nature, poetry, music, etc.

(elaborated from Rothschild, 2003b)

Identifying Resources

Resources to support a person in maintaining a feeling of 'OK-ness' include their own abilities, awarenesses, and action, together with other people, situations and happenings. When we are struggling with confused emotions, perhaps desperate, consumed with rage, stressed, stuck, bogged down by life's challenges, it can be all too easy to lose sight of our own strengths, skills, knowledge and personal resources. Without sufficient resources, a person's ability to function in life is undermined. How might these be marshalled?

In therapy, interventions which remind clients about their strengths and resources can be powerful and empowering. It's inspiring to see the way resources give *hope* and confidence that it is possible to grow your way out of challenging life moments. It can also be useful for the client (both during therapy and in the long term) to explicitly use the resources which help them to feel safe, at ease, empowered or even joyful. Indeed, one session of therapy might be enough to remind clients they are less helpless and more resourceful than they think.

In her **trauma work**, Rothschild suggests that clients may not have had enough resources at the time of the trauma; for instance, the person wasn't big or strong enough to run away or they lacked the support of a protective Other. She explains that 'that was then and this is now'. In this present, the person can be encouraged to recognise the resources they do have, and perhaps develop new ones, to help them as they work through their trauma.

Rothschild warns that before tackling any trauma face on, it is essential to ensure that a client feels safe and that they have some reasonably well-developed resources to hold on to (See box 6.2). Specifically, she discusses the use of *oases* (places and activities that divert from the trauma); *anchors* (comforting memories and calming images that can act as a braking tool when the therapy work gets tough); and the value of having a *safe place* to go to mentally, to reduce hyper-arousal. Others have taken up these ideas, for example in the field of 'resourcing and somatic therapy'.[3]

Box 6.2 Case illustration: Learning to self-regulate

Catherine was a very anxious woman in her early 30s who easily became hyperaroused during therapy. . . . Speaking very fast in an animated, high-pitched tone, her face flushed . . . Her legs and arms moved in an agitated, jerky manner . . . as she spoke wildly . . .. I noticed my predictable, implicit response of slight anxiety and pressure (*affect attunement*). My chest and throat had tightened, and I was breathing rapidly. . . . I began to concentrate at first on my body to slow myself down and to ground myself by breathing slowly into my belly . . . . I also created a slight distance by looking away. Feeling calmer and surer of my *stance*, I sensed when it was time to speak. My words were slow, deliberate and steady, as I suggested that she place the palm of her hand on her belly and breathe slowly into her hand. . . . I watched as she did so, and then suggested that she place her feet flat . . .. Her body stilled, she began to speak much more slowly, and to feel sad. (Nolan, 2012, p. 36)

The Value of Self-Help

It's worth reminding ourselves that most people cope, and survive the challenges in their everyday lives, without the help of a therapist. I sometimes worry that psychotherapy can foster an unhealthy dependence and we forget to respect clients' own creative capacities for self-healing and self-help.

RESOURCING: SKILLS AND COPING STRATEGIES   79

Norcross et al. (2003) have been active in this field of self-help, creating a manual of self-help resources to support clients (and therapists!) who wish to engage their own process outside the therapy. To this end therapists might suggest a client explores avenues outside therapy including:

- reading inspiring biographies and autobiographies (I've used David Karp's *Speaking of Sadness* which draws on many people's experiences of depression, and John Bayley's *The Iris Trilogy: A Memoir of Iris Murdoch* on dementia);
- reading popular self-help books about mental health (*I Never Promised You a Rose Garden* by Joanne Greenberg on schizophrenia; *Why Marriages Succeed or Fail* by John Gottman on marriage; *Courage to Heal* by Ellen Bass and Laura Davis on surviving sexual abuse);
- reading psychotherapy books (my favourites are Virginia Axline's *Dibs: In Search of Self*, Irvin Yalom's books, like *Love's Executioner*, Ernesto Spinelli's *Tales of Unknowing*);
- attending self-help groups (e.g. 12-steps, AA/Al Anon, online groups);
- watching commercial films and TV (e.g. *Sybil*, 1976, dir. Daniel Petrie, about Dissociative Identity Disorder, and *In Treatment* (HBO), to show psycho-therapy in action).

Du Plock (2006) similarly advances the technique of *existential bibliotherapy* as a potentially effective way for individuals to treat themselves. He highlights the value for clients of reading to create their sense of self rather than using self-help manuals to relieve specific symptoms. Bibliotherapy can be worked with actively in therapy; for instance, therapist and client can co-create lists of works which have had a profound impact.

Cooper and McLeod recommend the following personal development activity for therapists:

> Take 10 minutes or so, on your own, to make a list of the books, films or other arts materials (e.g. painting) that you have found helpful or 'therapeutic' in your own life. . . . Reflect on the circumstances under which you might wish to make suggestions to a client regarding reading material or viewing films. (2011, p. 104)

Looking more broadly, Jorm et al. (2000) conducted a survey into helpful interventions people identify to cope with anxiety and depression compared with the strategies they use in practice. They considered seeing a counsellor, physical activity, learning relaxation and seeing close friends to be the most helpful interventions. These contrast with the two self-help strategies used most often – alcohol and pain relievers. The lesson here is the reminder that the therapist is but one resource.

The case illustrations in box 6.3 remind us of the importance of self-help, engaging the world outside of the therapy room. As Deurzen-Smith (1997, p. 283) reminds us: "The work really has to be done in life, not in therapy."

80   RESOURCING: SKILLS AND COPING STRATEGIES

Box 6.3   Case illustrations: Finding and using resources

Reading

Rohan, a 25-year-old man, had been a regular substance user/abuser for 10 years. Rohan realised that because he had sedated and self-soothed himself for years, he did not know who he really was. He came into therapy (twelve sessions contracted) on an existential journey to explore his self-identity and to get in touch with his 'real' feelings. He was an avid reader and asked the therapist to recommend books which might help his search for self and assist him to better understand the therapy process. Later, Rohan was able to recommend other inspiring books to his therapist.

Joining a self-help group

Sunaina, aged 22, had been suffering with ME for five years. When she was sufficiently able she engaged therapy. However, in practice, she missed too many sessions and so the therapy proved insufficient to 'hold' her emotionally. The therapist encouraged Sunaina to use an online ME self-help group until she was able to fully engage her therapy. Sunaina found the forum extremely supportive and she appreciated all the information proffered, including tips on self-care, welfare benefits, self-help resources, and up-to-date research findings. She particularly valued talking with other ME sufferers and hearing their stories.

Reconnecting with past resources

Daniel, 43 years old, had been grieving the death of his father. After 15 months he remained depressed and found life pointless. He sought therapy to help him 'move on'. In addition to exploring Daniel's relationship with his father and normalising his grief, the therapist focused on nourishing his resources. She discovered that when Daniel was a teenager he loved going on hikes in the hills with his father, an activity he hadn't engaged for many years. She encouraged Daniel to reconnect weekly with his old hobby. In addition to enjoying the exercise and nature, Daniel discovered much solace in using his hike-time to 'be with' his father.

Experimenting

Becca engaged some short-term gestalt therapy, to help with her rageful outbursts and also to control those of her 8-year-old daughter. She was encouraged by her therapist to experiment with various techniques, including working with her breathing and saying to herself, 'This is a choice point' as she breathed. This expanded her options for her behaviour and she found she could begin to pause before she flew off the handle. Once she had mastered this, Becca modelled it for her daughter: 'breathe or have a tantrum, the choice is yours.' Both of their violent outbursts diminished.

Nurturing Insight, Awareness and Self-Understanding

Insight, awareness and self-understanding are especially valuable resources which we nurture in therapy. For instance, we might explore how a client's self-destructive behaviour is preceded by feeling swiped or shamed, or by a feeling of emptiness. Therapy can then focus on becoming aware of resources that can be tapped, allowing more choiceful responses. This more cognitive, teaching work occurs across different therapeutic approaches, though it might be languaged in different ways, for instance, as 'decontaminating the Adult' in *TA*, 'teaching emotional control skills' in *CBT* or 'broadening the field' in *gestalt* work.

Two routes to nurturing self-understanding are discussed here: feedback and information giving.

Feedback

Gentle, curious, supportive feedback can act as a useful mirror for the client. Through feedback, clients learn to become better witnesses of their own processes. They learn to appreciate the impact of their behaviour upon others (see box 6.4).

Box 6.4 Case illustration: Giving feedback

There are many times when you come into my office and I have the sense of you being sparkling and entertaining; yet somehow I feel far away from the real you. There is a certain effervescence you have at these times that is very charming but it also acts as a barrier, keeping us apart. Today it's different. Today I feel really connected to you – and my hunch is this is the type of connection you yearn for in your social relationships. Tell me, does my reaction feel bizarre? Or familiar? Anyone else ever said this to you? Is it possible that what I'm saying might have some relevance to what goes on with you in other relationships? (Yalom, 2010, p. 125)

Information giving

In addition to making such relational observations and giving feedback, in my own practice I often find myself becoming something of an information-giving teacher–parent. Commonly I return to three interlinked topic areas related to:

1. **The nature of mental health problems** Numerous clients over the years have approached me saying they have been diagnosed as having, say, 'a personality disorder' or 'Asperger's'. What exactly does this mean? All of us deserve more than a diminishing diagnostic label. We need to understand what

is being said about us, and if we have mental health challenges we need to find a way of living with that part of ourselves long-term. As part of exploring mental health issues, I have suggested that a client might benefit from going to their doctor if medication or another intervention might possibly help.

2. **Normalisation** Often clients simply need reassurance that they are not 'mad' or 'crazy', that their behaviour is not 'despicable', 'pathetic', 'hopeless', etc., and that they are not alone in their struggle. Here we have a significant role to play in normalising and de-pathologising the client's behaviour or responses. The therapist needs to let the client know that their confusion, panic, defensiveness, or bizarre fantasies come out of coping strategies developed in painful or challenging circumstances and that their experience is a reasonable, self-protective reaction. Normalisation involves both *acknowledgement* ('Given what you've just been through, it makes sense that you feel this way. Anyone would') and *validation* ('You are showing such strength in the face of repeated trauma') (Moursund and Erskine, 2004).

3. **Emotional literacy** I am using the concept of 'emotional literacy' here to mean the ability to understand one's own and others' emotions, and to handle and express them constructively. Already an implicit aim of most therapy, it applies more specifically when therapists teach clients about some elements of psychology and psychotherapy theory. I often find myself sharing TA theory, if it seems appropriate (see chapter 16). When working with someone in a co-dependent relationship, for instance, I might discuss both the drama triangle and the nature of co-dependency. Armed with such knowledge, some clients can then see and change their own problematic relational dynamics for themselves.

The information giving described in the examples above should be used judiciously, in an emergent way, in response to clients' needs. In relational work, we give information as part of opening up a dialogue rather than assuming some 'knowing' expertise. Often I will preface an explanation of theory by saying, 'This is one way of understanding it, if it helps. It's a way of looking at the process rather than "fact".' As Casement (1985, p. 218) acknowledges, there is a danger that "insight is intellectualised . . . and that the therapist appears more all-knowing than anyone really can be". He wisely suggests the value of presenting theory or **interpretations** in a tentative way, so as not to foreclose on clients' ideas and keep open the opportunity to play with ideas arising in dialogue. In opening up such dialogue, we set the scene for ensuring a more mutual sharing where we, in turn, are open to *learning from our client*.

In these ways theoretical and self-understandings are made available as helpful resources. Sometimes, however, it may be appropriate to take an explicit psycho-educational approach with the aim of developing client skills and nurturing practical coping strategies.

Skills Development: Psycho-educational Interventions

Some integrative psychotherapists routinely use *cognitive-behavioural* strategies in their work and focus on outcomes of teaching-learning skills. Others – particularly *humanistic-existential* therapists – prefer to focus more holistically and on process, resisting protocol-based interventions. Yalom makes the point strongly:

> [T]he flow of therapy should be spontaneous, forever following unanticipated riverbeds; it is grotesquely distorted by being packaged into a formula that enables inexperienced, inadequately trained therapists (or computers) to deliver a uniform course of therapy. One of the true abominations spawned by the managed-care movement is the ever greater reliance on protocol therapy in which therapists are required to adhere to a prescribed sequence, a schedule of topics and exercises to be followed each week. (Yalom, 2010, p. 34)

However, humanistic relational-centred therapists do still recognise the significance of clients' embodied-thinking-feeling responses and the value of intervening positively at one or other level. If only short-term therapy is possible given the context, then they may well embrace a more directive cognitive-behavioural type of approach. Whatever our theoretical orientation, we have an important role to play in challenging distorted, self-defeating thinking and encouraging the development of new behavioural repertoires such as anger management, anxiety management, social skills training, parenting skills training and assertiveness training (see chapter 11).

Box 6.5 illustrates a programme explicitly focused on resourcing an anxious client with a phobia about exams. The therapist acts as emotional support, coach and mentor. Initially, therapy had focused on exploring Tracy's phobia and what 'failure' meant, and links were made to her early high-achieving family scripts. Tracy remained crippled by her phobia, however, and it seemed that specific problem-solving coping strategies were needed to interrupt the vicious cycle of anxiety–avoidance.

Box 6.5 Case illustration: An anxiety management programme

Tracy was coming to the end of her first year of a physiotherapy course. While she had coped well with the continuous assessment component and was happy on her course, she found herself experiencing panic attacks when she thought about the end-of-year exams. She had given up a previous degree course for the same reason and felt destined to be a 'failure'. Inquiring further about Tracy's behaviour, thinking and emotions in relation to exams, the therapist recognised that Tracy seemed trapped in negative thinking. It

(Continued)

started with Tracy thinking, 'I can't cope with exams . . . I'm no good at them . . . I always fail . . . I'm going to fail this one . . . I can feel myself getting panicky . . . I won't be able to control it.' The cycle mushrooms into a full-blown panic attack.

The therapist suggested they explore *cognitive-behavioural* techniques, explaining that they would focus on changing her pattern of negative thoughts, so breaking this destructive spiralling anxiety–negative thinking–avoidance pattern.

Together Tracy and the therapist embarked on a *psychoeducational* programme to take place over the next few sessions.

1. **Education** The first step was to talk through the nature of anxiety. The therapist taught Tracy about the flight–fight–freeze responses to fear and how the key was to learn to 'get better at being afraid'. He emphasised that fear is supposed to be helpful (a certain amount was necessary for peak performance) and to protect rather than paralyse (or result in panic attacks). In addition, the therapist helped Tracy to feel some renewed hope and engage more deeply with the therapy by pointing out some of the latest research showing the effectiveness of cognitive interventions. Tracy was encouraged to recognise that her panic attacks on the previous course did not mean she would always struggle.

2. **Cognitive restructuring** Tracy was taught to think differently about her anxiety, for example to look on it as a 'potentially helpful friend' and not 'an out-of-control enemy'. Then, she learned to be aware of her thoughts and to stop the negative spiral (for instance, explicitly saying 'Stop!' and also searching for logical evidence to disprove these thoughts). Finally, she learned to replace the negative, catastrophic thoughts with positive (but realistic) ones. Tracy rehearsed a new sequence of thinking: 'I am not going to fail, I know I can do it, I have done it in practice. I have worked hard and I want to demonstrate my knowledge.' She was given some *between-sessions work*[4] of chanting this sequence every time she caught herself thinking about exams.

3. **Relaxation** Tracy also learned a range of relaxation techniques that she might practise to find ones that suited her in different situations (including breathing exercises, 'progressive muscular relaxation' procedure, and imaging techniques such as visualising relaxing on a warm beach). She learned 'grounding' mindfulness techniques, for instance, becoming aware of her feet planted firmly on the ground, then becoming aware of body and environment in the here-and-now.

4. **Finding resources** The therapist introduced Tracy to the idea of psychological, physical, interpersonal, spiritual and practical resources; they discussed what positive resources Tracy could draw upon. One particular

resource strategy she was encouraged to use was humour. She learned to laugh at herself and enjoy various antics (such as escaping to the toilet to engage some fast running on the spot, a strategy she found helpful for relieving tension). The therapist also encouraged Tracy to return to doing other physical activities she found relaxing, like swimming, yoga and dancing.

5. **Systematic desensitisation** Tracy eventually had to face up to the revising and actually sitting in an exam room under exam conditions. In conjunction with her therapist and her course tutor, Tracy prepared for this with a plan of action that broke down the task into manageable chunks (incorporating built-in rewards and applying her new cognitive and relaxation skills). (1) Tracy started by learning to sit down in her empty college exam hall comfortably. (2) She then managed two prepared mock exam questions supplied by her tutor, the first done at home and the other in the hall. (3) Next she successfully completed a full mock exam. Feeling thus empowered she faced her exams. While she had been anxious, she also now had the resources to manage her emotions.

Panic disorders and specific phobias like Tracy's have been shown in numerous studies to be extremely responsive to cognitive-behavioural techniques. Research evidence is growing to support humanistic and psychodynamic approaches as well (Cooper, 2008).

Instead of focusing on specific techniques or interventions, much current research explores the processes in therapy that are helpful, including the value of activating resources (see box 6.6).

Box 6.6 Research: Resourcing for people with primary cancer across the theoretical spectrum

The results of a study by Omylinska-Thurston and Cooper (2014) indicate that patients with primary cancers found a variety of processes helpful in their therapy. Referring to their experiences across a range of therapeutic modalities, it seems participants valued having the space to talk and express themselves in a relational, non-judgemental context which enabled them to be motivated and agentic. Those who had been treated within a *person-centred/humanistic* perspective emphasised the helpfulness of reassurance and normalisation, as well as working with a medically

(Continued)

informed person who had a specific knowledge of psychological adjustment processes following cancer diagnosis and treatment. Participants also described the value of *cognitive-behavioural* practices including relaxation techniques, problem-solving, and the use of self-help materials. Those who received *psychodynamic* treatment described the value of gaining self-understanding.

Concluding Reflections

In this chapter I have attempted a not entirely comfortable blending of *existential* and *cognitive-behavioural* discourse. The extent to which this integration is desirable, possible or necessary is a matter of debate. That research evidence supports the efficacy and effectiveness of different therapeutic orientations adds strength to the argument that therapists could usefully engage those therapy processes that have been found to be helpful, regardless of orientation.

The central concept of **resourcing** is important across *all* modalities, beyond theoretical dogma. We have a responsibility, in collaboration with our clients, to enable clients to grow their own resources and long-term survival strategies. So we might recommend self-help, or nurture awareness, or we may use psycho-educational interventions as part of empowering them to modify their way of being. This process as a whole can be understood as 'resourcing'.

I am committed to the existential celebration of "doing justice to the way clients live their lives, rather than to eradicat[ing] specific problems" (Deurzen & Adams, 2011, p. 1). I remain wedded to holistic *humanistic* values underpinning therapy which see the client as active, autonomous and entitled to search for life satisfaction. By increasing clients' resources and nurturing independence, we aim to enable them to find meaning and perceive themselves as possessing worth. Clients are not mere 'things' to be manipulated and 'done to' but human beings who can exercise choice and control over their life.

I find myself inspired on witnessing the journeys my clients take in their lives and the creative ways they help themselves. Strength, courage and inspiration can be found in many places:

The individual human is still the creature who can wonder, who can be enchanted by a sonata, who can place symbols together to make poetry to gladden our hearts, who can view a sunrise with a sense of majesty and awe. (May, 1983, p. 10)

Creative processes are brought to the fore in the next chapter.

Notes

1 This word has been carefully chosen. Initially I had been going to title this chapter 'Teaching'. But somehow that didn't capture the *being-with* process as it occurs in relational work and the self-healing capacity of the client. Somehow it was too 'doing-to', a potentially didactic one-way instructional intervention. The idea of resourc*ing* worked for me as it flags up the importance of resources and suggests a fertilising process where clients are co-creators, actively involved in their own growth.

2 Maslow (1954) argues that all human beings drive towards personal growth and self-fulfilment. We are motivated by a hierarchy of needs: physiological, for safety, for love and belonging, for esteem, cognitive and aesthetic, and finally for self-actualisation. Later he described a more spiritual sixth level of intrinsic values: goodness, truth, justice transcending self-interest. Baumeister (1991) suggests four ways of finding meaning: (i) to feel effective in our embodied existence; (ii) to feel of value and a sense of belonging in the social world; (iii) to feel a sense of self-worth and self-acceptance; (iv) to transcend the banality of our lives by living meaningfully and soulfully.

3 Ogden (2015) offers a different version of somatic therapy. In her **sensorimotor psychotherapy**, she suggests three phases of therapy: (1) developing resources; (2) memory (integrating the past); (3) attachment (and exploring interpersonal patterns). Her approach integrates interpersonal neurobiology (i.e., a somatic focus) with *cognitive* and *psychodynamic* approaches to trauma and attachment.

4 Ideally, **homework** assignments need to be structured to build on clients' strengths and to enable the client to succeed. Having a success experience in itself can be a helpful challenge to script patterns around 'feeling a failure' or 'being hopeless'. Opportunities for the task to be sabotaged need to be minimised and pre-empted. See Kazantziz, Whittington and Dattilio (2010) for a review of 44 studies regarding the therapeutic use of homework ('independent activities') in CBT. Their findings suggest 62% of patients improved in outcome studies – almost double the number of patients whose treatments that did not use homework.

7

Intuiting, Imagining and Interpreting

We discover the heart's intelligence in imagination, intuition, and song.
(Anderson, 2007)

In our therapy work we are guided by interpretive hunches, gut feelings, images and bodily impulses. When attending to our clients, we use all our five senses, together with other embodied, intuitive senses.[1] Elusive and unseen, the flows of energy that constitute these sensings lurk mysteriously in the *Between*, bypassing logic and reason. Such 'receivings' are the foundation of our clinical intuition and act as creative touchstones for inspirational transformation.

What exactly happens in those moments when we find ourselves able to intuit, imagine and interpret our client's experience? What is it that we sense and how do we make sense of it? How do we enable our clients to become more aware of their sensings so they can make sense of it all too?

Animated by such questions, this chapter focuses on our work with *imaginal possibilities* towards intrapsychic healing, specifically the use we make of **guided imagery and fantasy**, **metaphor**, **felt sense**, and **dream work**. Each of these is explored in some detail, and case studies provide illustrations of their use within the therapeutic context. I then attempt to pull the threads together by highlighting the **relational base of imaginal work**.

The exploration takes us towards the worlds of *eros* and *agape*, embracing a metaphorical heart–soul language informed by poetry and artistry as much as by psychotherapeutic theory and analysis. While the chapter addresses global

---

Relational Integrative Psychotherapy: Engaging Process and Theory in Practice, First Edition. Linda Finlay.
© 2016 John Wiley & Sons, Ltd. Published 2016 by John Wiley & Sons, Ltd.

INTUITING, IMAGINING AND INTERPRETING 89

processes, the particular theoretical lenses applied are *phenomenological/gestalt* and *psychoanalytical* (specifically Jungian).

Using Guided Imagery and Fantasy

'Guided imagery/fantasy' refers to a wide range of techniques including positive visualisations, fantasy exploration, rituals and imaginative story-telling. The therapeutic use of imagery has a long history spanning traditional shamanic healing and more recent practices in gestalt, Jungian psychoanalysis and CBT therapies. Contemporary integrative approaches rest on a substantial evidence base which demonstrates the valuable role of imagery in changing our perception, elaborating understandings and providing new narratives towards healing, resolution and integration (Hackmann, Bennett-Levy & Holmes, 2011). As Vedder (2002) notes, the metaphors, symbols and narratives produced by the imagination give us imaginary variations of the world (for instance, when working with a fear of snakes we might invite the client to envisage snakes differently using positive images), allowing us to see the world and its possibilities in new ways. Herein lies the transformational potential of fantasy-orientated practice.

Mindfulness-based therapy uses **guided imagery** techniques to work with anxiety and trauma and in the health care and pain management fields. They are used specifically in *cognitive* restructuring programmes too. For instance, symbolic stories and images can be used creatively as part of graded exposure programmes, for encouraging athletes to envisage a successful, winning performance, or in relaxation exercises, where a client imagines lying on a soft sandy beach, being warmed by the sun and listening to waves gently rolling onto the shore.

They can also be used in a quasi-hypnotic way in relational-developmental work. Processes out of our conscious awareness are invited into present experience. In *gestalt therapy*, for instance, guided fantasies and visualisations are used to bring bodily and affective experience into the here-and-now. Clients are asked to close their eyes (if they feel comfortable doing so) and – with the therapist's help – are guided to imagine a scene from the past, the fantasy-past or the future. For example, in the guided regression in box 7.1, Wahid talks to his (fantasy) 'mother', who died in childbirth.[2] He had always longed for his mother despite being brought up by his kindly but distant father and grandparents.

Box 7.1 Case illustration: A 'guided regression'

Therapist: Close your eyes and imagine you are a young child. You are going to sleep and your mother is beside you stroking your hair . . . Let yourself feel her touch . . . Tell her how it feels . . . [In the next few minutes Wahid describes his bodily sensations and feeling of warmth and

(Continued)

comfort. He experiences his mother's love and her delight in being with him. He imagines himself curled in her arms.] Tell your mother what it feels like to be in her arms. How does she feel? What does she smell like? Experience how special this moment is for you both. [**Wahid** is smiling and begins to chuckle saying she is reading him a funny story. He starts to cry.] Tell her why you are crying. [Wahid explains that he feels sad as he never had that experience.] Tell her what it was like for you to be a young child without a mother and what you missed. [Eventually Wahid starts to cry deeply for all those lost moments: 'I didn't want you to die. Why did I have to live and you die? If I hadn't been born you would still be alive. I'm sorry, I'm sorry I killed you.'] Let your mother reply to you. What does she want you to say? [After a silence, Wahid responds: 'She is telling me I'm a good boy and it wasn't my fault. It was her time and that she wants me to live as she celebrates my life. She tells me she is safe, at peace and in the arms of God.']

[After some time Wahid stops crying and looks at peace. 'She has gone now. It's okay.']

The therapist invites him to open his eyes slowly and look around at the group members (several are crying). The members gather around, and share their responses to what Wahid's work evoked for them.

Throughout his childhood he slept with a photograph of his mother under his pillow. Now in adulthood he struggles with intimacy in his marriage and has joined an ongoing therapy group to explore what might have been missing for him in his early relational world.

Engaging Metaphor[3]

Language is suffused with metaphor (Lakoff & Johnson, 1980), a figurative linguistic device which carries the speaker and the listener into a common universe of shared meanings where body, emotion, thought and culture merge. Metaphor can be understood as a barely whispered, indirect language of soul, a way of seeing a reality indirectly and differently which in turn allows new meanings to come into being (Romanyshyn, 2001). For example, the phrase 'Mary is all heart' uses a metaphor to express the depth of Mary's emotional capacity for compassion. The image of the beating human organ here provides a substitute for a literal statement such as 'Mary is emotional', or 'Mary has a lot of compassion'. It offers a different, richer, more evocative understanding of both Mary and her emotions.

There is a long tradition of engaging metaphor in therapy (see box 7.2; also Finlay, forthcoming). Not only are metaphors used by clients and therapists in

INTUITING, IMAGINING AND INTERPRETING   91

passing, they can be co-created and elaborated over time. Metaphoric statements can represent images or symbols which can be used to clarify or interpret experience. Burns (2007) goes so far as to advocate the use of 'metaphor therapy': using stories therapeutically to evoke, inspire and heal.

Box 7.2 Research: On metaphor and psychotherapy

The use of metaphors by clients can reveal bodily experiencing (Skårderud, 2007) and enable the sharing of experience. They can represent aspects of personal identity which can be explored, worked with and challenged: for instance, statements such as 'I am in pieces' or 'I am a rock' (Evans, 1988).

Used by the therapist, metaphors offer a reflective tool to enable insight. More directly they serve as interpretations, helping us make sense of unconscious fantasy (Reider, 1972).

Metaphors can also help celebrate accomplishments in therapy and be usefully employed towards ending therapy: for instance, the idea of having 'travelled a long way' or 'seeing things differently' or 'receiving a gift' (Rabu, Haavind & Binder, 2013). In her empirical investigation of therapists' use of spontaneous mental imagery, McGown (2013) highlights the potentially transformative nature of such imagery and suggests that professional development programmes should focus on developing therapists' capacity to use imagery.

In terms of empirical studies, Pollio, Barlow, Fine and Pollio (1977) provide extensive evidence of the significance of metaphor in therapy. Their content analysis of transcripts of sessions from a range of orientations, including existential therapy, rational-emotive therapy and analytic therapy with children, reveals extensive use of figurative language. In their comparison of gestalt therapy and psychoanalytic transcripts, they found that high levels of novel metaphorical language often preceded periods of insight. (Finlay, forthcoming. Reproduced here with kind permission of the publishers Taylor & Francis LLC (http://www.tandfonline.com))

Ogden (1997), using numerous *psychoanalytic* illustrations, argues for the use of *reveries* as metaphorical expressions of unconscious experience. He notes how his interventions frequently take the form of working with, and then playfully and in a non-literal way stretching and elaborating, the metaphors which analyst or analysand has introduced. He recalls once describing a patient's challenging marriage as an aircraft that had never taken off, as opposed to one that had crashed. The patient then used the metaphor to elaborate, 'It felt like I was just a passenger'. This new metaphorical imagery of sitting passively on a plane became the analytic object upon which analyst and client then focused.

92 INTUITING, IMAGINING AND INTERPRETING

The following extended case example of Alex (pseudonym) illustrates how metaphors are co-created via the embodied intersubjective relationship.[4] Revealing how the process is one of sensing and making sense, the case study shows how metaphors (along with associated imagery or embodied sensations) act as sensors or detectors of meaning which help us empathise with, interpret and understand our clients' experiences. In a sense they can become an emotional compass. Our visceral *Being-with*, and the use of metaphorical language which arises out of the relational space between, become portals to our clients' experiencing.

Case example 1: 'Vacuum-packed' Alex

I had seen **Alex** regularly over the course of three years for in-depth relational-centred psychotherapy. Initially she had come to me because of tensions in her relationship with her daughter. But the story we eventually found ourselves unravelling revealed intricate layers of grief, shame, abuse, abandonment and multiple trauma (some possibly intergenerational).

Alex had found a way to cope in relationships: she closed down her needs and worked hard to keep her environment safe by pleasing others.

These themes were crystallised in one session when a somewhat strange metaphorical image spontaneously emerged. Initially surprised and puzzled by the image, we explored it together. By the end of the session we were both in awe of how that image had so beautifully expressed Alex's experience. That it had come apparently out of the blue and in a serendipitous fashion seemed almost magical at the time.

The session began with a familiar conversation about whether or not Alex was 'strange' to want her solitude and whether her desire to withdraw from contact was unhealthy. Attempting to normalise her desire for space, I reinforced previous messages about how she had been entangled in damaging relationships which were exhausting for her. Alex noted that she felt her brain was 'shrunk' when in the company of others and could only expand when she was on her own.

In response, I found myself blurting out 'You're a vacuum-packed person!' We were both taken aback by these unbidden words. They stood oddly in contrast to Alex's way of being, which was gentle, loving and warm. More than this, the phrase was not one I had ever thought about or used before. I worried that Alex might have experienced the image as derogatory and dismissive. However, she took it well, noting the humour in both the image and my own consternation about using it.

Together we wondered what could have prompted this metaphor. It began to make sense when we recognised how Alex, when in the presence of others, felt sucked dry, without air, and made to shrink, to shrivel up. I asked if the image brought any associations to mind. Suddenly Alex gave an exclamation: she made a link with a storybook she had created in words and pictures with her granddaughter just a couple of days before:

INTUITING, IMAGINING AND INTERPRETING   93

A little girl was very attached to her small suitcase with a lion face on it called Lexa. They went everywhere together. One day, the little girl was going to go with her family on an aeroplane and she desperately wanted Lexa to go with her. But the girl's mother said Lexa had to stay behind as she was too big to take on the plane. The little girl was very upset. To comfort her child the mother tried to be helpful, saying that they would measure Lexa and if she was the right size and could fit on the plane, the two friends could travel together. As Lexa was being measured, she sucked herself in. She sucked more and more, making herself as small as possible. It worked! The little girl and Lexa happily went off together on the plane.[5]

I playfully shared an interpretation with Alex that Lexa symbolically represented *Little Alex* who was so desperate not to be left behind or abandoned that she made herself fit the plane (representing family demands, society's expectations). It seems that Alex has to disappear in order to attend to the requirements of others. Only when alone can she breathe and her brain expand; only when alone can she fully embody herself. The fact that the name Lexa was so close to Alex was all too much of a coincidence.

Our playful exploration reminded me of Winnicott's (1971, p. 3) 'squiggle game'. Similarly, Ogden points to the organising imaginative power of successive sets of metaphors which get elaborated by both therapist and client in therapy.

That the play with metaphor arises in both the interpersonal and the cultural[6] context is important. Together Alex and I developed a view of her way of being; had Alex been working with another therapist, a subtly different story would have emerged.

Our play with successive metaphors and story-telling imagery tapped a profound understanding, one that we would return to over and over. It also reaffirmed for me the magic of the relational encounter. It seems to me that somewhere in the relational field Alex's Lexa had been lurking, wanting to be seen. Tuning into her, I discovered the vacuum-packed person image. Had I not shared my image, I doubt Alex would have shared her storybook with its powerful thematic connections to her own childhood experience.

This experience with Alex reaffirmed the value of being spontaneous and sharing intuitions, even if in the first instance they seem odd and not particularly connected or useful. It also demonstrated the power of a metaphor to act as a key navigational touchstone in therapy.

Embodying a Felt Sense[7]

The *phenomenological* philosopher and psychotherapist Gendlin (1996) has drawn attention to the body's language and its innate wisdom. He advocates dwelling with our bodily meanings – *felt sense* – through a special technique called *Focusing*. Focusing is a means of attending to intuitive gut feelings, whether on the part of participant or therapist. It involves becoming aware of ongoing processes through relationship with one's own felt sense. For instance, we might ask a client to be explicit about bodily experience via such questions as 'How is what you are talking about making you feel in the middle of your body?' or 'What might that that body sensation be saying?'

We would then ask ourselves the same questions, in search of exactly the right words or images for this bodily felt sense of our client's. The insights gained from this can in some circumstances trigger an 'Aha!' moment: a sudden release of tension as a new way of capturing the experience in language is born. The possibility of transformation has opened.

With Focusing, as we become aware of different parts of our Self (for example, the part that feels envy, and the part that feels shame), we tune into the **felt sense** that enables us to be aware of our layered subjectivity. The felt-sense part of me who feels envy, or shame, for instance, is 'there' while 'I' am 'here'. Understanding in this way allows us to 'turn down the volume' choicefully on those unhelpful parts of ourselves. At the same time, still holding those parts in awareness means we can incorporate vulnerable aspects – including the less healthy parts - into ourselves as a whole (and this applies to being either therapist or client).

But Focusing is *more than* technique or simple awareness of non-verbal communication. It is a gentle, compassionate way of being which is respectful to one's own (and the other's) being and pace of movement. It helps us to listen; it encourages us to pay attention to our bodily gestures and to our experiencing at the border between what we are conscious of and what we are not quite aware of.

There is an intricacy to this inward experiencing, this exploration of the bodily sensed edge of awareness. It involves more than simply being in touch with one's body sensations. Focusing enables us to tune into **subtle bodily feelings**[8] that may be trying to tell us something. Time slows down, space opens up. Sensations, symbols and words emerge, fresh and alive. Initially the felt bodily sense is ambiguous and opaque but then words, an image or a shift is experienced. There is a sensation of a physical change and new awareness, insight or solutions arise. Now we are open to the wisdom of the body, which will guide us and surprise us as new solutions present themselves. (see www.focusing.org)

The extended case illustration below gives a feel of Focusing in practice.

Case example 2: Gillian

I had been seeing **Gillian** weekly for a couple of months. She had come for help with anxiety and panic attacks, specifically relating to swimming in deep water. Later that summer she was due to go on honeymoon to a beach resort, and she wanted to be able to enjoy her holiday.

The sessions – largely cognitively focused – were productive and useful, and we were able to establish a good working alliance. That she was prepared to engage open-ended, long-term relational work indicated her wish to go deeper, though how and why she wanted this was not clear to either of us at that stage.

Then during one session she mentioned her uncle, whom she described as a charming, charismatic, sympathetic character. His presence had brightened the family home one summer when she was about 10 years old. He took on the responsibility of reading to her at night and tucking her in. Gillian described his attentions as making her 'feel special'. She started to say something more and then went quiet.

During the ensuing silence I was at first curious, then concerned. The silence between us stretched out. Gillian seemed frozen in a nowhere land as she gazed sightlessly out of the window and I felt her withdrawal. I tried to reach out by asking what was happening to her. She replied that she didn't know and just felt 'empty'. At that point I, too, lost my words and joined her in feeling blank. A tickle of anxiety, related to my awareness that I needed to do something thera-peutic, pulled me out of the emptiness and helped me become aware once more of my own body.

Specifically, I sensed a large blockage in my throat. Seeing this as a pos-sible instance of somatic counter-transference, I focused more intensely on my bodily sensations. Were they mine or did they belong somehow to Gillian's experience? Could it be that my body was vibrating to something occurring between us?

When I focused on my throat, I experienced several different, even contradic-tory, sensations. My throat felt blocked up, as if full of unshed tears. It was pain-ful. But I couldn't clear it; I couldn't swallow; I couldn't speak. Nothing seemed to dislodge the lump.[9]

I shared with Gillian my sense that my throat felt blocked and how I was feel-ing the opposite of her emptiness, being choked up with unshed tears. She turned to me in surprise, saying that her throat too was feeling like it had a 'fist-size blob in it'. I invited Gillian to focus on her throat sensation. 'What might your blob throat be saying?' I asked.

'Get out . . . I don't want it', she eventually whispered. She tried to clear her throat and then said, 'It's not, it's not . . . c-c-coming out'. She started to get tearful and began to look visibly anxious. 'I don't want to speak any more. Stop this.' At this point I did not know whether she was still talking from her throat or expressing her own desire not to explore further, or pleading with me to stop her pain somehow. Uncertain about how to proceed, I made the decision to gently soothe and reassure her by saying we would proceed more slowly and only when she was ready.

It took two more sessions for her story of being sexually molested to emerge more fully. Together, we came to understand Gillian's sense of her *blobby* throat as partly representing the *re-membered* experience of the oral sex and partly her

96   INTUITING, IMAGINING AND INTERPRETING

own fearful pushing down of her desperate emotions relating to that unspeakable experience. (The hyphen in 're-membered' here is deliberate, to make the point that remembering is not just a cognitive function: experience gets replayed in the body.) That her closed throat had been linked earlier with a blank empty silence became more understandable.

I still re-member that sense of (my? her?) blocked throat. It somehow captured her trauma; her body had acted it out before she was conscious of it. Once it was acknowledged, we could work with it together, rather than remain trapped in that blank, silent space.

Eventually Gillian and I came to see subsequent experiences of what we called 'throat-block' more generally. It was a sign that prompted Gillian to dig a bit and speak about something she was blocking out or avoiding. Through naming and owning this process, Gillian found a new way of being present to her emotional world, and this proved empowering for her. As Faranda (2014, p. 66) notes, "through accessing this realm of affect, body, and image we are honouring a part of us that seems to communicate in ways that are more sensory, more visual, and less verbal."

Utilising Dream Work

After these sessions with Gillian, I became aware of images and dreams of sexual abuse which lurked in my imaginings. In particular, I remember experiencing a couple of nightmares related to shame, not being heard and not being able to speak. I linked all these images with my *re-membered* sensation of the blocked throat and the work with Gillian. What remained unclear is whether this blocked throat was symbolically too full (of tears, of semen?), or blocked as in preventing speech, representing the silence of holding in secrets and shame. Was the blockage a barrier that tried to keep the other out? Or was it holding the self in?

The image and sensation of our mutually blocked throats helped me to engage in reflective tentative **interpretation**[10] of multiple symbolic meanings (to do with both Gillian *and* myself). It highlighted the importance of attending reflectively to the images, dreams, and nightmares we experience, however bizarre and unconnected they may initially seem.

For Ogden (1997), reveries are metaphorical expressions of what unconscious experience is like, and using dream work with clients can open up meanings. The aim of dream work is to reflect on and engage the symbolic wholeness of the dream. Embracing a reflexive dialogue between conscious and unconscious (or that which is out of awareness) helps individuals to understand their current experience. Through dreams, unconscious, intersubjective experiences can be transformed into images and metaphors which are then rendered more accessible (see box 7.3).

INTUITING, IMAGINING AND INTERPRETING 97

> ### Box 7.3 Case illustration: A dream of loss and letting go
>
> The following account of a dream comes from a young woman whose brother had died in a skiing accident:
>
> > I am hiking alone behind the North Star Ski Resort when I come across some ancient caves. They are blue and cavernous and deep. I rappel down through chamber after chamber, following the blue light. When I reach the end, there is a room with nothing but a fireplace, which is lit, and a rocking chair. My brother is sitting in the rocking chair. He looks strange because he has a very long, gray beard and his hair looks scraggly. I also notice that his fingernails are grotesquely long. He looks very sad. Once again, I go through the feeling that he is not really dead, but has just been here the whole time. I am not angry, though. I ask him what he is doing here. He tells me calmly that he is 'stuck here' and that I need to tell Mom to 'let him go'. (Romanyshyn, 2007, p. 67)
>
> Romanyshyn (a *Jungian, existential-phenomenological* therapist) notes that this dream indicates how loss requires a transformation of one's relation to the other that has been lost. "In the losing we have to let go of what we have loved" (2007, p. 67). This 'interpretation' focuses on overall existential mood themes but could equally engage the archetypal meanings of the image of the 'wise old man' or the event of 'death/separation' or the 'cave' as signifying birth and resurrection.

How dreams are worked with in therapy varies according to the theoretical perspective adopted. For example, a contrast can be drawn between psychoanalytic and humanistic approaches (see box 7.4). In practice, however, integratively orientated therapists may well merge the two (see for instance Cannon, 2012).

- *Psychoanalytic* approaches view dreams as the 'royal road' to the unconscious, bearing unconscious messages which call for probing interpretation. The classic Freudian (1953) view is that dreams act both as wish fulfilment and as censors disguising the unacceptable material of unconscious reality. Freudian analysis aims to use interpretation to uncover the symbolism and work through the defended material. Therapists appropriate the unconscious in the lived world of consciousness in order to compensate for the limitations of consciousness. In more modern relational psychoanalytic version, dreams are seen to embody multiple purposes. A distinguishing feature is the use of *concrete symbolisation* to crystallise the organisation of the subjective world. The meanings of dreams cannot be interpreted and understood outside of the intersubjective context in which they arise (Atwood & Stolorow, 2014).

98   INTUITING, IMAGINING AND INTERPRETING

- In *humanistic* versions, the conscious/unconscious split is denied, and interpretations are avoided in that they are seen as arbitrary impositions of therapists' meanings. Dreams are seen to reflect a feeling tone and something of the dreamer's world, which may be currently in or out of awareness. The *dream world* is seen as accessible (not unconscious) and as experientially valid. In Spinelli's (2007) existential view dream work involves cooperative inquiry. He recommends a non-interpretive descriptive approach when working with dreams, seeing this as part of playfully engaging the relationship between the 'dream world' and the 'waking world'. Dreams thus offer an "existential message" and are the "royal road to integration", as the gestaltist Perls would say (1969, p. 66). Humanistic versions do not regard the therapist as having a privileged understanding of what a dream means. Instead of interpreting a dream, humanistic therapists want to encourage clients to find their own meanings using dream enactment and embodiment: the dream is used to *integrate* (Yontef, 1988).

Box 7.4 Theory: Contrasting Jungian and gestalt approaches to dreams

Jungian **approach**

Dream work is the cornerstone of Jungian psychoanalytic practice. Jung viewed dreams as an expression of the unconscious psyche and a source of wisdom, transformation and healing. His particular contribution was to view dreams as spanning both the personal and the collective unconscious in their ability to carry eternal archetypal[11] energy patterns:

> The dream is a little hidden door in the innermost and most secret recesses of the soul, opening into that cosmic night which was psyche long before there was ego consciousness, and which will remain psyche no matter how far our ego consciousness extends. (Jung, 1964/1970, paras 304–305)

Gestalt **approach**

In the gestalt approach, dreams are viewed as representing parts of self which can be brought into awareness and cathartically worked through in therapy. The client is invited to recount their dream from moment to moment, using the present tense as if the dream is actually happening. The dream can then be re-entered from the perspectives of the different characters or objects that figured in it, which can be seen as representing parts of self. The client–dreamer might also be invited to create a

> dialogue between the dream characters, using role-play. Or the therapist might ask the client if any particular bit of the dream draws the client or has more energy or a particular 'feeling tone', and that could become the focus. The point is not simply to stay with the dream but for the dreamer to experiment with new possibilities; a dream character may point the way.

Beyond theoretical debate, relational therapists regard dream work as *an essentially relational activity* (Gilbert & Orlans, 2011). Seen in these relational terms, there is a need to "approach the dream gently, respecting its integrity, treating it courteously, as we might an honored visitor from abroad" (Stern, 1972, p. 42).

Relational therapists like DeYoung (2003) argue against psychoanalytic preoccupations with inner symbolic worlds; they encourage clients to work with everyday relational experience in the world. As relational therapists, we also recognise that dreams may reflect aspects of the therapeutic work and provide space to explore what may be happening in the relationship. For instance, if the client is dreaming about unsafe spaces, might this represent a question about trust in and the safety of the therapy space? If the client dreams of a scary figure following a challenging session, might that figure represent the therapist and express the client's fears?

Noting that his notebooks are crammed with examples of clients' dreams about him, Yalom (2010) wryly observes that as he ages these dreams increasingly figure his absence and death.

The Relational Base of Imaginal Work

The use of imagery, metaphor, felt sense and dream work takes us into the realm of imaginal worlds. Here, reality and fantasy merge; imagination takes us beyond habitual body/space/time; visionary image transcends language; and the interpersonal transmutes into **trans**personal (Rowan & Jacobs, 2002; Samuels, 1989).[12] Entering this imaginal energetic realm, we find ourselves in the space *between* therapist and client, between consciousness and unconsciousness. Our intuition, imagination and interpretation become tools that help us make sense of the meanings arising in that nebulous, ambiguous space.

Working relationally mostly involves contact between therapist and client, though a similar process can occur in a therapy group when there is honest, sharing communication between members. And, for some, the relational connection occurs via an internal image of a significant other (see box 7.5). Here clients can use their imagination to express in fantasy what needs to be said, even if it cannot happen in reality (Erskine, 2015b).[13]

100 INTUITING, IMAGINING AND INTERPRETING

> **Box 7.5** Case illustration: Imaging a significant other
>
> Johnson (2009) offers an example of working with a depressed client who was struggling to stand up to his wife and ask for a separation even after decades of an extremely disengaged relationship:
>
> > In a key change event, I asked him to connect with the attachment figure who most loved him and might understand his pain. I then asked that he express his pain to this figure (his mother) while visualizing her with his eyes closed. I encouraged him to 'hear' and articulate his mother's loving empathic response. He was able, in his mother's voice, to reassure himself that he had been a good partner and must now listen to his own pain. He then gave himself permission to move into an assertive stance with his wife. This significantly affected his depression. Attachment research also supports the benefits of purposely evoking secure representations; this often leads to increased empathy and positive affect. (2009, p. 418)

In practice, I am struck by the way that imaginal possibilities emerge organically, playfully, creatively, reflexively and mutually through the embodied therapy relationship. Our therapeutic art lies in being open to imaginal visions, hearkening to their call and being ready for their touch.

In engaging imaginal possibilities **playfully**, **creatively** and **reflexively** (i.e. with self-awareness), we recognise that the various meanings contained in imagery, metaphors, felt sense, and dreams are often not self-evident. They need to be played with and worked through relationally. Ideally we should avoid jumping into hard interpretation and take time to dwell with multiple possibilities, resonances and associations. A relational stance avoids seeking to impose meanings from the lofty heights of specialist knowledge; instead, it concerns itself with opening up a dialogue by questions such as, 'What meaning or sense do you make of that?' or 'Help me understand how I feel dangerous to you.' As the dialogue progresses, therapists can then tentatively share their own intuitions and understandings. Any meanings need to be seen in the broader context of the particular individuals' histories, the therapeutic relationship and the wider culture.

As we strive to make sense of our sensings, the **embodied intersubjective relationship** (whether explicit or transferential) has a crucial role to play. The case examples presented in this chapter reaffirm the central interpretive role played by the body. Images worked with are not just visual, they can be visceral and may engage the different senses in multiple ways. Moreover, bodily experiencing remains a fundamentally *inter*subjective act, a mutual receiving and discovery.[14] When I am fully present and immersed in the therapeutic encounter, I am there with the client, sensing, moving, empathising, responding and resonating.

Concluding Reflections

This chapter has explored ways in which we intuit and interpretively enter the imaginal realm. Specific examples have been offered showing the process of using fantasy, metaphor, felt -sense and dream work. I have chosen to foreground *phenomenological/gestalt* and *Jungian* practice but I am aware of the wider potential applications of imagery work in cognitively orientated fields (see Hackmann et al., 2011).

Revisiting the different clients' stories above fills me with awe and wonder as I reflect on the mysterious, seemingly magical moments we sometimes experience in the therapy process. I feel inspired by the beauty of the layers characteristic of our relational encounters, moved by the subtlety and depth of relationships, and humbled by the potential for creative transformation.

In our search for the deepest possible therapeutic interconnection, we need to let ourselves go into it, to trust the process. For me, this means letting go of my being in order to *be-with* the other to the greatest extent possible. I ask myself, 'What might be getting in the way of understanding my client's world or being-with?' It means allowing those bodily experiences, images, gut feelings, symbols, reverie and intuitions that characterise metaphorical sensibility to emerge in unexpected ways. It involves thoughtfully choosing to share (or not share) emergent embodied images and intuitions, however weird or uncertain. It includes embracing the uncanny and the inexplicable as we tune into our primordial interconnection: a space where it can sometimes be hard to disentangle what belongs to oneself, what to the Other. As the phenomenological philosopher Merleau-Ponty says, "To the extent that I understand, I no longer know who is speaking and who is listening" (1964, p. 97).

While imaginal possibilities can be informative, evocative and transformational, they remain opaque, layered and subject to revision. As we know, meanings are only ever part-truths and can never be truly captured. Reflection on meaning always "miscarries at the last moment" (Merleau-Ponty, 1968, p. 9). Much remains beyond words, linguistic games, and therapy techniques. Todres, an existential psychotherapist and phenomenologist, picks up this point in his exploration of the mysterious ambiguous relation between language and Being. As he sees it,

> The 'unsaid' (i.e. implicit meanings), lives always exceedingly as that which the said is about. Speech in a broad sense is pregnant with this excess . . . The shape of understanding is first 'wet through' by the insight of intimate participation and this can come to language in tentative ways. (2007, p. 19)

One of the greatest gifts we give our clients is being attentive to what is emerging in the embodied, intersubjective space *between*. Here, we can work together, using our mutual sensings to make sense of experience, create new narratives and find new ways of being. In this space, there is much to be gained if we remain open to the possibilities opened up by adventures in metaphor and tantalising engagement with dreams and imaginings.

Notes

1 More precisely, the idea of embodied, intuitive senses collapses kinaesthesia (sense of movement), proprioception (inner sense of body in space), and what is sometimes called the 'sixth sense' (including emotions, cognition, intuition and forethought). Anderson (2007), in her **intuitive inquiry** work, notes there are many ways to be intuitive, including through levels she calls the unconscious, direct psychic, sensory-feeling, and empathetic identification, and also through the openings offered by our emotional or historical wounds. Anderson has also developed a Body Insight Scale to identify and measure different aspects of body awareness (Anderson, 2006).

2 Care needs to be taken with such practice that both therapist and client understand the fantasy nature of the exercise ensuring *distorted or false memories* are not being created. Here, both therapist and client were clear that this imagined mother is an idealised fantasy version who becomes sufficiently 'real' at an experiential level that her presence is a source of comfort, validation and healing.

3 Much of the material in this chapter has been drawn from my paper on metaphor use in psychotherapy (Finlay, forthcoming) and has been reproduced here with kind permission of the publishers Taylor & Francis LLC (www.tandfonline.com). I am also grateful to Professor Maria Gilbert, editor of the *British Journal of Psychotherapy Integration*, for giving me permission to draw on the Alex and Gillian case studies from Finlay (2012).

4 Although my practice is primarily existential-phenomenological, my use of some relational psychoanalytic concepts reflects my integrative practice, which allows a blurring.

5 I have taken the liberty of paraphrasing Alex's story, aware that I have not done justice to the original.

6 In some Far Eastern cultures it is possible that Alex would be seen as a good, dutiful daughter, wife and mother. In Western culture the idea of being a 'people pleaser' is mildly pejorative; Alex had internalised this more critical version.

7 In this section I explicitly discuss the phenomenological technique of 'focusing'. Other *TA/gestalt* ways of using the body are discussed in Erskine, 2015a.

8 In a similar but different way, *Jungian* theory identifies the 'subtle body' as the imaginally experienced unconscious-soul energy matrix between two people which is outside 'normal' space/time. Jung suggested that the less access we have to our unconscious thoughts and feelings, the more likely it is that they will be crystallised physically. In becoming denser, the patterns are pressing up against the limits of our conscious mind. This somatising process is a step towards embodiment and towards wholeness.

9 We can also see this shared bodily experiencing at the level of culture. In the Western world, the idea of *feeling choked up with tears* is a routine, even clichéd, metaphor. It is perhaps not surprising that I reached for this symbolic interpretation in trying to understand my bodily being. But in attending to the layers of emotional and cultural symbolism of a *blocked throat*, I want to be cautious about imposing any fixed meanings and interpretations: for me they are best co-created and seen as both emergent and dynamic.

10 Interpretation can be understood as operating at different levels of intensity, from simple mild metaphorical association to empathetic interpretation from within, as in *phenomenological* disclosures of meaning, to more radical probing interpretation from outside where theoretical constructs are important to make sense of meanings as in *psychoanalytic* symbolism. In my own phenomenological practice, I prefer not to impose meanings and instead work with clients to explore their meanings. Rather than shape the client's story, I prefer to offer opportunities for them to find their own truths.

11 Jung spoke of multiple archetypal figures but the primary ones are: Mother, Child, Wise old man, Animal, Anima/Animus and Shadow.

12 Rowan and Jacobs (2002) define **transpersonal** as mystical (even spiritual) experiences that go beyond the usual ego boundaries and involve

an expansion of consciousness beyond the limits of body/time/space. See also: Rowan (1993 online) for a description of the transpersonal emerging through the active imagination, personal mythology, visualisation, guided fantasy, dream work, and meditation.

13 Erskine (2015) suggests that the *gestalt* empty-chair technique can be useful to allow clients an opportunity to have these imaginal conversations to complete 'unfinished business'.

However, for some, direct interpersonal contact between client and therapist may be more effective, particularly if the client cannot visualise the Other, perhaps lacking the internal support.

14 By 'mutual', I do not mean symmetrical in the sense of parity of contribution (Aron, 1996). Rather it is an acknowledgement that two people cannot encounter each other without each impacting on and being impacted on by the Other (Finlay & Evans, 2009).

8

Challenging

All effective helping is a mixture of support and challenge. . . Challenge without support is harsh and unjustified, support without challenge can end up being empty and counterproductive. (Egan, 2010, p. 211)

Bob was a 45-year-old man who felt shame and isolated himself in reaction to any interaction that was not totally positive. He was consistently reluctant to experiment with self-nourishment.

P[ATIENT]: [*whiny voice*] I don't know what to do today.

T[HERAPIST]: [*looks and does not talk*]

P: I could talk about my week. [*looks questioningly at therapist*]

T: I feel pulled on by you right now. I imagine you want me to direct you.

P: Yes. What is wrong with that?

T: Nothing. I prefer not to direct you right now.

P: Why not?

T: You *can* direct yourself. I believe you are directing us away from your inner self now. I don't want to cooperate with that. [*silence*]

P: I feel lost.

T: [looks and does not talk]

P: You are not going to direct me, are you?

T: No.

P: Well, let's work on my believing I can't take care of myself. [patient directs a fruitful piece of work that leads to awareness of abandonment anxiety and feelings of shame in response to unavailable parents] (Yontef, 1993, pp. 156–157)

Relational Integrative Psychotherapy: Engaging Process and Theory in Practice, First Edition. Linda Finlay.
© 2016 John Wiley & Sons, Ltd. Published 2016 by John Wiley & Sons, Ltd.

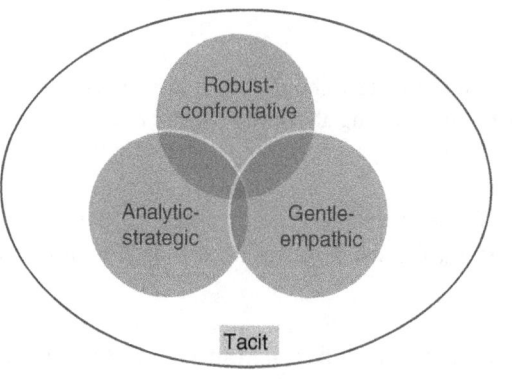

Figure 8.1 Types of challenge

In the dialogue above the therapist subtly challenges through refusing to direct (and potentially rescue or infantilise) the client.

In everyday usage, the word 'challenging' can carry aggressive, even negative connotations: it summons images of argument and discord, even of battle. In the therapeutic context, however, challenging involves a spectrum of responses, from hard-edged, *provocative* confrontation to tender, compassionate, *evocative* challenge.[1] For example, being met by nothing more than a silent, loving gaze can prove hugely challenging for some clients – and might be the only challenge needed for healing.

This chapter discusses four general styles of challenge: **robust-confrontative**, **analytic-strategic**, **gentle-empathic**, and **tacit**. Figure 8.1 indicates the interconnectedness of these styles and how they may mix or remain separate within an overall context of tacit challenge. Numerous examples are offered throughout the chapter. The primary focus is on *gestalt* approaches to challenging, although *cognitive*, *TA* and *relational psychoanalytic* approaches are also touched on. In the final section, I reflect on the ingredients of what makes for effective **challenge in a relational context.**

Robust-confrontative Challenging

Robust-confrontative challenges are designed to grab attention, provoke and create tension, express open disagreement, or set a firm limit or boundary. They constitute the most muscular style of challenge, used when dysfunctional, self-damaging, self-defeating or dishonest behaviour requires direct confrontation.

Yet even in this relatively robust form, confrontation still tends to occur in an empathetic, compassionate way that gives the client sufficient space to make their own choices (McGuire-Bouwman, 2006). Challenges only work in a relational context if the client knows the therapist has their best interests at heart. Consider these two relatively mild examples of confrontation:

THERAPIST: I'm finding it hard to concentrate and getting a bit lost. You're rambling a little. What's that all about? Does my response remind you of anything?

106   CHALLENGING

or

THERAPIST: You said earlier that you wanted to talk about your marriage. But we've just spent the last twenty minutes talking about this job application. Is this what you want to focus on? Might you be avoiding something here?

However, in some contexts more abrasive forms of confrontation may be required, as in this intervention by a therapist working in an adolescent unit for 'troubled teens':

THERAPIST: What the hell are you doing, Cassie? Look at yourself and the choices you're making! You're sleeping around, having unprotected sex. Why? What are you getting? If it's love you're wanting you're looking in the wrong place. You're just a trophy f*** for those boys.

Early *gestalt therapy* was characterised by similarly robust interventions. Check out Perls's charismatic robust-confronting approach in his infamous, though dated, interview with 'Gloria.'[2] In this excerpt, he accuses Gloria of being a 'phoney'. He pushes her to get angry and get 'real' (in other words, not deflect her anger with a smile). In the *psychoanalytic* world, too, some therapists embrace confrontation alongside more empathic interventions.

According to Masterson (1976), a strong, boundaried therapeutic presence and realistic but firm confrontation is the main intervention in the early 'testing and resistance' phase of working with 'borderline' clients:

Confrontation . . . throws a monkeywrench in the patient's defense system by introducing conflict where there previously had been none. The patient had been regulating his internal equilibrium or making himself feel good by acting out in ways that were harmful, but because he denied the harmfulness he felt no conflict. When the therapist points out the harm the patient can no longer act without recognizing the harm. . . . As the therapist brings to the attention of the patient's observing ego that which had been split off and denied, the patient often responds with anger at the loss of a [coping] mechanism. (Masterson, 1976, pp. 100–101)

Box 8.1 Case illustration: Challenging body work

During a professional development workshop, one group member – **Suki** – asked to do some work on integrating her emerging new identity as a peace activist/worker. She tentatively owned her dream to be a 'peace warrior' but then, unused to owning her power, she teetered with shame. The group facilitator suggested she stand up to embody being this 'peace warrior' and invited her to stand holding a shield in one hand and a raised sword in the other.

> Suki complied but, being in an ungrounded place, she looked weak and unconvincing.
>
> The facilitator's response was to provide robust challenge, forcefully urging her to get some 'chi' into her 'floppy arm'. After a while Suki became angry with the facilitator. Together they were able to harness that energy into a more convincing 'peace warrior' posture. Suki was reminded how empowering her anger could be and how it could be used to counteract her shame.

Sometimes, a client may need to be confronted, but this needs to be done selectively, within the context of a therapeutic alliance. I might say, 'You say you can't, but don't you mean "won't"?' or 'How many times are you prepared to keep going back to being abused by her?' Therapist self-disclosure can also offer a useful – if occasionally risky – model of presence and openness. In the past, I shared with a client that I felt 'used' by her in the same manner as a soothing medication, which was then discarded until she needed me again. Exploring this further, we realised how she herself had felt used and then abandoned in all her significant relationships. It was the start of her deciding to relate in new and different ways.

Building on Masterson's work with **personality adaptations** (see box 8.2), gestaltist Yontef (1988) agrees that therapists need to be consistently and energetically present to contain regression and interrupt acting out when working with individuals with *borderline* disorders. Boundaries (containing and limiting) need to be strongly maintained but in a non-judgemental, and realistic and rational, rather than authoritarian way (for example, encouraging awareness of logical consequences of behaviour). These individuals need to be encouraged to take self-responsibility rather than make excessive demands for support (e.g., the client rings the therapist at all hours). "The borderline patient needs a therapist who energetically, reliably, explicitly, consistently and insistently presents the demands of the environment for consideration" (1988, p. 473).

However, in the case of clients more inclined towards *narcissistic* and *schizoid* styles, confrontative interventions are likely to be too shaming and intrusive. The therapist needs to work more analytically or empathically, making use of the other forms of challenge. Yontef recommends that therapists offer narcissistically inclined individuals gentle, warm, soothing, affirming responses, and that challenges initially focus on clients' experience in an attempt to validate the core self. The aim is to enable the person to feel safe enough to show their grandiosity or depletion. Hopefully, in time, they will open up about their unmet needs; through learning self-support and how to keep perspective, they will become more available for contact.

108   CHALLENGING

> ### Box 8.2 Theory: Personality or character disorders
>
> Yontef (1988) describes borderline and narcissistic 'character disorders' in the following ways.[3]
>
> **Borderline** persons have "intense emotions" and are "emotionally labile". They are prone to "impulsive, addictive and acting out" behaviour without regard for "consequences, ethics, safety or legality" (p. 460). They often have entangled close relationships and disturbed boundaries involving intense confluent attachment where they are dependent, demanding and manipulative. Without a solid sense of object-constancy, separations are experienced as abandonment and can result in psychological disintegration. Commonly the person 'splits', for example lurching from feeling the Other is all 'good' to feeling they are all 'bad'. At a more subtle level, the splitting is seen in splitting connectedness/incompetence and autonomy/competence. Competence means abandonment so the person remains 'incompetent', in need of help.
>
> The **narcissistic** person is "one who is easily wounded, has low self-esteem, is very dependent on the attention, approval, respect and love of others to maintain a sense of themselves . . . [and] any semblance of equilibrium. . . . The narcissistic person fills with shame and erupts in rage, despair and/or panic and at those times appears inconsolable" (p. 429). This person may lurch between a sense of self-centred grandiosity (with associated contempt and devaluing of others) at one end and a sense of feeling deflated, depleted and despairing (involving extreme shame and self-rejection) at the other.

Analytic-strategic Challenging

Analytic-strategic challenging occurs when therapists (1) work more cognitively (at Adult level in TA terms), (2) give honest feedback, and (3) invite the client to take responsibility for life choices.

Working **cognitively**, the therapist attempts to enable clients to be aware of their creative self-protective responses, perhaps underlining how reasonable – even rational – they were in the circumstances. A secondary level of challenge involves suggesting they may now be able to do something different.

Challenges can usefully be offered through **feedback**, with a focus on observable behaviours (such as a tapping toe or the incongruent smile) and on how the client's behaviour makes us feel. Such challenges are usually more fruitful than those made on the basis of interpretations and assumptions about internal processes, because they are less open to dispute. 'I'm noticing you have just clenched your fists and I'm wondering if that is in response to what I've just said . . . What are your clenched fists saying?' is likely to prove more effective than 'You're feeling angry with me, aren't you?' (See box 8.3).

CHALLENGING 109

> **Box 8.3** Case illustrations: Providing feedback dialogically
>
> THERAPIST: I'm noticing that we're falling into a pattern here. I'm giving you practical suggestions and you've always got a 'Yes, but' reply telling me it's not going to work.
>
> CLIENT: Maybe. Yeah, I guess so.
>
> THERAPIST: I find myself wanting to argue with you. But also the anger I feel is mainly on the surface. Underneath I think I'm feeling rejected; that I can't offer you any right answers. How are you experiencing what we're doing?
>
> CLIENT: Hmmm . . . you're reminding me of my mother when she nagged me and wanted to control everything.
>
> THERAPIST: Ah, I think I understand a bit now why I have this sense of you pushing me away. Was that what you had to do with your mother to stop her controlling you?
>
> THERAPIST: [noting that her new client keeps reading incoming texts on her mobile phone, and holding her irritation in check] Bethany, I'm noticing your attention seems only half on what we're talking about and half on your phone. It feels like you're only half here.
>
> BETHANY: [sullenly rolls her eyes and puts away her phone]
>
> THERAPIST: Your reaction just now suggests you might have felt told off by me?
>
> BETHANY: Whatever.
>
> THERAPIST: I wasn't trying to tell you off. I was curious. I felt you were telling me you preferred to be with your friends and not me.
>
> BETHANY: I guess so.
>
> THERAPIST: I appreciate your honesty.

When inviting a client to take **responsibility for choices**, we might say, 'You're at an important choice point. Do you want to carry on avoiding and hiding or do something different?'

Another example is the client who feels forced to ring his ageing mother every week:

CLIENT: I resent having to ring her every week. She just winds me up and brings me down.

THERAPIST: I'm curious then about why you ring her every week without fail. You could choose not to ring. What would that mean to you?

Such analytic-strategic challenges can open up an exploration of how the client *feels* (feeling pressured to make that weekly phone call in the case above), *thinks* (unable to see choices), and *behaves* (lacking assertiveness and the ability to resist making the call). This multi-level approach to challenge can also be found in more gentle-empathic variants.

Gentle-empathic Challenging

Gentle-empathic challenging involves a more emergent process. It arises out of an *ev*ocative mode of influence where the therapist attempts to bring about a shift of awareness, perhaps in both client and therapist. This contrasts with the *pro*vocative-confrontative mode discussed above, which involves a forcing, jolting process designed to achieve an action or re-action (Nevis, 1983).

Gentle-empathic challenging is shown in the following examples:

1. CLIENT: [deflecting] It's not a big deal.
   THERAPIST: It *is* a big deal! It seems HUGE to me.

2. THERAPIST: You're telling me this incredibly difficult, sad story and I'm very impacted by the tough time you had. At the same time, I'm noticing you smiling as you tell this story. What is that smile saying?

3. CLIENT: I've always been a failure.
   THERAPIST: *Always?*

4. THERAPIST: You say you hate your mother and I hear something of the rage that underlies that. Yet I also see you being incredibly generous to her and caring. Is there a little love there too amongst the anger?

As these varied examples show, this form of challenging involves attuning to and verbalising feelings. At the same time a challenge is issued, one which calls attention to something that doesn't quite fit. A 'Say more about that' nudges the client to explore matters further.

The target of such challenging is often a client's self-defeating expressions of feeling and emotion and self-limiting internal responses. In response to a client who is viciously castigating themselves, a therapist might say, 'You're being *really* hard on yourself'. The client could then be encouraged to remove themselves from damaging internal dialogues, for example to step outside their usual perspective via imaginal work: the therapist might ask the client how they would respond if they came upon a parent in a supermarket berating their child so harshly.

As with other forms of challenging, the key is to offer the challenge in a way that doesn't shame the client or put them on the defensive. In their version of **relational TA**, Hargaden and Sills (2002) recommend that therapists offer challenges in validating, empathic ways.[4] This, they suggest, will open the way for deeper enquiry and focus on how the client's sense of 'lack of OK-ness' has been internalised and become part of a relational template. Therapists can confront by pinpointing any persistent, if subtle, discounting (of self or of the therapist or the therapy).

Box 8.4 offers an example of a **relational gestalt/TA** dialogue. Here, the therapist (Richard Erskine) subtly challenges his client's (Herbert's) expectation of being criticised by *refusing* to criticise him. Erskine understands that indicating anything remotely like disapproval of Herbert would only reinforce his crippling view of himself and his world.[5] In the dialogue therapist and client discuss Herbert's critical introjects and their links with his alcoholic behaviour.

CHALLENGING   111

> **Box 8.4** Case illustration: Decommissioning an introjected Critical Parent through empathic challenging
>
> HERBERT: Well . . . if you haven't criticized me yet, ya, well I'm waiting for it.
>
> RICHARD: . . . Herbert, how am I going to criticize that deep sadness that permeates your life? The sadness that goes with that belief, 'I'm an outcast'. The sadness underlying the belief, 'I'm misunderstood'. That sadness underlying the belief, 'people are out to use me.' The real depression that goes along with 'What's the use?' That 'life is a struggle'.
>
> HERBERT: Life is life. What are you going to do about it but carry on.
>
> RICHARD: Well I think what you did is, you drank, not to feel that hurt.
>
> HERBERT: I like to drink.
>
> RICHARD: And what happens when you get the booze in you? What happens to that hurt?
>
> HERBERT: I start feeling like I'm somebody. Like somebody important . . .
>
> RICHARD: Well, Herbert, you've been somebody for me. And you haven't been drinking while we've been talking.
>
> (Erskine & Moursund, 1988, pp. 285–286)

With reference to Herbert's story, the authors suggest that when individuals are not given permission to exist and have their needs attended to, they find artificial solutions like drinking alcohol. The unfinished gestalt is temporarily closed by drinking; for a short while, the emptiness is filled. But this solution then becomes a new problem. In Herbert's case, drinking makes him feel important, but his drunkenness invites others to treat him as unimportant.

Often the growing edge for our clients (and ourselves) is what happens at the 'contact boundary' of the therapeutic relationship. This contact is both internal, in terms of getting in contact with feelings or needs which may be partly out of awareness, and external, which concerns becoming aware of the people in and the demands of the environment around (Erskine et al., 1999).

It is at this contact boundary that *resistances* to challenges (and change) are to be found. By resistances I mean those times when invitations to encounter feelings or explore experience are abruptly declined. When a client blocks something or avoids exploring it further, some **humanistic** therapists view this as a positive choice rather than seeing it in **psychoanalytic** terms as defensive resistance. (I take the humanistic line and see it as indicating a need to go slower in order to assimilate new ideas. If a client indicates their wish to avoid something that at the moment feels too overwhelming, I might invite them to simply stay with that awareness and see what happens. And perhaps the client is simply making a healthy choice to focus on something different from the things that have caught my

112 CHALLENGING

attention. The therapist's role then is to respect and support the client's choice while continuing to challenge by encouraging them to become even more aware of the options available.)

Tacit Challenging

Silent, tacit challenges are ever present in the therapeutic encounter. Just sitting in the therapy room is a challenge for some. This applies particularly with clients new to therapy who, fearing the unknown, find it difficult even to come to therapy. Once inside, they are asked to put aside lifelong habits and injunctions, such as 'we don't talk about our feelings'. And so it starts, the uncomfortable therapeutic challenges begin, immediately confirming doubts about entering the room in the first place.

A different example is the therapist's decision to put a withdrawn client into a group in order for him to have the emotionally corrective experience of an alternative 'family'. The therapist's hope is that the client will gain a sense of attachment to others and learn new ways of expressing himself in a safe situation: one where conflict is managed without anyone getting hurt. In this way, the group environment becomes both a safe 'container' and a tacit 'challenger'.

Clients can also find it challenging to be in the presence of a supportive, compassionate therapist: the potential nourishment of the therapeutic relationship can itself be troubling. How challenging might it be for a client full of self-critical bile to be looked at with kind eyes?

Box 8.5 Case illustration: 'What do you see when you look at me?'

Katya is a 30-year-old woman who grew up in a war-torn Eastern European country. Her parents were killed in the war when she was a child and she went to live with distant relatives who turned out to be physically and emotionally abusive. She eventually emigrated to the UK, where she found a reasonably secure job and a husband. Following a miscarriage, however, she felt depressed, isolated and estranged from her social relationships. This prompted her therapy, where she faced multiple layers of trauma, grief and shame.

After several months, she was expressing and exploring some of her pain, but she remained dissociated and was often unable to sustain eye contact with her therapist.

THERAPIST: Can you look at me, Katya?
KATYA: No, It's errr, too hard.

> THERAPIST: What's hard?
>
> KATYA: I'm, I'm afraid of what I'll see.
>
> THERAPIST: What are you afraid of seeing?
>
> KATYA: I don't know. Your disgust. You say nice things but I think I will see that really you're err, judging me.
>
> THERAPIST: So you're already believing that I'm judging you. How about checking it out to see if you're right, to see what I'm really saying?
>
> KATYA: No, no, I can't. I'm too scared to look.
>
> THERAPIST: What might happen if you look?
>
> KATYA: I'll see you don't like me; you'll think I'm bad.
>
> THERAPIST: But if you think that I'm feeling that anyway, what have you got to lose? Please, will you try to look at me? [Katya takes a peep as the therapist smiles gently] And what did you see?
>
> KATYA: Umm, You look. . . kind.
>
> THERAPIST: Yes, I think that is what my eyes are saying. And they are saying something more. Will you look again?
>
> KATYA: It's so hard. It's hard to look. [Katya looks up and holds the therapist's loving gaze momentarily and then starts to sob]

The example in box 8.5 shows the painful double-bind Katya is in: it was scary for her not to be seen, *and* it was scary to be seen. Expecting a judging, critical face, she felt exposed and wanted to disappear. But her hiding away from eye contact then created an endless loop where she could not receive positive messages to counterbalance her shame. As a result she felt more diminished (Yontef, 1993).

The therapist's loving compassion invoked a *juxtaposition*[6] response (Moursund & Erskine, 2004). Here the nourishment of the therapeutic relationship is contrasted with the violence of her earlier family relationships. For Katya, the pain of receiving a loving gaze was a major challenge to her sense of being bad and deserving of judgement. Part of the challenge was that receiving the love she had so longed for triggered another layer of grief for all the loving she had never had.

Aside from being a shame response, Katya's lack of eye contact suggested she might be distancing herself from parts of herself to avoid re-encountering the many layers of grief that she had buried. She desperately wanted – and needed – to have a loving relationship with a parental figure (the therapist), for this was what she had been missing for much of her life. Yet in order to meet that need she risked getting hurt (replaying being abused) and re-awakening her grief (which she had kept at bay over the years by dissociating). Her dissociation can be understood as a way of keeping her experience of loss and emptiness out of her awareness. Facing it now in therapy was painful (Moursund & Erskine, 2004).[7]

Katya's story illustrates just how challenging therapy can be. Even before we open our mouths to speak, our very presence as therapists taps evocatively into clients' longings and needs that may have been long buried or denied.

Key Principles of Effective Challenging

The process of challenging is layered and complex. Much depends on the specific context and the people involved. However, there are some general (and interlinked) principles that probably apply across all challenging relational interventions.

1. Therapists need to believe in the **value of** challenge, and acknowledge the vital role it plays in nudging someone towards new ways of thinking, feeling and behaving. There are times when we need to say difficult things to clients, and some degree of challenge is necessary for forward movement.

   That said, it is not uncommon for less experienced therapists to be reluctant to challenge. In addition to lacking confidence and nursing fears about what might happen, such therapists may well have some residual archaic anxiety stemming from a "thousand confrontation agendas" from their own past, situations where their child was "too vulnerable, unskilled and insecure to confront its parents" (Heron, 2001, p. 61). With this double layer of anxiety, it's not surprising that we find it easier to be supportive and empathic than to invite conflict or negative transferences. Maintaining positive, idealising transferences feels safer. However, by so doing we may end up colluding with the client's avoidance strategies and blind spots. It is worth remembering that clients are often more robust than we think; that 'pussyfooting' around is likely to be more damaging than a straight, honest, well-meaning comment (Heron, 2001).

2. Challenging should be **relational** and always performed in the context of a therapeutic relationship. In the early stages of therapy, when trust is being established, it is usually advisable to avoid muscular, provocative challenges. In his *existential-relational* model of practice, Spinelli (2015) argues that in early phases simply attending to a client and attuning to them in a 'staying-with' way may constitute a sufficient challenge. For one thing, 'staying-with' may offer the client the rare experience of being with another who doesn't immediately set out to diminish, reject, dispute or try to change their world view. That alone may have profound impact. Later, once sufficient trust has been established for the therapist to express disagreement, more explicit challenging can be engaged towards exposing 'what is there' for the client.

   Yalom (2010) also emphasises the relational when he recommends that we phrase our challenges and feedback in terms of wanting to get closer to the client but finding that their behaviour is making that difficult by creating a distance.

3. Challenges should be issued in the **client's interest** rather than being prompted by our own feelings of frustration, impatience or irritation. This ethical imperative is probably obvious but it can be hard to find the right balance. Caught in powerful counter-transferences and projective identifications (see chapter 14), we can all too easily fall into confrontational, critical ways of being (which in other circumstances, and with a cooler head, we could have

avoided). It is therefore important to be aware of our *urge* to challenge in more destructive, self-serving ways. Then we can hope to frame our challenge constructively, so that it can be non-defensively received.

That said, there are times when the therapeutic moment may require a more spontaneous, forceful, honest challenge. I remember witnessing a piece of work in a personal and professional group where the therapist suddenly pushed her chair away from the client and exploded: 'I am not going to do this work! I refuse to be manipulated! This is your toxic mother talking and I am not prepared to be annihilated by her!' This proved a pivotal moment for the group member, who became much more aware of the power of her toxic internalised 'mother' to damage and manipulate. She began the process of learning that whenever she became 'swipey' her 'mother' might be around. Armed with this awareness, she could then choose to close this 'mother' down.

4. Challenging needs to be engaged in with **empathy** and compassion. Clients need to know that our challenges spring from caring concern. All challenging needs to be integrated into the wider therapy process and designed to help clients develop alternative perspectives, internal processes and actions:

> All challenges should. . .be based on understanding, be caring (not power games or put downs), be genuine (not tricks or games), and be designed to increase the client's self-responsibility (not expressions of helper control). . .Empathy should permeate every kind of challenge. (Egan, 2010, p. 252)

When giving such challenges, it can be useful to use the 'on the other hand . . .' type of intervention. For example, 'I can feel something of how hard it is for you to talk about that. On the other hand, I think it would be helpful to put it into words.' Or, 'I'm hearing you say you're calm. On the other hand, I see your foot tapping and I'm wondering if your body is saying something different?'

5. Our aim is to use a proportionate amount – an **optimal** level – of challenge. Too much challenge, or challenge delivered when the person isn't ready to receive it, can be shaming, undermining, and overwhelming; it can fuel defensiveness and resistance. Too little challenge and we end up colluding with cosy stagnation. Ideally we establish an appropriate balance, perhaps via feedback or confrontation, together with a non-judgemental compassion designed to develop awareness and courage.

6. It can help to ask **permission** to challenge. For instance, 'I'd like to offer you a challenge. Are you up for it?' Yalom (2010) discusses this in terms of giving *feedback* to clients. Here he recommends first enlisting the patient as an 'ally' and asking permission to offer a here-and-now observation. Then he explains that his observations are relevant to the person's reason for being in therapy, saying, for example, 'Perhaps I can help you understand what goes wrong with relationships in your life by examining our relationship as it is occurring' (Yalom, 2010, p. 118).

116   CHALLENGING

7. It is useful to encourage *self*-challenge (Egan, 2010). As our aim is to facilitate self-awareness and taking responsibility for choices, it makes sense to use probes which give the client the opportunity to think through situations for themselves. As Yalom (2010) notes, once clients recognise their role in their problematic life situation, they begin to understand they have the power to change it. Consider this intervention for instance: 'You are sharing your different stories of online dating with me and I'm seeing a bit of a pattern where it seems you tend to end up feeling used and betrayed. Is this a familiar pattern? Would you be willing to think about your own role in this?'

8. It can help to challenge unused **strengths** rather than weaknesses (Egan, 2010), given that challenging needs to avoid putting too many demands on the person so they feel overwhelmed, shamed or hopeless. For instance, instead of challenging a client for being an unhealthy 'rescuer', it may work better to note the client's huge caring ability when it comes to others but not for herself.

    As another example, consider the situation where a supervisor wants to challenge a shy, anxious trainee to speak up more in the supervision group. A negative intervention like 'You're being passive and letting the others take your time' is likely to be received badly. Instead, the supervisor might say, 'I really appreciate the way you're beginning to speak up and share your view quietly. I get the feeling that you feel good about that and would like to do it more often? How might you do that and what do you need from us to help you?'

9. Challenge issued with shared **gentle humour** can be as forceful as a shout and, sensitively done, need not be shaming. A client tended to deflect away from contact with the therapist by turning her head to the side. Noting this pattern, the therapist mirrored this, much to the client's amusement, who then exaggerated the movement in recognition of its familiarity. Thereafter, the therapist's use of this head turning offered a shorthand prompt challenging the client to stay in contact. The client smilingly accepted this challenge where a verbal one might have felt too critical.

10. Finally, it is only fair that we ourselves stay **open to being challenged** as therapists. The challenge here could be from our clients, our colleagues, or even our 'internal supervisor' (see box 8.6). How else are we to grow and develop? Additionally, being open and non-defensive towards challenges from clients is a useful way to model this behaviour.

> **Box 8.6** Case illustration: Being challenged in supervision
>
> **Rekha** raises in supervision the matter of a client she is struggling with. The (white) client had made aggressive, Islamophobic comments and was generally full of critical bile and scorn. While Rekha felt some irritation at being stereotyped as a Muslim when her family background is Hindu, mostly she just felt diminished. She felt subtly attacked as being inferior and, as a

CHALLENGING   117

result, felt silenced. She was unable to do much more than just listen and she recognised that she had become ungrounded and unable to hold on to her presence. After the session, Rekha recognised that she should have challenged and disavowed the racist views and was annoyed at herself, as in other contexts she would normally say something.

The supervisor agreed that there had been a missed opportunity to challenge. At the same time she acknowledged the difficulty of maintaining a compassionate empathic presence in the face of a client's scorn, particularly when something repellent is being said. After the supervisor admitted that she too would have found that session very difficult, the two of them discussed some interventions that might have worked.

Rekha and her supervisor were able to recognise that Rekha, who had shown herself well able to challenge other clients, was in some sort of *process* with her client. The supervisor thus shifted the focus onto what was happening *within* the relationship, onto what it was that had silenced Rekha so effectively. Had Rekha feared some sort of aggressive backlash? Was this fear connected with something from her own developmental history? Or would that aggression represent something of Rekha's client's experience of being caught up in a drama triangle? Perhaps the client herself had been silenced with a 'don't speak out' injunction. Was Rekha perhaps picking up her client's own anxiety and shame?

The supervisor proceeded to do some teaching from a Kleinian psychoanalytic perspective, suggesting two other possible interpretations: (1) The client might have been deriving some unconscious pleasure from the relief of expelling painful, conflicted parts of self by projecting them onto the 'Other' (Muslims). (2) The client might have been engaged in an unconscious identification with her punitive authoritarian parents, whose views she had introjected.

At the end of the session Rekha felt both supported and challenged. With her supervisor's help, she had developed greater awareness of the nature of relational work and had deepened her theoretical understanding.

Concluding Reflections

This chapter has focused on the possibilities opened up by well-timed, sensitively engaged therapeutic challenge. Such challenge invites a relational examination of intersubjective processes and behaviours.

The different styles in which therapeutic challenging can be conducted (vigorous-confrontative, analytic-strategic, gentle-empathic and tacit) can help reveal inconsistencies and blind spots which keep clients stuck in self-restricting, self-damaging ways of being. In its tacit form, our very presence as compassionate therapists offers a profound ongoing challenge. Whatever the form, *challenge remains a necessary and ever-present component of therapeutic process.*

The *art* of relational integrative therapy is to find that tricky balance between **challenge** and **support** – a balance which we tailor for each individual. It's about balancing competing pressures and needs regarding setting limits and allowing freedom, using pressure and communicating acceptance, being sure and being tentative, taking risks and ensuring safety, imposing oneself and allowing the other, to name just a few of the tensions. We make these judgements intuitively and routinely throughout every session, simultaneously recognising that what is challenging for one person may be water off a duck's back for another. Ultimately, we must all find our own particular preferred styles of *being-with* clients; our challenges must be in tune with the emergent relational context, the theoretical models we adopt and our personal values.[8] And, of course, we won't always get it 'right'.

I like gestaltist Philippson's (2012) metaphor that, in the face of a closed door, you can wait, knock or push it. The decision to challenge depends on how much (self and external) support both client and therapist have. He recommends waiting if the client is terrified, and knocking to check how someone is doing. Pushing the door open is best when the transference would be too destructive if the therapist waited, provided the therapist would not be acting out of anger.

Where clients embrace our challenging and learn to reframe their actions and take responsibility for them, some healing integration can take place. It is to this topic of integration that we turn next.

Notes

1 This distinction between *pro*-vocative and *e*-vocative interventions or 'modes of influence' was originally discussed by the gestaltist Nevis (1983).

2 See https://www.youtube.com/watch?v=8y5tuJ3Sojc. The extract is one of three fascinating films in a series made in the 1960s called 'Three Approaches to Psychotherapy'. This contrasted Albert Ellis's rational emotive behavior therapy, Carl Rogers's person-centred therapy, and Perls's gestalt therapy. Each therapist was invited to treat the same client.

3 Note that with the use of the term 'disorder' Yontef (1988) is referring to more extreme forms of personality adaptations. Most of us can periodically dip into narcissistic or borderline ways of being. He is clear that he is not offering recipe treatments. It is important to still treat

the individual person and make contact with openness. I agree. We should not discard the person's *complexity* and our own *unknowing* by putting people into predetermined boxes.

4 Hargaden and Sills (2002) contradict Eric Berne's idea that 'decontamination' precedes 'deconfusion'. They argue that a person needs a reasonably solid sense of self to avoid feeling attacked or irrelevant in the face of challenge.

5 This case study actually represents a *Parent interview* dialogue (McNeel, 1976) between the therapist and his client, Jon, whose internalised father is called Herbert. Thus, the intervention of challenge or confrontation is layered, targeting both the introjected Parent and the Parent's (Herbert's) critical introjects (see chapter 16).

6 'Juxtaposition' has been understood and described in different ways. In general, it refers to

the noticing of two contradictory ideas or ways of being which are present in the same frame, e.g. from the past and in the present.

7 Different therapists understand disassociation in subtly different ways. *Psychoanalyst* Stern (2003) understands dissociation as refusal to interpret experience, which exhibits itself as defensively avoiding verbal and symbolic articulation. Taking an *existential relational psychoanalytic* view, Stolorow (2011, p. 54) sees dissociation as a defensive "tunnel vision" that narrows experiential horizons and keeps emotional worlds apart so as to exclude the terrifying, the prohibited, and the emotionally unbearable. For Stolorow, that experiential horizon includes a temporal dimension where the person feels alienated and estranged from others: "torn from the communal fabric of being-in-time" (p. 56).

Similarly, the *humanistic* and *gestalt* view is to see dissociation as a 'creative adjustment' (Evans & Gilbert, 2005) developed to survive otherwise unbearable trauma. It can become dysfunctional when the environment is no longer traumatic but the person still lives as if it is.

8 While all the forms of challenging discussed in this chapter can be applied across the theoretical spectrum, commonly, *person-centred* therapists tend to prefer to engage more tacit forms of challenge; *TA-orientated* and *psychodynamic* therapists tend towards analytic challenges; and *gestalt* therapists have traditionally enacted more robust forms of challenge. The challenge of being an integrative therapist requires us to examine our personal and theoretical values towards developing preferred styles of challenge.

9

Integrating

The client is becoming whole. Contact with the self, with all its complexities and capacities, so long split and fragmented, is being re-established. Feelings and thoughts and perceptions rush in, often with surprising intensity. And each of those long-repressed, long-hidden parts of self has a kind of fragility, like a flower bud freshly opened or a butterfly newly escaped from its hard cocoon. (Erskine et al., 1999, p. 172)

The aim of integrative psychotherapy is to facilitate a sense of wholeness in a person's being and functioning, at intrapsychic, mind–body, relational, societal and transpersonal levels. We strive to enable our clients to gain insight into their experience and to have a sense of feeling 'at home' with self, at ease with others. There are of course limits to the extent to which any of us can be deemed 'whole', but integration remains the driving spirit of our project – particularly with longer-term work.

Being relational we insist that, ultimately, healing integration occurs through relationships (with the therapist and with others). Therapeutic relationships act as catalysts enabling client's growth through fresh insight, reflection and the experience of relating at depth. It's the new experience of being in relationship which allows previous ways of being to be understood and laid to rest, and new ways of being to be brought into life. DeYoung (2003, p. 152–153) explains this elusive process:

That's why therapy begins by focusing on the here-and-now therapy relationship and on changes for the better in that relationship: in order to create a space within which integration and insight will eventually find a home. . . .

Relational Integrative Psychotherapy: Engaging Process and Theory in Practice, First Edition. Linda Finlay.
© 2016 John Wiley & Sons, Ltd. Published 2016 by John Wiley & Sons, Ltd.

INTEGRATING   121

> [R]elational therapy becomes first a place where a client feels better as she feels understood, then a place where she sometimes feels worse than ever . . ., and finally a place where new interpersonal confidence can emerge, along with new insight and self-integration – providing a sturdier, more durable kind of feeling better.

This integrating, healing therapeutic journey towards feeling more at home with self and others is the focus of this chapter. Chapter 1 discussed *theoretical* integration; the focus in this chapter is on clients' integration.

The first section briefly lays out the nature of the **integrating process**.[1] Four therapeutic journeys are then described to springboard theoretical discussion. **Jayne**'s story is presented first. This example from my own practice demonstrates the process of integrating intrapsychic *parts of self* (selves) into a new integrated whole using an integrative existential-phenomenological, gestalt and TA-orientated approach. The second story – **Kjell**'s – has been taken from Rothschild (2003a); it illustrates how therapy worked towards a layered relational integration of many dimensions including *body/mind*, *past/present/future*, and *self/other*. The underlying theoretical approach taken by Rothschild arose out of a blending of 'somatic trauma therapy', CBT and attachment theory. The third story – **Norbert**'s – taken from Ruppert (2008), describes the use of family constellation work drawing on both psychoanalytic and systemic thinking as well as attending to *mind/soul* connections.[2] The final case study comprises a letter written by a client. Here, **Steven** describes what integration means for him.

The Integrating Project: Levels of Integration

The answer to the key question 'What are we are striving to integrate?' is that it is multi-layered and interconnected (see figure 9.1). There is a layer related to *intrapsychic integration* (e.g. conscious–unconscious) where disowned or unacknowledged parts of self are brought together. Then there is the integration of **body–mind** and *relational-social integration* (or self–other) where our relationship with our self and others in the social world become more connected. Lastly there is *transpersonal* integration, which taps spiritual aspects including intergenerational integration of ancestral history.[3]

Any or all of these levels can become the focus of therapy in which we seek to enable clients to make insightful connections and become aware of experiences that may have been out of awareness. Integrative insight comes in many guises and involves links being made between past and present, conscious and unconscious,[4] thought, feelings and behaviour, and self and other. The insights might be emotional or intellectual, sudden or gradual. The process is one of trying to make sense of experience and perhaps moving from terror or despair and meaninglessness to curiosity, positive connections and meaningfulness (see box 9.1).

122   INTEGRATING

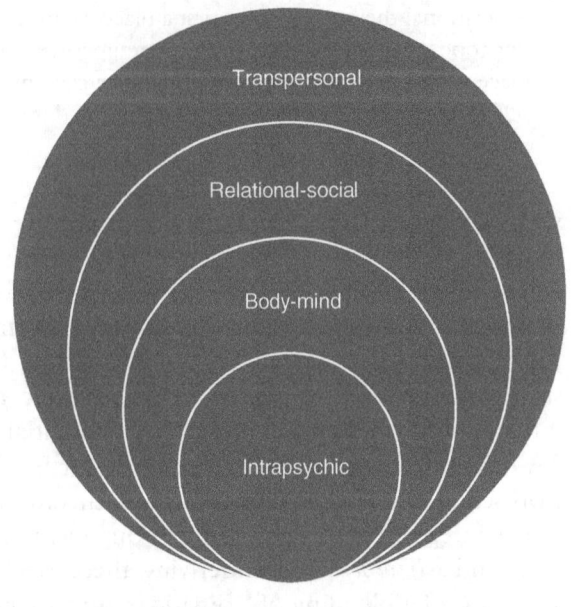

Figure 9.1   Levels of possible integration

Box 9.1 Case illustration: Integrating insight

Joe was in a state of paralysing indecision about whether or not to take up a wonderful opportunity to work in Africa. This was enacted in his procrastination about sorting out his visa and inoculations. Deadlines were looming and Joe was on the cusp of missing his opportunity through inaction.

Recognising that conflicted internal dialogue was probably the root of Joe's indecision, the therapist invited him to put his rival internal voices on different chairs around the room. He was prompted to sit in each chair in turn and express that perspective. Soon he was immersed in a dialogue between his 'voices' and he gained significant insight into the motivations, drives and uncertainties that were impacting his behaviour. After some negotiation between the 'voices' (for example, his Nurturing Parent self contracted to take care of his anxious Child self), a consensus was reached. Joe got his visa and vaccinations in time and enjoyed his adventure in Africa.

A year later the therapist received a letter from Joe. He expressed his gratitude and let her know his Africa trip had been a great success. He also wanted her to know that he now regularly used this technique of using different chairs for talking with his different 'voices' to help him make decisions.

The different layers of insight and integration we celebrate are relevant to both our client and to ourselves. We are all engaged in an ongoing integrative project: it's not something that ever ends as there is always more that could be integrated. Our work with clients involves working *with* them in a learning-exploring space, towards making sense of their lives; we don't integrate clients – not ever. Instead we collaboratively engage a gentle integrating *process*. The integrating work with ourselves is the ongoing work we engage in our own therapy and when we are reflexive about our practice in supervision or through other CPD activities.

How exactly we effect this integration is possibly unexplainable. The mystery and the magic of our work rely on artful dimensions of practice which emerge beyond theory, technique and method, and also on the capacity of our clients to recognise and embrace their own journey. In an attempt to nurture integration, I might simply act as a **witness**, a mirror or a sounding board. For instance, I might say, 'I am curious about the way you are missing out — here.' Or 'Your voice gets soft when you speak of —.'

Another avenue to enabling new awareness can be to **invite comparisons** between the therapy context and outside. Are there things that a client can say in therapy that they feel they couldn't say outside? What would help them say it outside, assuming that would be desirable? How might they take their learning from one situation into another? Would a 'homework' task be helpful? It is through such opening up that integration in different relational contexts beyond the therapy room evolves.

Working with a client at the contact boundary we often encounter 'resistances' which may signal a titanic battle between the segment of the client that is struggling to emerge and become whole and the segment that seeks to remain partial, hidden or entrenched, between the side that wants change and the side that feels safer with the status quo. In our role as therapists, it is part of our work to name this battle, to try to bring it to the **client's awareness**. For example, if a client says, 'Part of me wants that, the other part is scared', it might be helpful to engage role-play or empty-chair work acting out the two sides of the internal dialogue (which often occurs just out of awareness).

Enacting such dialogues allows clients to attend to what they are saying and begin to **make connections**. In time they may be able to hold the polarities which represent their experience more comfortably. Such enactments may begin the process of integration as clients become increasingly aware of their process. Then, as old ways of being and thinking are transformed, they are revised and revisited, and further new connections are made (see box 9.2). This learning spiral both occurs in the therapy space and is rehearsed in the world outside (Erskine et al., 1999).

All the previous chapters in part I of this book identify ways in which we might be present with our clients, bringing our empathy, intuition, challenge, resources and knowledge, and our heart and soul, to bear towards the complex and layered task of working towards integrating experience. However, there are no easy formulae that can be applied to increase insight and effect change. Integration

> **Box 9.2** Case illustration: Making connections towards integration
>
> A client sends an email to her therapist acknowledging her new awareness:
>
> > I had a huge 'aha' moment that I wanted to share with you. I thought about your challenge to me that I wasn't taking in what you were saying. I suddenly realise you're right and recognise how hard it is for me to accept your compassion. I'm so not used to it. It's confusing and challenges those voices in my head that tell me I'm unlovable and defective. I yearn for loving compassion but when I get it, I feel sad. I realise what it is that I have been missing all my life. I wanted to explain this to you; to explain why I push you away, just like I push other people away. It's safer isn't it, to have people at a distance? So they don't really see you. But by letting people closer, they can see me better and that's nice too. So I want to let you closer if I can, however scary it is!

cannot be forced and it is not something that the therapist does. Instead, as relational therapists we believe that the embodied intersubjective **therapeutic relationship** lies at the centre of the process of integration, techniques and method being secondary. Any integration that comes through therapy emerges out of a gentle, constantly evolving, negotiated and dynamic co-created being-with relational process to which both therapist and client contribute (Evans & Gilbert, 2005). Using *relational psychoanalytic* terms of *attachment theory*, we could say that clients are given a second chance through a new attachment relationship. Experiences which were not processed or contained in early attachment relationship had to be split off. The new therapy attachment allows space to integrate those dissociated bits through a form of re-parenting (Wallin, 2007).

> Genuine integration and healing happen only when a new experience of relationship allows the old feelings to be understood more gently and thus be laid to a better rest. . . .
> Relational therapy knows that the bumps and grinds of life and the therapy relationship will produce plenty of new/old memories, transferences, feelings, and thoughts to integrate, but unless there's a new relational way to be with it all, nothing will change in how a client can feel and think about herself. (DeYoung, 2003, p. 152)

Thereafter, the client takes their learning out into the **wider world of relationships**. Movements towards integration occur as a result of work within the relationship which are then re-worked outside over time. The work continues beyond the therapy room. It is not enough to dwell endlessly with a person's intrapsychic confusion. We need to be attentive to that intertwining of body–self and world. And it is the client who has to find their way, to make sense of their way of being in the world. If the client can apply learnings in the therapy room to the world outside, and vice versa, then the movement towards integration can occur.

The four stories below capture something of the breadth and depth of what integrating processes might involve.

Jayne's Story: Integrating Selves[5]

In her first therapy session Jayne explained that she had lost everything and she felt lost. Her husband's irresponsible spending had left her without house or money at a time when the slow process of emerging from suffering ME/CFS (myalgic encephalomyelitis/chronic fatigue syndrome) was leaving her easily fatigued. Previously she had worked in the probation service – a stressful job which had contributed to her current poor health. She had moved into rented accommodation near her mother. She seemed depressed and appeared to have few resources. I wondered if she might be contemplating suicide.

My aim was to create a safe therapeutic space in which I could be as present as possible, and invite Jayne to be present as well. Jayne's challenge was to hold on to her own self, as I soon discovered.

'The therapy has helped,' Jayne told me as we started our second session; she felt better already. She continued sharing her life story; it proved full of long-standing relational problems, in particular her tendency to sabotage relationships and run away from intimacy. She acknowledged that she often fell into the pattern of being needy and dependent when she became involved with men. She also spoke of hearing loud, critical voices in her head. At this point she presented as anxious rather than depressed; her world appeared threatening rather than empty.

A sassy, vivacious, intelligent, highly competent and professional Jayne appeared unexpectedly at our next meeting and I began to be puzzled by these dramatically changing presentations. I felt a little anxious in the face of her unpredictable, labile way of being. That I couldn't *feel* her feelings in those early sessions, and resorted to 'head-level' formulations, nudged me to speculate that Jayne might also be cut off from her embodied emotions. Amongst all these varied presentations (fronts, selves?) where was the 'real Jayne'? Perhaps real Jayne was truly 'lost'; had she ever existed even? I couldn't help but wonder about diagnostic categories such as dissociative identity disorder. But she herself was conscious of the different 'selves' that emerged in different contexts, and this led me to reject this formulation. Seeking to bracket my previous knowledge, I resolved to continue to remain gently present with her, listening and responding to whatever was figural for her in the moment at each meeting.

Jayne's different 'selves' or 'subpersonalities' (Rowan, 1990)[6] formed the centre of our attention over many months, during which I 'met' or was told about several selves including:

- Ice Queen Jayne, who was distant, brutal, unemotional and powerful: she picked men up for one-night stands but never got involved;

126   INTEGRATING

- Work Jayne, who was highly competent, conscientious, sharp, judgemental and organised;
- ME Jayne, who was weak, vulnerable, needy and terrified; and
- Mum Jayne who was insecure and a relentlessly selfless people-pleaser (like her own mother).

We explored how these different subjectivities might have originated in response to her different relationships. Of particular significance seemed the early childhood insecurely attached relationship with her highly critical, feckless father who disappeared regularly, effectively abandoning his family.

One time Jayne arrived full of self-critical bile. The gains we had made over the weeks seemed to have completely disappeared; I hardly recognised her and was taken aback. Responding to my felt-sense that something didn't fit, I eventually asked who she was today. I might have punched her; with a deep outbreath she recognised that she had unwittingly embodied the critical side of her mother. This was a good lesson which showed her how easily she could fall into confluence with her mother. She learned to boundary her internalised 'Critical Parent' mother without rejecting the loving nurturing part of her – a holding of polarities which seemed important.

Our therapy project over the course of three years involved Jayne's search for a way of being which she liked, respected and could hold on to. Within our safe therapeutic space, she could test out and rehearse responses. 'New Jayne' grew slowly as Jayne created and learned about aspects of her evolving self. She had always been attractive, but now she was claiming a gentler, more natural look, matching a manner that was softer and less critical of others. Gradually, as her ways of being became less extreme and more integrated, she explored her darker side. Her deeply felt sense of loss, aloneness and abandonment by everyone she allowed close helped her understand her tendency to cut off from relationships in a pre-emptive, self-protective manner.

Latterly, we worked on integrating her 'Child self', that part of her whose anxiety spiralled overwhelmingly when she felt rejected by friends or lovers. She initially struggled to accept, and have compassion for, this 'weak' self. She would berate herself, trying to deny her feelings, while engaging in potentially self-destructive self-soothing activities. Over time, she learned to recognise that part of her self which was anxious (and why) and see it as a part, not the whole, of herself.

As we entered the ending phase of therapy, her continuing challenge lay in carrying (with compassion) her fragmented selves as a part *of* herself, while also holding them apart *from* her new, more integrated and better-functioning self. While she continues to work on how to stay with less comfortable emotions, she has learned not to abandon herself and she is aware of her ability to make active choices about how to be-with others.

The integrative process we engaged in therapy was one where Jayne and I together tried both to enable different parts of herself to come together and to help her to make an **existential choice** about the person that she wanted to be. The emergence of a new softer Self was a transformation that we could not have predicted. But as Jayne experimented and tried out this new way of being (first with

INTEGRATING   127

me and then with others), she found that it felt good, it fitted her somehow; and she was able to be in more direct contact with her world. In a metaphorical sense, she had brought parts of self together in a more open and contact-full personality.

Central to Jayne's story, though less explicit, is the story of our evolving **therapeutic relationship**. It could be said that Jayne explicitly *used* me in an instrumental way to try out new ways of being. In a way this is true, and that kind of instrumentality possibly applies to most if not all therapy, particularly during the early stages of the relationship. But I did not *feel* used. Instead I felt we were in partnership, co-creating playfully Jayne's evolving self. At times it even felt like a friendship, for instance when we laughed together about the excitements and tribulations of her online dating experiences and when we discovered a shared love of the same style of clothes from a particular designer dress shop.[7] She taught me things as I taught her; we enjoyed each other's company; and we both grew with and through our contact. There were moments in our open and honest relating where it felt like a true human-to-human meeting. This kind of meeting is beautifully expressed in Buber's concept of 'I-Thou' (box 9.3).

Box 9.3 Theory: Buber's *I-It* versus *I-Thou*

Martin Buber (1878–1965) was an Austrian-born Jewish theologian, educator and existential-phenomenological philosopher. In his best-known work, a short philosophical essay titled *Ich und Du* (1958), Buber argues that the more spiritual dimensions of human relationships are linked to the relationship between God and man.[8] He writes romantically of the potential of the *I-Thou* **relationship**, seen as one where each person is accepting of and open to the other, recognising the I-ness of me and the you-ness of you. The *I-Thou* relationship is one of mutual regard; it is free from judgement, narcissism, demands, possessiveness, objectification, greed and anticipation (Hycner, 1991/1993). Persons respond to one another creatively and in the moment, eschewing instrumental and habitual ways of interacting (as found in the *I-It* **relationship**).

The *I-Thou* relationship is mutually revealing because to recognise the value of the other's personhood is to help renew one's own authenticity and personhood. In the authentic, open relationship of *I-Thou*, each person gives of him- or herself without attempting to perform, or to control the impression being created. The direct experience of such 'presence' of ourselves with another is both comforting (in showing us we are not alone) and threatening (because it challenges us to be *more*).

Treating others as 'Thous' rather than 'Its' has important ramifications. For Buber, the Holocaust represents a terrifying example of the ethical consequences of seeing others as 'Its'.

(Continued)

128   INTEGRATING

> For Buber, our communication is not just conversation: it is a reciprocal exchange which opens up awareness; it is where we can grow through each other (to the ultimate point, as he saw it, of having a conversation with God).
>
> The meaning of Buber's notion of **interhuman** is to be found in the dialogue between: "All real living is meeting" (1958, p. 11).

Kjell's Story: Integrating Experience

The dialogue in box 9.4 has been taken from Babette Rothschild (2003a). She describes working with a client, Kjell, a married man in his fifties who was suffering from the traumatic effects of having been shot at by a sniper. The descriptions in italics show both something of the tentative emergent quality of the interaction and the delicate pacing of the interventions which move towards integrating mind (emotions and thinking) and body.

Box 9.4 Case illustration: Somatic trauma therapy

I paced the telling of his story so that he could digest the pieces.

KJELL: Three years ago I was shot at by a sniper. I was driving in my car; he was on an overpass. I wasn't hurt – he just shot out my rear windshield. I called the police, but as no one had seen the sniper and he left no evidence, they couldn't do anything.

THERAPIST: What's happening in your body?

KJELL: Only a little tension.
It appeared to be okay to go on.

THERAPIST: Okay. What were the next steps?

KJELL: (*with shaking voice*) I stopped going out so much.
Kjell began to cry. A central issue had emerged.

THERAPIST: I see you are crying. Can you tell me what's happening – what you are feeling while you are crying?
I wanted Kjell to be able to think and feel at the same time – the goal of mind/body integration. Though I could observe him crying, I didn't know what emotion he was feeling.

KJELL: All mixed up.

THERAPIST: What feelings are mixed up?

KJELL: Being by myself. No one could help me. No one knew who it was. I didn't know if it could happen again.
Still no emotion was named.

THERAPIST: And so you are feeling?

KJELL: Like lost, completely lost.

> *He was describing his experience, not identifying an emotion. I decided to try to ask more specific questions.*
>
> THERAPIST: What are the sensations in your body?
>
> KJELL: Like I am covered with a film.
>
> THERAPIST: How do you experience that?
>
> KJELL: I feel a bit numb. And you are a little blurry.
>
> *He was experiencing slight dissociation from his body. That probably was why he couldn't identify his emotions.*
>
> THERAPIST: Have you ever told anyone about what happened?
>
> KJELL: My wife, but it scared her so much I never mentioned it again. And the police, but they couldn't do anything, so I gave up.
>
> THERAPIST: It sounds as though you were quite isolated during that time.
>
> KJELL: *(eyes watering)* I didn't know who to talk to. The police couldn't help me. I didn't want to scare my wife more. Because she got so scared, I was afraid to tell – and scare – anyone else. I didn't want to make a big deal out of nothing.
>
> THERAPIST: What were your feelings then?
>
> KJELL: I felt really scared.
>
> *He could identify his past emotion, which would help him to connect to his current emotion. He began to cry.*
>
> THERAPIST: Say that again.
>
> KJELL: I was really scared.
>
> *Kjell cried more deeply. The sobs subsided after a while.*
>
> THERAPIST: What are you feeling as you cry?
>
> KJELL: Scared.
>
> THERAPIST: How are the feelings of being scared then and being scared now different?
>
> KJELL: *(taking a deep breath)* Right now I can relax. Then I was just always wound up.
>
> THERAPIST: Can you feel that difference in your body now?
>
> KJELL: Yes. I can breathe!
>
> (Rothschild, 2003a, pp. 183–185)

Kjell's story touches on layered integrating process related to mind–body, self–other, and past–present. His therapy proceeded with the aim of encouraging insight and making a bridge to his daily life and relationships as part of working on his feelings of aloneness. For Kjell, his sense of isolation had become more traumatic than the incident itself of being threatened by the sniper. With the therapist's prompting he went on to recognise that he was protecting everyone close to him by keeping his experience secret. She helped him reach out to his wife and brother for support by inviting him to imagine telling his brother about his experience. As he imagined the scene he realised that he felt a sense of relief, and anger about protecting others when he needed support himself. Making this connection helped him to reach out in real life.

There are two significant therapeutic dynamics at play here in this short example: a focus on (1) *somatic responses* (2) in the *present moment*.

Firstly, the explicit focus of therapy was on his **somatic responses** which allowed him to release anxiety from both his body and his mind (Rothschild, 2003a). Kjell started by describing his trauma in a distanced, dissociated manner and the challenge was to get beyond the disconnectedness. One of the key aims of integrative psychotherapy is to facilitate the integration of the client's body, self and world. It involves sensing and making sense towards connecting up the person's experience into a coherent narrative. With our holistic gaze we are always mindful that body, mind and spirit of the self are intertwined with the world. The client's broader social-life context needs to be an ever-present horizon for the work.

This process of attending to the intertwining of body–self–world is particularly figural in cases of trauma and dissociation where painful feelings are sequestered, kept away, perhaps with the person becoming emotionally numbed and unavailable for interpersonal contact. Yet ironically that dissociation itself brings challenges: when the feelings are left unintegrated, reduced awareness occurs and contact with others is only ever partial or perhaps based on pretence or performance. As the person disconnects from others, they are robbed of a vital source of support and their sense of isolation or disconnection grows. The person may have a vague sense that something is wrong and feel some disturbance, but that too is pushed down. While the unwanted feelings stay mostly in the background, they can confuse, say, by erupting at unexpected, unwelcome moments in nightmares, flashbacks or meltdowns. This can be what brings the client to therapy in the first place.

DeYoung (2003, p. 111) describes it well with her concept of *radioactive memory*:

> The picture is more like scattered fragments of radioactive memory – body memory, event memory, emotional memory, and/or interpersonal process memory. These fragments lie strewn across your client's internal landscape, disconnected from each other and from your client's awareness, but still emitting powerful, disturbing signals.

The therapist's role here is to offer that vital support, witnessing and opportunity to be in contact. The therapist can affirm the client's experience, help them name the feelings and radioactive memories and, ideally, face the shame that comes with secrets and hiding. It's a question of working slowly with the person to piece together the fragments, to find pattern and meaning, to find a way for the person to be more fully present to themselves and with others in the world.

I know from my own therapeutic work that in situations where I do not feel emotion in my body, I could be manifesting my client's own dissociation. I might then share this (self-disclose) with my client, implicitly inviting them to bring to awareness their own embodied – or cut-off – self. Alternatively, I might find myself feeling somewhat helpless, seemingly unable to find a helpful response to my client's distress. Perhaps my sense of helplessness is reflecting their own helplessness and my urge to do something mirrors their own desperate search for a quick, soothing solution? What is needed from me, I suggest, is to model the process by staying with that distress, however uncomfortable it feels.

Secondly, Rothschild invited Kjell to tune into the **present moment** (Stern, 2004[9]) to begin to make sense of differences between his responses in the past and now. Relational integrative psychotherapists tend to focus on experience in the face-to-face and here-and-now of the therapy (while simultaneously holding in awareness both past and future horizons). Before engaging trauma in the past, the individual needs to be sufficiently grounded in the here-and-now. Without this grounding, the person could well be re-traumatised from encountering fragments of the past.

Depending on our theoretical preferences we vary in the degree to which we focus on past experience. In my own *existential-humanistic* practice I appreciate how habitual ways of being in the world can take hold and may link to past experiences but, unlike many more *psychoanalytically* orientated therapists, I would spend less time dwelling in the past; I prefer to focus on current ways of being and what they tell us. The past manifests in the present. Current awareness (insight) offers the opportunity to challenge habitual patterns and open up to fresh possibilities.

Norbert's Story: A Transpersonal Integration

There are times in therapy when we aim for more than insight. Sometimes active role-play, enactment or a ritual ceremony offers the opportunity to symbolically complete unfinished business. This type of work is predominant in fields of *gestalt therapy* (see chapter 13), dramatherapy and psychodrama. It is also the basis of work with *constellations*.[10]

The following case study is taken from Ruppert (2008, pp. 192–193) and indicates the *intergenerational* focus of family constellations work.

Norbert came to a constellations seminar because his relationships with women always went wrong. He is a good-looking, sensitive, intelligent and friendly man in a secure job. However, in relationships with women he becomes childlike . . .

In his constellation it became clear that his bonded connection with his mother was impaired. His mother seemed like a small child, unable to access her own mother who, it seemed likely from the behaviour of the representatives in the constellation, had been sexually abused by her father. The representative for Norbert's mother also seemed terrified of her father and it seemed that the cause of this fear was that her father had been active as a doctor in the Third Reich in Germany during the war. As a small child she had noticed how Jewish children in her neighbourhood suddenly disappeared.

The solution for Norbert lay in speaking out about the sexual abuse and in confronting the abuser as represented in the constellation. It turned out to be one of the few times that I have experienced in a constellation a culprit as represented actually feeling remorse for his deed, and this enabled the representatives for the grandmother and her father to approach each other. This in turn allowed some contact between the representatives for the grandmother and her daughter, Norbert's mother, who was then able to connect to the representative

132 INTEGRATING

for her husband (Norbert's father) and address the issue of Norbert having experienced her as absent, and so cheated of her love. However, the representative of Norbert's grandfather continued to find excuses and justify his crimes as a Nazi doctor whenever he was confronted in the constellation. Norbert was finally able to tell the representative for his grandfather, 'Grandfather, you are mad and you nearly made my mother and me mad with fear.' Norbert was able to access his feelings and approach the representative of his mother with love.

Ruppert's version of constellation practice engages explicitly with trauma and intergenerational bonding. He argues that the solution to shame and guilt is to express the feelings, out the family secrets, and own remorse and acts of restitution. A key principle of constellation work with multigenerational trauma is that "the healing of psychological injuries must be sought through maintaining sight of the entire trauma-disturbed bonding network in which the individual is engaged" (2008, p. 29). He goes on to assert that "healing only happens when the soul is really touched" (p. 304).

This story of touching 'soul' reminds us that our work often involves an ineffable **spiritual dimension**[11] that is hard to capture but should not be ignored. When we work towards healing and integration by engaging the presence of souls in our ancestral heritage, spirituality is present. When we set out to create a quiet, interconnected space in which to meet ourselves and where the client is invited to meditate on meanings and life, spirituality is present. When we feel love and compassion for a client, and when we experience an expanding awareness and empathic intersubjectivity, spirituality is present.

Steven's Story: Healing through Relationship

A letter to my therapist

When I started out, the reasons I was going to therapy in the first place felt terrifying, like some uninvited visitor that I didn't want, like or dare to even glance sideways at. The process was so full of fear that at times it felt all-consuming and I feared for my own safety. I wasn't sure I could endure it, it occupied my thoughts every minute of every day, making my stomach feel tight as if I was recoiling from myself. The feeling of panic would come in waves and at times I felt physically nauseous at the rise and fall of these sickly emotions.

I wanted to feel safe but feeling safe meant taking risks, to reveal things, to feel as vulnerable as one could possibly feel. (When you have spent a lifetime learning that vulnerability means you will be attacked, ridiculed and ultimately your weaknesses and flaws used against you – trust is a huge ask.)

Fear and lack of trust were in the way. I could go forward or I could go back. Going forward was like reaching out in the dark and trusting the next branch would appear without actually knowing whether it would or not. Going back meant certain death. So forward I went.

Branches appeared in the form of consistency, calmness, kind eyes and compassion. As nice as it sounds, not always pleasant. Compassion sometimes feels like shards of light entering a room that has been blacked out for decades. Painful at first, unnatural – I don't really want to take a moment and feel what I have been missing because those shards of light are revealing just how much was there that I haven't received.

And then of course there is still that thing over there in the corner that I'm terrified of; I try to accept it but it doesn't work as I'm too frightened of it. But then something interesting happens: little by little I feel a bit more grown up, the person opposite me is talking to me as if I am capable, intelligent and as if I have a future. This is music to Little Me's ears, and Little Me decides to sit still for short periods of time and trust that things are being taken care of. There is an adult in the room that I can trust and the adult is me.

My thinking is more rational, forgiving and strong; part of me is able to recognise that Little Me is afraid of that thing over there in the shadows and offers the Little Me some comfort in kind words, hugs and compassion. The uninvited guest starts to feel less like a terrifying stranger and its presence is acknowledged. I sit with it for short periods and try to get to know it.

Then the people out there start to change too or I notice things I didn't used to. I'm hearing positive comments and seeing love from my friends. More than this I'm 'feeling' these comments and I'm feeling this love. And I feel less afraid. That thing over there in the corner becomes less ugly.

I tell myself that I'm safe and try sleeping with the light off. I deserve a good night's sleep – and I get one :-). I trust Adult Me to take care of Little Me.

I recognise, through the eyes of the person sitting opposite me that my circumstances were not normal and in witnessing this I am able to forgive and understand the little me. I am responsible but I am not to blame. I am not inferior or unlovable – it is not me that was lacking but my environment. I know this intellectually *and* emotionally.

The light and the shade make up the whole – 'everyone' has light and everyone has parts in shadow. I am proud of myself for having the courage to look at it.

It feels as though I was dealing with adult-sized issues/responsibility – abandonment, neglect and other things but still a child myself. I found ways to comfort myself based on my age, inexperience and what was familiar to me. BUT I'm doing my best with what I have been dealt in life and I haven't abandoned myself.

So this is where we have arrived so far.

I just wanted to say Thank you.

So Steven tells of his (continuing) journey of healing and transformation.

I find this an extraordinarily evocative letter which captures many key elements of relational-developmental integrative processes. I particularly appreciate the way he has found love and self-compassion, in part through internalising his therapist's compassion. Significantly, he owns his own growth while recognising it has been co-created.

His words remind me that both love and the human spirit animate our therapeutic encounters. "A therapy of contact-in-relationship creates one of the closest and most intimate of all human connections", say Erskine et al. (1999, p. 148) They emphasise the therapeutic importance of accepting and staying with clients' expressions – including their gratitude – rather than assuming that there must be some hidden agenda or that it's 'just' transference. They also remind us that the need to express (and receive) love is present in every healthy relationship including therapy.

Concluding Reflections

This chapter has explored the layered nature of our process towards integrating intrapsychic, mind–body, relational-social and transpersonal-spiritual dimensions. At its most basic level, integration comes when a client opens themselves to seeing (themselves and their world) in a different way, when they have a moment of **insight**. Integration also involves the **holding of polarities**. Here the client accepts their ambivalent emotions towards others and owns both their light and dark sides. But perhaps the deepest integration comes when clients move beyond acceptance of polarities towards some kind of **transformation**, a new way of being and a sense of meaningfulness.

Beyond science, theory and technique, the magic and mystery of our therapy is most in evidence when we witness another and make connections towards healing and renewal. We may be unable to specify the exact process of integration, but it can be sensed and observed. I love seeing that moment of epiphany and unity, of belonging, and of self-acceptance. This is never a stagnant end point – instead it's the springboard forward. It's as though the security of finding 'home' opens us to new 'adventure', to a new readiness to face the unexpected. A new energising potential comes into being, a new sense of well-being. Perhaps it is also the process of facing our sense of not feeling entirely at home, which – although an anxiety-provoking experience – also opens up this path of movement[11] (Todres & Galvin, 2010).

And as we engage with our client's integrating project, do we not also need to continue to do the same for ourselves and in our wider relationships? Of course there is never a point at which any of us can claim to be completely integrated. There will be parts of ourselves that remain hidden, not entirely accepted; there will be times where we fall into disconnection between our body and our mind, or our past and our present, or between self and other. There are those moments where our clients touch our own vulnerabilities and we momentarily disappear from ourselves and our clients. We remain work-in-progress and maybe we also find we receive some healing from our clients.

So we travel together and commit to a gentle *integrating* process for our clients . . . and for ourselves.

Notes

1 I use the word 'integrating' deliberately to emphasise that a process is involved; none of us ever achieve full integration!

2 In *family constellation work*, 'soul' refers to the intergenerational interconnectedness of people that goes beyond kinship (Ruppert, 2008).

3 See Siegel (2010) and his version of **interpersonal neurobiology** in which he identifies eight domains of integration between the brain, body, emotions, parts of self and relationships.

4 *Relational therapists* have challenged the traditional psychoanalytic focus on insight that carries assumptions that the therapist somehow has privileged access to the client's unconscious material and that it is the therapist's role to interpret this material. Instead, insight is seen as emerging organically through an active collaborative therapeutic relationship. Insights come when the client feels safe and there is a reduction of shame, as well as with the curiosity and creativity that are unleashed through an attuned relationship (Messer & McWilliams, 2007).

5 I'm grateful to Professor Maria Gilbert, editor of the *British Journal of Psychotherapy Integration*, for giving me permission to reproduce this case study here from Finlay (2012).

6 The idea of **multiple selves** is contested and understood differently across different modalities. Traditional *humanistic* theory champions the idea of a private, unique, authentic, core Self, while post-modern variants celebrate plurality. *Psychoanalytic* theory accepts each person as being psychologically made up of unconsciously introjected parts of others, while *social constructionist* approaches see selves emerging discursively in different social contexts. An integrative position is to acknowledge relationally-derived parts of self (which may be experienced subjectively as distinct identities).

7 In Kohut's terms, we might see the transferential relationship between Jayne and myself as meeting her self-object needs for 'twinship'.

8 In the original German Buber talked of *Mensch* (human being, person) and not *Mann* (exclusively male person).

9 The *relational psychoanalyst* Stern (2004) states that the past is phenomenologically silent. While it can become a live issue, its influence on our feelings and behaviour in the present is largely invisible. He argues that repeated patterns of interaction provide the basic building blocks of psychic formation which structure a child's representational world. However, this can be brought into awareness and re-worked. A not dissimilar argument is advanced by neuro-psychologists. The *neuro-phenomenologist* Damasio (1999) discusses how neural patterns in the brain are constructed of mental states and emotions. His research shows that representations of emotion are contained in the subcortical nuclei of the brain stem, the amygdala, the hypothalamus and the basal forebrain. These representations are implicit and not available to consciousness, but once activated a particular emotion can be worked with to create new neural patterns.

10 The practice of constellations is integrative in spirit, both in integrating *psychoanalytic* and *systemic* theoretical insights and in focusing on intrapsychic, relational-social and transpersonal elements. While constellations work is not always conducted in a relational way, I've included this example as the focus is fundamentally concerned with relationships and relationships are seen as both the cause of and 'solution' to problems.

11 Spirituality might be explicitly integrated into therapy in terms of: (1) working with clients' religious views and spiritual development directly; (2) use of spiritual techniques, e.g. meditation and visualisation; (3) acknowledging a transpersonal dimension as in transgenerational work; (4) facilitating a spiritual approach to life, as in AA's 12 steps, for example; (5) therapists' own use of spiritual practices.

10

Ending

Termination is a jolting reminder of the built-in cruelty of the psychotherapeutic process. (Yalom, 1985, p. 373)

Imagine ending therapy after three years of intensive work. You launch your client off into an uncertain future like a parent launching a teenager off to university. As intimate bonds are wrested apart, both of you carry some mix of excitement and trepidation, joy and sadness, hope and disappointment, and relief and frustration. This ambivalent cocktail renders the space between you poignant and clammy with half-acknowledged emotion.

How do we manage the process of preparing for and making that farewell? What responsibilities do we have as therapists to control the process? What entitlements must we respect about the client's role in both process and event? How do we prepare for and cope with our own loss, particularly if the client has deserted us angrily or unexpectedly, challenging our professional competence? How might we celebrate the client's transition into healthier, more fulfilled ways of being?

Just as endings are an unavoidable part of everyday life, they are found in every corner of the therapy relationship. While they can be a routine and unproblematic part of our work, they can also be powerful and poignant – for both client and therapist – particularly when longer-term relational work is involved. Such endings require delicate timing and layered negotiation. We seek a mutual, celebratory experience but sometimes there is a premature stopping which we are required to respect and accept whatever our wishes.

Relational Integrative Psychotherapy: Engaging Process and Theory in Practice, First Edition. Linda Finlay.
© 2016 John Wiley & Sons, Ltd. Published 2016 by John Wiley & Sons, Ltd.

Ending 137

The challenges of separation and loss that come with endings can lead us to avoid, resist and deflect from the experience. But if we (client and therapist alike) can enter that space and embrace it, we will then be more open to new beginnings and the possibility of transformation. The key is to face the reality of transition, welcoming both the pain of ending and the excitement of new journeys. Then, when our client is ready to be on their way, we need to let them go.

This chapter sets out to explore the processes and challenges of ending therapy. In the first section I examine the process of **deciding to end**, which is partly dependent on whether the decision is mutual, forced or unilateral. The second focuses on working through **loss**, **separation** and **grief**. The last two sections home in on the processes of **embracing the transition** and **stock-taking**.

Deciding to End

The best decisions to end are *mutual*. But endings may also be *forced* by circumstances out of our control and, sometimes, there are *unilateral* endings where either client or therapist decides to quit. Each of these scenarios is discussed below.

In general, whatever the form, there is a process to engage, followed by our role to respect clients' decisions (especially in private practice) and, when we don't agree, to make the best of it. We would aim to review the situation jointly and, hopefully, leave the client richer for the experience. For instance, I might say something like, 'It is been a privilege to work with you. I appreciate your hard work and courage.'

Mutual endings

Mutual decisions often emerge organically, perhaps when both client and therapist suddenly find the ending becoming figural. Then the process begins. That first tentative peek into a future that doesn't include therapy can be pivotal.

If no moves are forthcoming from the client, I might put out feelers to gently open a dialogue. For instance, I was seeing a long-term client who was due to go to university later in the year. The client was shocked and dismayed to recognise that it would not be possible to continue therapy (at least in the same weekly form). I reassured her that we would find a way to continue if we both decided we were not ready to end therapy and that we had eight months to work it out. It was important that she didn't feel I was suddenly going to leave her world – that would have replayed her history of abandonment in early life.

Endings may be built into the therapy contract, say when we contract to meet a client for six or 12 sessions. Knowing that horizon, we would work towards ending from the first minute of contracting. However, even though the date is fixed there is still an ending process to go through and decisions to be made about how to end and evaluate the therapy.

Making the decision to end longer-term therapy where it is not predetermined raises more thorny issues. It's not as if we end at the point when eternal happiness is assured; clients will always have stuff they could work on. Often therapy just becomes stale or some impasse surfaces. Is the client simply holding on out of habit? This might be the moment for a challenge to be issued: engage or move on. In group therapy situations, sometimes several members decide to leave around the same time. The tricky bit is deciding if the decline in energy and motivation signals that clients are ready to move on or if there is still some useful work to be done.

Forced endings

Forced endings are not uncommon. At times, of course, the decision is taken out of both client's and therapist's hands. Illness or health issues, financial stress, moves to other locations, loss of funding or organisational changes may all precipitate an end to therapy. In these cases it is important to avoid sudden, unexpected endings where possible as these can evoke archaic traumatic experiences in clients. Careful discussion is needed to determine if and how therapy might continue, perhaps with a different contract or by using social media, providing that a secure connection and confidentiality can be assured. If the client would benefit from seeing another therapist, options could be discussed.

If a client is marking time and not making any progress, the therapist may decide to enforce an ending. At the very least, a strong challenge needs to be issued. It may turn out that the client fears making changes and this could prove a useful new focus of work (Moursund & Erskine, 2004).

Professional ethical guidelines usually state that therapists must ensure they are both competent and sufficiently supported to carry out their role. If a therapist feels out of their depth, or otherwise unable to practice adequately for physical or mental health reasons, they need to consider carefully whether or not it would be in the client's best interest to be referred to another professional. As Adams (2014) points out, one of the consequences of insufficiently attending to ourselves may be that we let our clients down harder than had we acknowledged our limitations and vulnerabilities in the first place.

Unilateral endings

Over the years a number of my clients have just stopped coming; perhaps they left a previous session saying they would contact me but didn't. I like to think these clients intended to come back but found, as time passed, that they were coping with life, and therapy became a distant memory. Some perhaps were voting with their feet because the therapy I offered was not sufficiently helpful or else some dramatic life change occurred. And, yes, I suspect that they simply weren't ready to engage more fully. Whatever the motives, abrupt endings leave both client and therapist with solitary 'ending work' to do to manage regrets about the incomplete process together with any lurking feelings of shame and rejection.

Murdin (2000) suggests that three emotional states are probably figural when a client stops therapy unilaterally: they leave with *anxiety*, with *aggression* or in *silence*. Each of these signals a possible **resistance** where the respective flight, fight or avoidance responses can be seen as serving important protective psychological functions.

Whatever the underlying dynamics, we have to respect the client's decision to leave while encouraging them to talk about their reasons, assuming that proves possible. The ending process can then be engaged in such a way that the client feels supported and validated, perhaps leaving a door open for future work when the client is ready. (I do not always make this promise, particularly if there are warning signs about their motivations.) Clearly we should not seek to keep hold of reluctant or disengaged clients out of our own narcissistic needs (Moursund & Erskine, 2004).

In this situation of stopping, rather than ending, it is important not to be passive or let therapy fizzle out through shame. As relational therapists, we recognise that a client's behaviour may mirror their usual ways of being in relationship outside of therapy, and that they may be re-creating a pattern of avoidance or a borderline pushing-away process. It might be important for us to challenge the behaviour or do some chasing. For instance, I usually prompt the client informally after a few weeks have passed, say with a text reminder. If, after another month or two, there is still no response then I might send a formal discharge letter acknowledging the client's choice and wishing them well.

The opposite of clients stopping is clients seeking to hang on: 'Does therapy have to end? Could we keep in touch? Can we carry on in another way?' Behind these 'bargaining' questions other questions lie. Is the ending right? Does it make sense to hang on to the relationship so as to avoid an ending? If so, why? *What needs, and whose, would be met by continuing in some way after ending?*

In general, my own response is to affirm that either we are still in therapy working on something, or else we should end. Letting go usually needs to be as respectful and clean as is possible with the prospect of future re-engagement offered to gentle the parting process. Messing up the transition with undermining messages like 'Come back if it doesn't work out' (which effectively says 'You can't cope without me') are less than helpful; it's much better to enable the client to own their choices and growth.

That said, some clients or relationships benefit from an ongoing attachment; it depends on the nature of the relationship and the work engaged. I know one therapist, who works with children and young people, who actively invites clients to keep in touch just to let him know how they are getting on. Such an offer can, of itself, mediate grief and any sense of abandonment which may be experienced.

Working through Loss, Separation and Grief[1]

An ending is "always a 'petit mort', a little death that has to be respected" (Romanyshyn, 2006, p. 31). Endings hurt. How can they not hurt given the inevitable loss involved when we say goodbye? More than the loss-feeling

140   ENDING

of the absence of a presence, there is the presence of an absence. We can feel empty, alone, even abandoned. In this experience, clients and therapists alike face the challenge of separation and resulting grief from severing a special bond. The ending of therapy (particularly long-term therapy) can trigger some re-experiencing of past loss, rejections and unresolved grief (see Joyce, Piper, Ogrodniczuk and Klein, 2007, for a review). The key process in the ending phase of therapy is to enable a client to work through any arising pain; in strategic terms, it's about allowing the client to deal with 'unfinished business'.

The **grief** that is evoked for clients when therapy has gone well comes from recognising both something they have never had (e.g., an affirming loving parent figure) and something they are losing (our healing caring availability). It is natural to feel sadness when losing a special relationship. There may also be some resentment and anger felt towards a therapist who is perceived as having stopped caring: and perhaps even envy or jealousy towards clients who continue. There may also be associated despair and loss of hope. More than the loss of a valued relationship, the client must abandon current hopes that their hurt will finally be gone. The final goodbye churns such feelings afresh.

The process of working through this potential grief and loss – and then letting go – involves exploring complex layers of denial, anger, bargaining, depression, acceptance, fear and hope (see box 10.1). In working with **denial** or **acceptance**, we might have to remind clients about the agreed contract and the nature of ending. We then have a role in accepting the expression and exploration of feelings of **anger**, **depression** or **anxiety** while bringing into client's awareness transferential elements which may indicate unfinished business. **Attempts to bargain** may be a part of this as the client seeks to hold on through other means ("Can't we just be friends and go for an occasional coffee?").

Box 10.1 Case illustration: The process of ending therapy

During the final (withdrawal) phase of the counselling process with Gary he went through a period of regressed neediness and doubt about his ability to manage in the 'real world' without my weekly presence. For instance, during one session he recycled some of the introjected messages that he was a bad person and spent several days in a rather depressed state feeling that he had accomplished nothing in his counselling. At other times he felt pleased and grateful for the many things he had learned. . . .

Gary was also genuinely sad that his relationship with me was ending, and I felt sad too. For a while he thought of coming into training with me. In following this through with the help of guided fantasy, for example, a day in the week of a counsellor, he became aware that this was more to do with his desire to hold on to me . . .

> This became the last enactment of his pathological confluence played out with me. Working through the fear of being abandoned by me, the wish to reject me before I abandoned him, as well as the remnants of feeling engulfed was the bulk of the slow, careful work with Gary in this phase. (Clarkson, 1999, p. 158)

If a client isn't taking the opportunity to talk spontaneously about feelings around ending themselves, then they might need encouragement and such spontaneity is not merely something which occurs in the final session. Instead we might be working through such issues in any or all sessions. Deurzen and Adams (2011) go as far as saying that at least *one-sixth* of therapy time should be spent considering endings.[2]

Beyond sessions being devoted to endings, Moursund and Erskine (2004) recognise that the 'little endings' within each session can be helpful rehearsal and opportunity to face up to places which hurt. In this context, clients can sometimes struggle with ending sessions, as demonstrated by the way they try to take control prematurely by ending the session abruptly, or avoid the ending by attempting to extend the time. This pattern of avoidance and contact disruption offers another form of opportunity for clients to learn to face the pain of endings and to repair some damage. *It is important that therapy doesn't add to the list of our client's experiences of unsatisfactory endings.*

Embracing the 'Transition' into the World

The concept of **liminality**[3] (from the Latin *limen*, 'threshold') captures those periods when we transition from one stage to another. In this space 'between' we are fully in neither one place and time nor another. At this threshold space is ambiguity and uncertainty; we mostly have a choice: do we go back, stay stuck or move on?

Therapy can be understood metaphorically as potentially transformational liminal space with individuals journeying towards self-realisation or individuation, and from confusion and fragmentation to greater integration and maturity. Just as trauma and negative experiences stay with us from our past, clients will hopefully carry positive messages of therapy (and ending) with them across the threshold into the future. In relational work, more than learning particular skills or insights, clients hopefully internalize the nourishing relationship which can allow them to feel differently about themselves and others. At best they learn to be more connected with others in their relational world, moving away from over-dependence or self-sufficiency and into human interconnectedness.[4]

The ending phase of therapy is a pivotal liminal transition zone. The client is neither where and who they used to be, nor where and who they will be once

142   ENDING

therapy finishes (see Steven's story in chapter 9). Our job is to help them prepare for life after therapy, to bridge their therapy world with the real world (the final 'They-focused' phase, as Spinelli (2015) in his *existential* model calls it).

In a real and present way, during this phase the content of therapy sessions may well shift markedly away from the client's private inner world and therapy relationship, onto the more public relationships outside of therapy (concerning family and colleagues, social roles and responsibilities, and wider cultural norms and expectations). Clients' decisions to act in some way are not just probed in terms of individual needs, but viewed against the requirements, restrictions and reality of their wider life world. Personal freedom cannot be uncoupled from interpersonal-social dimensions (Spinelli, 2015).

Our therapist's role here is to affirm gains and choices, and to help the client anticipate future challenges by arming them with sufficient resources or strategies to cope. The emphasis is on **letting go** and on promoting the client's autonomy[5] rather than their dependence on the therapist; the spirit is more one of empowering hope. This is not the time to go back and dig about in early trauma, or do further developmental work. If this is what we find ourselves doing then it might be useful to question whether or not the therapy should be ending. (See box 10.2 where a therapist reflects on a somewhat messy long-term process of ending.)

Box 10.2 Case illustration: To end or not to end?

The ending of therapy with Ellie proved a somewhat messy, staggered process. We started with some short-term work focused on her conflicted relationship with her persecutory (grown up) daughter. Ellie soon recognized her part in the drama triangle and, feeling satisfied with her gains, Ellie sought to end therapy. But within the month she was back, in crisis and paralysed in her rescuer-victim position. I soothed and supported (rescued?) her, and set her on her way again. And once more, she returned in crisis.

Eventually we both agreed that longer-term, committed, in-depth relational work was required. Over the next couple of years we found ourselves unravelling a story layered with profound grief, shame, abuse, abandonment and multiple trauma (including some intergenerational trauma).

It took two more years, for Ellie to be ready to begin to consider ending therapy. This time the process involved a slow 'weaning-off' over many months. Ellie started to come fortnightly, then monthly. At last Ellie said she felt safe enough to consider coming in just six months' time for a "check in rather than therapy".

Now Ellie is clear that she no longer needs therapy and she carries me with her instead. In times of stress she is able to get some comfort from imagining my eyes and remembering my 'holding'.

For my part, I miss her. I enjoyed being with her. Her courage and the depth of the work she did still impacts me profoundly. And I also celebrate her new found freedom and independence. I believe she is currently enjoying her retirement and travelling the world, and I'm happy for her.

The *transtheoretical model* of Prochaska and DiClemente (1982; see figure 3.1) provides a useful way of conceptualising transitions. In terms of the ending process, clients may start out in 'precontemplation', being not yet ready to think about leaving. They then move into the 'contemplation' and 'preparation' stages when they can think about ending. In the 'action' phase they face the process of ending, while the 'maintenance' stage calls for attention to be paid to resourcing for the future. The therapist's first role is to gently nudge the client into awareness and readiness. Then we actively work with what is needed to end therapy satisfactorily. The final, possibly critical, task is to let go and help the client assume ownership of any growth and change.

Also with a cyclical focus, in *gestalt therapy* ending work is equated with the *withdrawal phase* of the gestalt cycle. The interruption to contact most characteristic of this phase is 'confluence'. With confluence, there can be a healthy merging and empathy, where the client sees the therapist as a separate independent person with different needs from themselves. But there can also be a reluctance to withdraw and separate, and this interruption to contact can interfere with a satisfactory conclusion of the cycle.

Clarkson (1999) points out that issues of attachment and separation may well need to be re-worked in this transitional withdrawal phase, perhaps at a different level than previously. The issues that may emerge include the experience of primitive fears of abandonment, or perhaps the desire to reject – 'kill off' – the therapist before being symbolically 'killed off' themselves. Clarkson suggests that engaging gestalt rehearsals and experiments around boundary work can helpfully emphasise self-agency and *self-support*:

Rehearsal might involve role-plays or guided imaginary narratives to practise handling potentially difficult situations (cognitively, behaviourally and emotionally) as part of building resources for the future. Old ways of being are left behind as new ways are birthed. A person might, for instance, practise asserting herself in a staff appraisal meeting. A client who is estranged from her brother might rehearse a scene of their meeting at an uncle's funeral.

Boundary work might focus on exercises related to disagreeing, rejecting and defining self as different from the therapist and others. Such exercises also reaffirm a sense of self. For instance, a useful *homework* assignment[6] might be to encourage the client to look around her environment (both inside and outside the therapy room) and state preferences in all aspects of life. 'I prefer living just outside town; ice cream is my favourite dessert; I don't like prejudice; I like modern art. . . .'

Stock-taking

Stock-taking involves processes of reviewing and evaluating, processes which ideally have been taking place from the beginning of therapy. In the ending phase it is foregrounded explicitly. It might even be done more formally by using various evaluation and outcome measures.

144 ENDING

> ## Box 10.3 Theory: Outcome measures
>
> 1. **CORE-OM** (see www.coreims.co.uk/download-pdfs) The CORE-OM is a 34-item generic measure of psychological well-being and distress, encompassing: well-being (4 items); symptoms (12 items); functioning (12 items); risk (6 items).
> 2. **Outcome Rating Scale (ORS)** (Miller & Duncan, 2000) This copyrighted and licensed tool plots changes in how the client is feeling in four respects: individually (personal well-being); interpersonally (family, close relationships); socially (work, school, friendships); and overall (general sense of well-being).
> 3. **Session Rating Scale (SRS)** (Miller, Duncan & Johnson, 2000) Also copyrighted and licensed, this four-item tool focuses on: relationship (feeling heard, understood and respected); goals and topics (extent to which work was done as planned); approach or method (therapist approach and fit with client); and overall (whether something was missing or felt right in the session).
> 4. **Relational Depth Inventory (RDI-R2)** (Wiggins, 2013) This 26-item scale measures experiences of relational depth in particularly helpful moments or events during therapy; for example, 'I felt my therapist understood what it was like for me' or 'I felt a kind of magic happened'.
> 5. **Working Alliance Inventory (WAI)** (http://wai.profhorvath.com/) This non-standardised but copyrighted and licensed research tool (with different long and short versions), invented by A.O. Horvarth, allows therapist and client to compare scores on statements like 'I trust/like my therapist', 'We work together on mutually agreed goals'.

The myriad outcome measures available (published or informal) form a continuum from **objective** measures utilising set criteria and measurements of behavioural change at one end to **subjective** feedback focus on emotional responses at the other. Some are completed by the therapist, others by clients.

Box 10.3 outlines three validated and scientifically researched generic measures: CORE, ORS and SRS. These are amongst the most widely used across the UK and North America. The last two tools, RDI-R2 and WAI, are of particular interest to relational researchers as their focus is on evaluating the client–therapist relationship.

All of these measures, and many others, can be used for research purposes as well as for evaluating practice (see box 10.4 for a selection of current research findings related to ending therapy). Preliminary research, for example, indicates that RDI scores can predict post-therapy outcome scores and that an experience or moment of relational depth is a significant predictor of positive therapy outcomes. Similarly, research on the use of tools like WAI shows that establishing a working alliance early on in therapy (e.g. between the third and fifth sessions) is predictive of positive outcomes (Hovarth & Bedi, 2002).

Box 10.4 Research: On ending therapy

A meta-analysis of 125 studies on psychotherapy dropout in the US showed the mean dropout rate was 46.86%, with higher dropout rates for African-American (and other minority), less educated and lower-income groups (Wierzbicki & Pekarik, 1993). Of those who drop out of therapy, approximately a third do so because they feel their problems have eased, a third because they are dissatisfied with their therapist, and a third face issues like lack of finances and time (Pekarik, 1992). Studies of outpatients in mental health facilities suggest that approximately a quarter to a half drop out after the first session (Brogan, Prochaska & Prochaska, 1999).

In another study of thousands of clients and more than 200 therapists, Brown, Dreid and Nace (1999) found that if there was no improvement (or perceived benefit) by the third session, there will not be much improvement later. Clients who worsened by the third visit were twice as likely to drop out of therapy than those reporting progress.

Other research (e.g., Marx & Gelso, 1987) suggests that clients who have a history of loss and significant grief often experience the ending of therapy as something of a crisis as well as an opportunity for development. Research (e.g., Roe, Dekel, Harel & Fennig, 2006) also suggests that clients feel more positively about ending when they are satisfied with their progress. For most clients, the final stages of therapy are associated with a sense of pride, accomplishment, satisfaction and general health (Quintana and Holahan, 1992). The majority (69%) appreciate the opportunity to discuss reactions to termination (Marx & Gelso, 1987).

At a more informal level, I often spend the last couple of therapy sessions inviting clients to **reminisce** about pivotal moments and to review their journey overall. 'What have you *gained*? How have you grown?' 'Do you have any *regrets* or bits of unfinished business for the future?' 'What will you miss and what do you *take away* with you?' These are questions that we might usefully focus on ourselves as part of giving the client useful feedback. In addition, I might also say that I appreciated the opportunity to work with them and their openness to do the work.

Sometimes such reflective dialogues can be enabled and made more concrete through structured exercises or **ending rituals**. In groups, for instance, we might enjoy a group song or imaginary gift exchanges done in mime. One of my favourite experiential group activities is where each individual has a blank piece of paper taped onto their back. Group members then acknowledge in writing something positive they experience about that person. I have known some individuals still have their 'strokes' piece of paper years later!

One particular ending ritual worth considering further is *gift giving* (and accepting). Sometimes clients seek to express their gratitude and mark the end of therapy through giving a gift to their therapist. Rules about whether or not gifts are allowed depend on the institutional, cultural and relational context and the contract. Some institutions rule against accepting gifts but the value and motivation for the gift giving also need to be taken into account. Spinelli (2007), for example, is clear that in his private practice he has no hesitation in accepting small gifts and, interestingly, with longer-term clients, he may well offer one himself.[7]

It probably goes without saying that it is vital for relational therapists to monitor and review the health of their **relationships** with clients. Our clients are our best source of feedback and validation. Formal tools like the RDI and the WAI (see box 10.4) offer a useful focus for (mutual) reflection and dialogue, even if some therapists find the use of questionnaires distancing.

And sometimes the feedback is unsolicited. See the extract in box 10.5, which comes from a letter a client wrote to her therapist when therapy ended.

Box 10.5 Case illustration: The jewellery box: Maruna's letter

Words can't express how much you mean to me. When I first came to you I wanted you to take away my anxiety. I hoped you'd do it in a couple of sessions. In the end we took two years. I'm glad now that we had that time. That was the time I needed to learn how to help myself and care for – rather than harm – myself. If you had just taken away my anxiety, I would have been dependent on you. Instead, you were just always there for me, supporting me, caring for me, teaching me.

I have some special memories of our tears, our laughter, your TLC, your understanding. Our time together was precious. I will remember it forever. Looking back it's like looking at jewels in a jewellery box. You taught me that I was worthy of being kept safe. You never judged and you allowed me to be Me. This was a Me I had never let myself know. And now I can say that I like Me! This was a magical gift you gave me – the most precious jewel which I will carry with me always.

With love and heartfelt gratitude always,

Maruna

Concluding Reflections

While there are no one-size-fits-all formulae for how to end therapy, some general principles are worth following:

1. If at all possible, engage the ending process over time to give your clients (and yourself) time to work through issues.
2. It can help to engage an explicit and mutual/relational exploration around loss and hope, need and resources, emptiness and satisfaction, autonomy and dependence, regrets and appreciation, and so on.
3. The shift away from clients' inner worlds towards the interpersonal-social life world of work and relationships offers a useful focus towards preparing for life-without-therapy.
4. Where possible, clients should be left richer for having had contact with us. We might, for instance, give them some positive feedback about changes observed, or recognise the client's new resources and their effort and courage to face and work on their issues.

Space has not allowed enough exploration of the power and poignancy of what it means to be on the threshold between being in and being out of therapy, between past and present selves, and between the therapy relationship and separation. However, I have tried to indicate how the combination of processes of separation, mourning and mutual reflection render the ending transitional phase potentially rich with opportunities for growth (Whitaker, 1985).

Part of our role as therapists is to help clients face the pain of the goodbye as part of embracing life. And then we are obliged to let go with *grace*.[8] The prize comes as clients celebrate their growth, and take the good experience, of both the therapy and the ending, into the rest of their lives. This sharing can also be part of our own healing too.

> Saying good-bye hurts. Grief hurts. But to be allowed to say good-bye with gratitude and love as well as with sadness and loss is a privilege. (DeYoung, 2003, p. 203)

Notes

1 In this section I am referring especially to what can be evoked in longer-term relational work. A six-session *brief therapy* contract is unlikely to prove too problematic. However, it still involves an ending, and that, itself, can evoke pain. This is easy to forget when we are caught in the treadmill of attending to many clients.

2 This formula is a useful heuristic. For six session contracts, we would aim to spend at least the

final session on ending processes and looking ahead. The implications for longer-term work are more dramatic if we recognise that seeing a client for three years probably deserves at least six months of ending process.

3 The concept of liminality was first elaborated by anthropologist Van Gennep (1960) to describe the central role of formalised practices that bring about social or spiritual transformation

through symbolically engaging various death and re-birth rituals.

4 Theory from **self-psychology** expresses this process in terms of clients having different experiences of self-object support that helps when times get tough. When self-object needs are met the person can develop a capacity to feel and empathise with and to nurture others.

5 Stern (1985) and others have described how a sense of self emerges in stages depending on the relationship with caregivers. One of the crucial relational patterns is the infant's expression of 'self-agency' (i.e., feeling able to impact the environment). Applying these ideas to therapy, we could say that we have a significant role in promoting client's agency and their sense of competence and empowerment.

6 In contrast to some *gestalt* and *cognitive-behavioural* therapists who are comfortable with the idea of homework, Spinelli (2015) takes an *existential* view critical of the idea of the therapist assigning some task from a position of higher authority. Recognising his unease with the idea of homework, he might still recommend between-session exercises while emphasising that the client is free to refuse or amend the task.

7 Spinelli talked of giving a relevant CD or book or even a hug. Recently a therapist colleague shared that she had given her client a bookmark with a particular symbol on it which had been significant in therapy.

8 I like Heron's notion of therapist **grace** which he regards as involving five attributes: warm concern for and acceptance of the other; openness and attunement to the other's experiential reality; a grasp of what the other needs for his or her essential flourishing; an ability to facilitate the realisation of such needs in the right manner and at the right time; and an authentic presence. "This combination of concern, empathy, prescience, facilitation and genuineness is . . . the spiritual heritage of mankind" (2001, p. 11).

Part II

Theory Applied to Practice

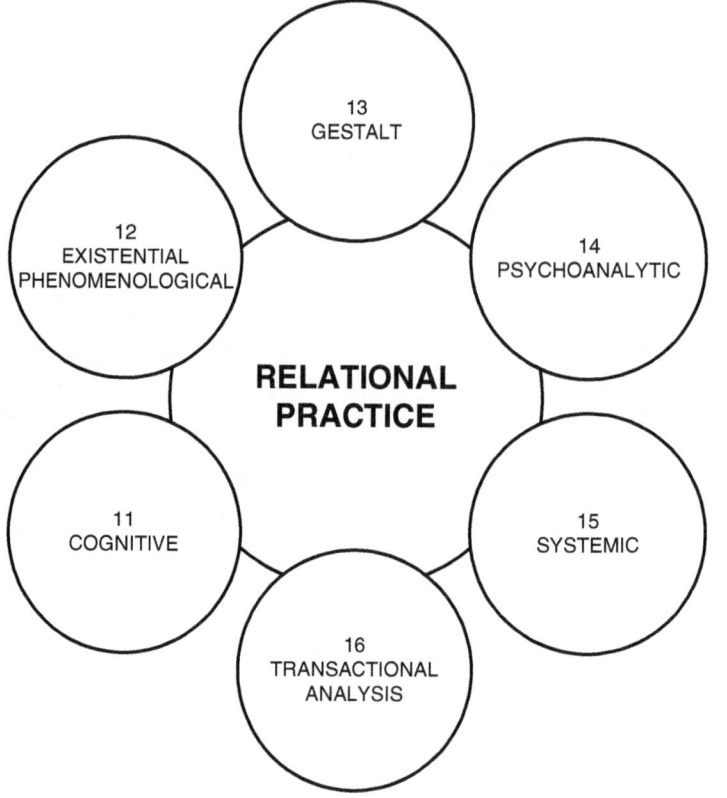

Chapters 11–16: Six theoretical perspectives and their relationally focused overlap

11

Cognitively Orientated Therapy

When your whole life is driven by doing, formal meditation practice can provide a refuge of sanity and stability that can be used to restore balance and perspective. (Kabat-Zinn, 1990, p. 60)

Approaches to psychotherapy across all modalities work with clients' thoughts and beliefs. Therapists are joined in a concern to enable clients to develop new ways to think about themselves and their worlds. In *transactional analysis* the focus is on nurturing or decontaminating 'the Adult' and helping clients recognise the nature of any distorted or childlike 'magical' thinking; in *psychoanalytical* work, the focus is on exploring conscious versus unconscious experience. Therapists engaging *humanistic* approaches seek to make sense of clients' experience and meanings along with nurturing a more positive self-concept. In *systemic work* therapists home in on the contextual dynamics influencing thinking–feeling–behaviour, while *cognitive-behavioural therapy* (**CBT**) focuses on the dysfunctional nature of clients' thoughts influencing behaviour.

Some relational integrative psychotherapists regard CBT as being overly reductionist and mechanical, and feel dismayed about its wholesale application. However, such views may cloud judgement of cognitive techniques and achievements. It seems more helpful to recognise the knowledge base of this field, and the important insights, techniques and tools it provides. Whatever our opinion of CBT, we cannot deny the fact that, as therapists, we all work cognitively.

Relational Integrative Psychotherapy: Engaging Process and Theory in Practice, First Edition. Linda Finlay.
© 2016 John Wiley & Sons, Ltd. Published 2016 by John Wiley & Sons, Ltd.

Numerous integrative models and approaches have evolved to acknowledge the potential contribution of cognitive therapy. These include DBT, CAT, REBT and mindfulness-based CT, discussed below, along with many others.[1]

This chapter focuses on how a cognitive orientation can be brought into relational integrative work. In the first section, I lay out some basic **principles underpinning the cognitive tradition**, with particular attention to *CBT* theory. I go on to explore the currently popular movement of **mindfulness** which, through its focus on consciousness, offers an alternative route to cognitive working. In the third section of the chapter, I look at explicitly **relational integrative** cognitive work in practice. Finally, I reconsider the place of CBT in therapy, touching on some of the critical debates underlying the **evidence base** of our profession.

Principles Underlying the Cognitive Tradition

The cognitive tradition encompasses a diverse range of theories, models and techniques spanning the fields of cognitive science, CBT, mindfulness and positive psychology (see box 11.1). All share the view that cognition (i.e. our ability to think, attend, perceive, remember, problem-solve and reason) underlies human activities, and that changing cognition alters feelings and behaviour.

Box 11.1 Case illustration: Positive psychology

Interest in **positive psychology**[2] has exploded over the last decade or so. The movement focuses on ways to achieve satisfactory, happy lives rather than treating mental illness and pathology.

Applied to therapy and research the focus has been on: (1) examining how people experience happiness (and other positive emotions like interest, anticipation, hope); (2) identifying what gives us a positive sense of well-being and meaning; and (3) investigating the beneficial nature of immersion in pleasurable activities ('flow experience'). Such theorising has led to the so-called 'happiness formula': pleasure + engagement + meaning = happiness.

Spearheaded by both a *humanistic* interest in maximising human potential and a scientific *cognitive* approach, much research has demonstrated the value of this positive focus (see: https://www.authentichappiness.sas.upenn.edu/). Seligman, Park, Peterson and Steen (2005), for example, studied the impact of making a deliberate attempt at least once a day to reflect on the good things in one's life. Specifically participants were asked to reflect on personal strengths and write down three things that went well each day and on why they went well. This exercise in positive thinking was found to have a significant impact on happiness levels. Such findings have also energised the mindfulness meditation movement.

The *cognitive-behavioural therapy* approach itself spans two distinct psychology traditions: the central role played by cognition, and the application of learning theory to the modification of behaviour.[3] When the two are blended in practice the focus is on replacing clients' problematic maladaptive behaviours, thoughts and beliefs with new adaptive ones; and dominant negative, self-defeating, unrealistic, distorted thoughts with more positive, rational ones. For instance, a woman with an eating disorder might say of herself, 'Once I'm slim, I'll be happy' or 'I'm fat so I'm an awful person'. Through CBT she would be encouraged instead to say, 'I can be happy even if I'm overweight' or 'I may be overweight but I am still an okay, worthy person'. To give a different example: a father who says, 'I should have stopped my daughter driving that night; it's my fault she got killed in the accident' might be enabled to move to 'I didn't kill her; the accident did'.

When viewed through a CBT lens, the extreme emotional distress characteristic of disorders such as depression and anxiety is seen as primarily the result of unrealistic, negative *schemas* which impact on feelings, behaviour and physiological responses. For instance, anxiety can spiral when negative thoughts ('I can't do this. I need to leave. If I don't I'll have a panic attack') lead to bodily hyper-arousal (increased heart rate and palpitations), which in turns triggers 'catastrophic thoughts' ('I'm having a heart attack'), which escalate the initiating anxiety. CBT argues that controlling one part of the system – that relating to cognition – eases other parts.

In Box 11.2, a cognitive-behavioural therapist discusses her perspective on Abi's eating disorder (binge–vomiting behaviour).[4]

Box 11.2 Case illustration: Applying CBT to binge–vomiting behaviour

The vicious cycle of Abi's binge–vomiting behaviour is aggravated by her distorted attitudes to weight, diet and dieting. It is important to consider the antecedents of her bingeing; what sets it off? It seems that she has learned to handle stress by bingeing. What then are the pay-offs for this behaviour? The biochemically tranquillising effects of bingeing may help distract her from other worries. Also her weight control is a key factor in her vomiting. Her fear of gaining weight acts as a possible negative reinforcement when combined with her distorted understanding of diet.

My recommended intervention would involve three elements:

- helping Abi to examine and modify her attitudes towards food, dieting, and her body: in other words, helping her to see that she is not fat and evidence shows she will not gain weight if she sticks to three well-balanced daily meals;

(Continued)

154 COGNITIVELY ORIENTATED THERAPY

- encouraging her to recognise the antecedents and pay-offs of her behaviour;
- re-training her to acquire new dietary habits, for example by keeping a diary in which she records everything she eats and her associated thoughts and feelings.

Abi should become more aware of triggers and the way she is using her bingeing–vomiting. In the process the therapist can positively reinforce any reduction in bulimic behaviour (Finlay, 2004).

These principles have been applied widely in therapy, generating numerous protocols and techniques designed to relieve symptoms of anxiety and depression, to manage anger, and to teach social skills and other coping skills through assertiveness training, meditation, etc.[5] CBT principles have been corralled in such integrative programmes as short-term *brief therapy*[6] work, which offers a directive, structured, time-limited, resource- and solution-focused approach to therapy based on a *psycho-educational* model.

Two of the most widely applied and researched models of cognitively orientated psychotherapy are Beck's Cognitive Therapy (CT), and Ellis's Rational Emotive Behavior Therapy (REBT).[7]

Cognitive therapy

Beck's theory (1967, 1976) proposes that depressed people are prone to distorted, negative, self-defeating thinking that leads to low mood and passivity (see table 11.1). According to Beck, three main beliefs typically dominate, to do with Self, present/experience, and future (see figure 11.1). For instance, on being made redundant, a person may feel this is their personal failure, that they always lose jobs, and that the situation is hopeless.

Beck's cognitive therapy recommends that:

- the individual is first helped to become aware of their *automatic thoughts*, e.g. 'I'm a terrible person';

Table 11.1 Patterns of faulty thinking

Faulty thinking	Behaviour
Arbitrary inferences	Drawing conclusions with insufficient evidence
Selective thinking	Seeing only the negatives
All-or-nothing thinking	Seeing everything as good or bad, success or failure
Catastrophising	Exaggerating a minor thing into a disaster
Overgeneralising	Drawing sweeping conclusions from one incident

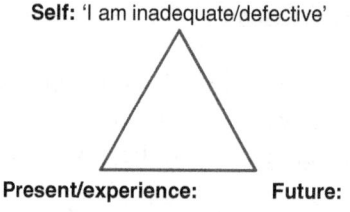

Self: 'I am inadequate/defective'

Present/experience:
'All my experience results in failure'
or 'People hate me because I'm defective'

Future:
'The future is hopeless'

Figure 11.1 Beck's 'Cognitive Triad' (1967, 1976)

- they learn to challenge these thoughts by testing them as *hypotheses* rather than accepting them as facts. Through this process, they come to discover what errors of logic are being made, e.g. 'I'm terrible because I never do anything right';
- therapy focuses firstly on *stopping the negative spiral* of thoughts (for instance, explicitly saying 'Stop!') and then searching for *evidence to disprove* these thoughts, e.g. 'I sometimes do things right'.

The person is then ready to try to replace the negative thoughts with positive but realistic balanced ones, using the technique of *cognitive restructuring*, e.g. 'Its human to make mistakes; it doesn't mean I'm terrible.

Rational Emotive Behavior Therapy (REBT)[8]

Ellis (1973, 2000) offers his humanistic version of cognitively orientated psychotherapy, one which similarly aims to challenge irrational beliefs, inferential distortions and life philosophies (e.g., 'Once I'm slim, I'll be happy'). Therapy is highly directive, with well-defined goals geared to challenging unrealistic expectations and changing behaviour through both cognitive restructuring and behavioural methods of self-reward. Therapy includes homework assignments, anti-procrastination exercises and skills training.

Ellis argues that people mistakenly blame external events for unhappiness and that it is our interpretation of these events that lies at the heart of our psychological distress. He relates this to his *ABC model*, where A is the Activating event (something that happens in the environment), e.g. a failed test; B is the Belief(s) held about this event or situation, e.g. 'I must pass or I am worthless', and C is the Consequence (the emotional or behavioural response to the belief), e.g. the person feels worthless.

For Ellis, it then becomes a question of challenging unhealthy patterns and helping the person respond more rationally. They would be encouraged to recognise that failing a test is disappointing but not a comment on self-worth. New ways of approaching study and revision could then be practised.

Mindfulness

Most psychotherapy encourages clients to step back in order to observe and describe their experience and become more aware of their process. We seek to nourish a capacity for self-awareness, encouraging clients to be observing, rational and reflective.[9]

Recently, cognitively orientated therapists have sought to integrate self-awareness via mindfulness techniques. Mindfulness training offers a therapeutic distancing from uncontrollable emotional states ('hot cognitions'), and clients learn to be more self-compassionate.

Arising from spiritual traditions such as Buddhism and Hinduism, mindfulness means to be **present**: to be aware of what we are doing and where we are. Through such techniques as meditation, breathing exercises and yoga, it attempts to help us become more aware of our thoughts and feelings so that, instead of being overwhelmed by them, we're better able to manage them. If we are concentrating on being mindful, there isn't much room left for troubles. Being present *to* experience involves living each moment to the full, something which can feel calming as well as conducive to clarity and awareness of choice.

Puddicombe (2011) describes the process of brushing one's teeth in a mindful manner, alert to the sound of the brush, the physical sensations involved in moving arm and hand, the aroma of toothpaste. "By focusing on just one of these objects at a time," he argues,

> the mind will start to feel a little more calm. And in that calmness there's every possibility that you might notice the tendency to drift off into thought, or to hurry to get on to the next thing. Or you might notice that you apply too much or too little effort to the brushing process. You may even notice a feeling of boredom. ... Having this increased awareness is the difference between having a stable, calm and focused mind, or a mind that feels out of control. (p. 108)

The aim of mindfulness is to change one's relationship with thoughts and feelings – and thereby with oneself. It encourages individuals to be more present in each moment, rather than lost in thought or caught up in emotions. This involves developing the art of allowing the mind to roam in a non-judgemental, effortless way; while aware of passing thoughts, the individual does not attempt to stop or change them. Practising mindfulness techniques, such as sitting or walking meditations, can give people greater insight into their emotions and boost their concentration and sense of well-being.

A growing pool of empirical **evidence** demonstrates the beneficial impact of mindfulness on stress, anxiety, depression and addictive behaviours (Shonin, van Gordon & Griffiths, 2014). It has been shown both to boost the immune system and to have a positive impact on physical problems like hypertension and chronic pain (http://bemindful.co.uk/about-mindfulness/). Mindfulness-based

COGNITIVELY ORIENTATED THERAPY   157

cognitive therapy is now advocated by NICE in the UK (NICE, 2009) and the American Psychiatric Association (APA, 2010).

Davidson et al. (2003), for instance, carried out an experiment on a group of highly pressured workers. These were randomly divided into two groups, one receiving meditation training and the other acting as a control group. The striking results showed that those who received the meditation training were happier and that their brain activity had shifted towards the left side of the brain. When both groups subsequently received flu vaccinations, those who had received the meditation training developed a stronger immunity to the flu virus.

Given these positive benefits, it is not surprising that the therapy world has shown an interest in mindfulness – as a technique if not as a spiritual practice. Faris and van Ooijen describe their use of mindfulness-based cognitive strategies within their ***relational integrative model*** (RIM; a postmodern, systemic relational integrative model blending CBT, psychodynamic and humanistic approaches):

> [M]indfulness allow[s] clients to really tune into themselves in a deeply authentic way, to come back to a more genuine sense of self without the need to continue to adopt a mask ..., as well as to learn to dis-identify from self-critical, attacking and negative patterns of thinking, which will have the effect of giving a greater sense of choice to how they then act and relate. (2012, p. 100)

They suggest a focus on meaning, insight and experience (see figure 11.2), illustrating that mindfulness approaches constitute a move away from a focus on the content of thinking to *process*, i.e. becoming aware of thought patterns instead of changing negative thoughts.

Increasingly, mindfulness is being integrated into ***cognitively orientated therapy*** programmes. An example of this is its growing use in **anger management** (see box 11.3).[10]

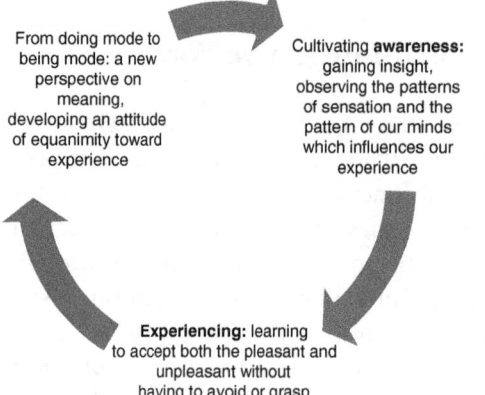

From doing mode to being mode: a new perspective on meaning, developing an attitude of equanimity toward experience

Cultivating **awareness:** gaining insight, observing the patterns of sensation and the pattern of our minds which influences our experience

Experiencing: learning to accept both the pleasant and unpleasant without having to avoid or grasp

Figure 11.2   Mindfulness perspective (Faris & van Ooijen, 2012, p. 100)

158 COGNITIVELY ORIENTATED THERAPY

> ### Box 11.3 Case illustration: Mindfulness-based CBT programme for anger management
>
> The following 10-week anger management programme is summarised from Kelly (2007).
>
> 1. Introductions of therapist and client and of the method; assessment
>   *Homework*: generating personal goals
> 2. Agenda setting and theory about anger
>   *Homework*: assertiveness work sheet contrasting aggression with assertion
> 3. Body Scan technique
>   *Homework*: practise Body Scan to become more mindful of breath and body
> 4. Handling obstacles experienced during Body Scan and doing a Sitting Meditation
>   *Homework*: listing anger triggers, noting connection between thoughts, behaviour, feelings
> 5. Introduction to 3-Minute Breathing Space technique
>   *Homework:* Anger-Provoking Events Calendar activity to track anger-provoking situations and emotional and behavioural reactions
> 6. 3-Minute Breathing Space technique as a coping mechanism
>   *Homework*: use of Breathing Space technique and sitting meditation practice
> 7. Introduction to Acceptance, Allowing and Being exercise
>   *Homework*: practising meditation and breathing techniques
> 8. Problem-solving exercise to resolve conflict
> 9. Review, reinforcement, and connections made between CBT and mindfulness practice in relation to managing anger
> 10. Feedback and evaluation of outcomes

Working in a Relational-integrative Way

Relational integrative therapists argue that the efficacy of cognitive techniques is increased when they are applied in a relational context which attends to broader, more holistic, emotional and interpersonal functions. The challenge lies in finding ways to engage cognition and consciousness relationally without reducing clients to their behavioural symptoms and therapy to one-size-fits-all protocols.

It should also be recognised that many, if not all, cognitive practitioners strive to work in relational integrative ways that are responsive to individuals. It's not uncommon to see CBT counsellors, for instance, also embrace a *person-centred* approach of warmth, genuineness and empathy. That an *actively collaborative* psycho-educational approach is usually favoured increases the relational component, as for instance when we invite clients to participate fully in treatment as part of their taking responsibility for choices.

Cognitive-type therapies are also often included as part of a wider intervention. For instance, Lacey (1983) pioneered an outpatient treatment for women with bulimia nervosa. This involved ten sessions each of supportive, cognitively orientated (using contracts, diary, homework) individual sessions and insight-directed group therapy. Lacey and his team at Newbridge House, Birmingham, UK, later developed a multidisciplinary approach to working with clients with eating disorders. This includes:

One-to-one therapy Providing CBT or psychoanalytic psychotherapy, depending upon which approach best suits the individual.

Family therapy Seen as essential and recommended by NICE for all young people aged below 18 who have anorexia.

Dietary advice Providing meal prescriptions for all patients throughout treatment and in general supporting patients' acceptance of food and normalised eating.

Group and occupational therapy programme Providing a supportive practical and relational context in which to explore thoughts, feelings and challenges.

Dramatherapy Providing an innovative approach to self-discovery and healing.

(adapted from www.newbridge-health.org.uk/therapeuticrecovery/)

Beyond such eclectic multidisciplinary work, more formally structured (and validated) approaches to integration can be found in a range of models and approaches. *Cognitive Analytic Therapy* (CAT) from the UK and *Dialectical Behavior Therapy* (DBT) from the US are two notable examples of integrative cognitively orientated therapy.

Cognitive Analytic Therapy

This time-limited therapy was developed by Ryle (1990) in the context of the UK's National Health Service aim to provide affordable, effective psychological treatment. CAT represents a collaborative approach which combines ***psychoanalytical*** and ***cognitive*** therapy theories. It argues that we actively construct our realities, while acknowledging that our sense of who we are has been shaped developmentally by a process of internalising others (attachment figures) and disowning parts of ourselves which we may project onto others.[11] All this is seen to result in 'self-states', or parts of self, that reflect important inner patterns of relationships. Therapy is concerned with integrating these parts into a whole by helping clients develop a capacity for self-reflection.

CAT is usually conducted over a 16-week time frame. The introductory sessions, concerned with assessment, culminate with the therapist offering a 're-formulation' letter (see box 11.4 for an example which highlights a client's

160   COGNITIVELY ORIENTATED THERAPY

engulfment–abandonment issues). Remaining sessions then focus on exploring the issues and working towards change. The last couple of sessions allow attachment and separation issues to come to the fore; both client and therapist have the opportunity of writing a 'goodbye letter'.

Box 11.4 Case illustration: A therapist's CAT 'reformulation' letter to a client

Dear Phillip

I said I would write down some of the themes that have emerged in therapy so far. You came into therapy describing recurrent feelings of failure and difficulties in being with other people. So far, we have examined these problems in relation to what you recall as an unempathic family in which you felt compelled to be the perfect son to a father whom you described as controlling and authoritarian. When you were 8 you were sent away to boarding school and this seems to have compounded your feelings of emptiness and aloneness. Perhaps at an unconscious level you have experienced this as a punishment for failing to be the perfect son …?

… In relation to both your professional and personal life we have examined the need for you to remain in some way separate and different from both your family and work colleagues. With your family this seems to have taken the form of you appearing unreachable. At work it may have taken the form of what you have described as 'dropping clangers' – something that alienates and distances you from your colleagues. … [Y]our self-worth is very low and you seek to restore self-esteem by working hard to regain the attention and admiration of others. …

One way of looking at these issues would be to see them as a set of polarized choices or dilemmas. …

- Either I strive to feel safe from others by being in control, or I risk being compliant and controlled.
- Either I push others away, exist on my own, feeling in charge but rejected, or I am with other people, feeling engulfed, invisible and taken over.

(Crossley & Stowell-Smith, 2000, pp. 211–212)

Dialectical Behavior Therapy

Developed originally by Linehan (1993) in the US as a way of working with people with borderline personality disorders, DBT offers a structured dynamic integrative approach. It is a form of ***behaviour therapy*** in which the therapist attempts to acknowledge the person's feelings and experience (particularly their sense of vulnerability and desperation), and to teach new coping skills.[12]

DBT theory suggests that, in response to invalidating environments, the emotionally vulnerable child will not have the opportunity to accurately understand their feelings and will not learn the skills of handling emotions. The child's behaviour typically oscillates between the opposite poles of emotional inhibition, in an attempt to gain acceptance, and extreme displays of emotion, in order to have their feelings acknowledged and their needs met. Patterns of self-harming tend to develop as a means of coping with intense and painful feelings. This can escalate to suicide attempts; the person feels unworthy and life does not seem worth living.

DBT focuses on offering validation. For example, acknowledgements that an individual has valid reasons for 'cutting up' validate their experience and past behaviour. At the same time, the therapist will seek to challenge the individual to find other strategies to manage stress in the present. Therapist and client together identify and put into practice alternative behaviours which are less self-damaging and which move the client in a life-affirming direction.

DBT thus demands, on the part of the therapist, an intricate and subtle dance between acceptance and challenge, a dance aimed at both supportively accepting the patient and confronting them with new possibilities. Therein lies DBT's central 'dialectical tension': acceptance is balanced by change and change is seen to occur in a context of accepting 'what is'.

Evidence-based Practice?

All therapists, irrespective of their modality, would surely argue for the value of their approach, the reputable nature of its theory, and the soundness of the evidence which demonstrates its effectiveness. However, the question of what constitutes *legitimate* evidence is much contested. Some therapists – *cognitive-behavioural* ones in particular – favour 'hard' empirical research evidence based on systematic and measurable tests (such as those found in systematic reviews or outcome studies). Others value the equally systematic but 'soft' qualitative research evidence of clients' and therapists' experiential narratives accounts. For many therapists, the evidence accumulated from their practice and their many years of experience (perhaps of being a client as well as a therapist) bolsters confidence in their work.

Whatever one's preferred route, there is no question that in the current climate therapists are increasingly being exhorted to demonstrate the effectiveness of their work. One of the understandable but problematic results of the **evidence-based practice** movement has been the growing tendency to set different psychotherapy treatments against one other. This drive to find evidence to value some modalities over others, or to prioritise one particular approach, has proved divisive and unhelpful.

Within this specific policy and research context, empirical **outcome research** on integrative treatments has expanded considerably over recent years. Much of this has been fuelled by the controlled research undertaken within the *brief therapy* and cognitive or behavioural fields, which routinely use standardised behavioural measures to set out pre- and post-therapy results (see box 10.4).[13] (Much research originates in the US, whose managed care context demands cost-effective, short-term therapy with 'proven' results, often to the detriment of longer-term work conducted at greater depth.)

Critics of such reliance on outcome research point out that, since the early 1970s, substantial and compelling research has demonstrated that the specific type of therapy a client receives has no significant impact on outcome (Luborsky, Singer & Luborsky, 1975; Wampold et al., 1997) – the infamous 'dodo bird' verdict. Hubble, Duncan and Miller (1999) explain this lack of evidence in support of any one modality or technique over others by suggesting that clients are resourceful and can be the architects of their own change processes, creatively using whatever healing opportunities are offered. Further, much of the research suggests that relational dimensions present across all modalities are more important than specific techniques (Cooper, 2008; Norcross, 2011).

Critics are concerned that short-term behavioural gains measured by outcome research may be reductionist ones that do not represent clients' holistic experience and may not be sustained long-term. While therapies such as CBT supply outcomes which seem to measure a reduction in symptoms, long-term change involving shifts in narrative may prove much harder to capture. Paradoxically, a client who starts therapy being dissociated and ends having greater awareness of their feelings may actually show an *increase* in anxiety or depression on behavioural scales, while, in existential terms, their life may be more satisfying.

The debates surrounding the role, form and quality of evidence find reflection in the findings of current research (see box 11.5). There is now a considerable evidence base in favour of cognitive and cognitive-behavioural methods. More than others, these approaches have consistently been shown to be effective for a wide range of psychological difficulties (see Cooper, 2008, for a review). Research indicates that clients respond well (and quickly) to cognitively focused therapy, particularly when symptoms of anxiety and depression are measured. However, the evidence for other modalities and for integrative approaches is also growing and compelling.

Many argue that outcomes research is the way forward for integrative psychotherapy. These voices urge practitioners to use outcome measures routinely in their practice (see Miller, Duncan & Hubble, 2005). The evidence suggests that use of easily filled out questionnaires like the SRS (a measure of therapeutic alliance) or the ORS (a measure of outcomes) improves outcomes and increases client satisfaction and retention. Such practices offer the client respect, engaging with them as interested *service users* rather than passive recipients of health care.

Box 11.5 Research: Comparing CBT with other approaches

Cognitive therapy versus relaxation therapy and medication

When Clark et al. (1994) compared the outcomes of cognitive therapy, relaxation training and use of the drug imipramine, cognitive therapy emerged as the most effective of the three, measured immediately after the therapy and 15 months later.

CBT versus narrative therapy

Lopes et al. (2014) compared the outcomes of *CBT* and *narrative therapy* in a controlled clinical trial. Sixty-three moderately depressed clients were assigned to either CBT or narrative therapy, and the BDI-II[14] and Outcome Questionnaire were used as outcome measures.

The two therapies were more or less on a par in terms of effectiveness. Discussing these results, the researchers observed that the narrative therapy route seemed to require more resources than a client might have at the start of therapy and that these took time to learn. In contrast, CBT offered clear behavioural instructions that could be immediately implemented, resulting in more rapid compliance and change. They also pointed out that, on average, roughly a third of clients dropped out of therapy (slightly higher for the narrative group). For them, this highlighted the importance of the therapy relationship and the need to ensure that clients are well engaged in therapy.

CBT versus CBT with existential integration

Gebler and Maercker (2014) studied the efficacy of a standard *CBT* group for chronic pain, compared with a programme for the same group which integrated an *existential* perspective. One hundred and thirteen patients suffering from chronic pain and attending an interdisciplinary treatment centre in Germany were evaluated. Outcome measures, including ones for pain-related disability and pain severity, were applied at the conclusion of the group and at the follow-ups conducted three months and six months later.

The results indicated that the programme which integrated an existential perspective resulted in a significant reduction in pain-related disability compared with the results achieved by the traditional CBT group-programme. Both groups showed significant improvement post-treatment but the CBT group did *not* show sustained improvements over the long term. Existential aspects seemed particularly important for patients with a spiritual orientation. The findings support the importance of an existential and integrative approach to chronic pain and the relevance of meaning-making in the context of loss.

Concluding Reflections

In the process of writing this chapter, I have become aware of a slight shift in discourse and tone, perhaps triggered by my entry into the world of CBT. The therapy that I have been describing in this chapter seems more structured and systematised, less intuitively spontaneous than the approaches explored elsewhere in this book. Still, I hope I have managed to represent the field with integrity, conveying its breadth, complexity and relational richness.

CBT has, over the past fifty years or so, emerged as one of psychotherapy's success stories. Indeed, in certain circles and for some clients CBT is synonymous with counselling and psychotherapy. Its hegemony seems assured for the time being. Part of the success of CBT programmes lies in the way outcomes can be behaviourally measured in terms of symptom reduction. The fact that the efficacy of the treatment can be relatively easily demonstrated has spawned a mass of validating research. In the context of market-driven, cost-cutting impulses to find cheap, effective, quick-fix solutions, CBT has found a secure niche.

Even outside this specific political context, CBT – with its associated scientifically validated technical procedures and manualised protocols – has its passionate devotees. But it also has equally passionate detractors. A gap has opened up between therapists offering CBT and advocates of more holistic approaches, with the latter at times tending to stereotype CBT as reductionist, formulaic and unsuited to relational ways of working.

I remain saddened by this chasm. That numerous splits exist in our profession is perhaps inevitable, given our differing ideological frameworks and the way that new theories and practices supplant traditional forms. But I am disturbed when I hear comments like 'CBT is the enemy', or that humanistic, psychoanalytic approaches are 'subjective waffle'. (Such partisanship now seems to be taking hold among integrative practitioners who seek to reify particular models as superior or claim theirs is *the right way* to do integrative work.)

I prefer a more open relational-integrative position: one which respects diversity and informed pluralism, and is sensitive to the needs of individuals and particular social-cultural contexts. As for our attitude towards research, while my heart lies in qualitative, humanistically orientated research, and in nurturing greater acceptance of its legitimacy, I strongly support the growth of *both* outcomes- and process-orientated research. I would urge all integrative psychotherapists to engage with, and be aware of, the breadth of published research now available to us, irrespective of whether we incorporate any in our own practice.

For any integrative practitioner with a knee-jerk reaction against CBT, it bears emphasis that CBT techniques are part of our tool bag of therapy resources. We can and do work cognitively! The challenge for us lies in finding ways to integrate cognitive elements *holistically*, *relationally* and *mindfully*.

Notes

1 Neuro-linguistic programming (**NLP**), constructivist self-development theory (**CSDT**) (McCann & Pearlman, 1992), eye movement desensitisation and reprocessing (**EMDR**) (Shapiro, 2001), mentalization-based treatment (**MBT**) (Fonagy & Bateman, 2006), cognitive-behavioural analysis system of psychotherapy (CBASP) and mindfulness-based stress reduction (**MBSR**) are a few more that come to mind.

2 The term 'positive psychology' was first used by Abraham Maslow in his 1954 book *Motivation and Personality*. Martin Seligman – a former president of the American Psychological Association – reignited interest in the concept in 1998, fuelling a lively scientific research movement which aspires to inform social policy and influence practice.

3 Behavioural techniques include exposure therapy (also called 'systematic desensitisation'), which is done *in vivo*, *imaginally* or via *virtual reality*; and the systematic teaching and learning of skills ('shaping') through positive reinforcement or through 'time out' from positive reinforcement (such as being asked to stand in the corner). These psycho-educational techniques are particularly evident in work with children and in the field of learning disabilities.

4 Space does not permit the inclusion of a full account of how therapists of different theoretical persuasions would view Abi's binge behaviour. An *existential* therapist, to give an example of a radically different account, might suggest that Abi was hyperaware of her body as an object while being disconnected from her subjective body. Questions might be asked about whether she has the necessary space, protection and support to 'be' and to accept herself. A *gestalt* therapist might find the symbolism of the bingeing to be a form of retroflection; might she be pushing down anger while engaging a self-soothing feeding behaviour in an attempt to fill a need which is not met by the environment?

5 See for instance clinical resources (protocols, handouts) for working with traumatic bereavement: www.guilford.com/companion-site/

Treating-Traumatic-Bereavement/
9781462513178.

6 Brief therapy is a strategic, solution-based (rather than problem-orientated) integrative way of working. The focus is on a specific problem, with the therapy using direct, proactive intervention, e.g. taking a *psycho-educational* approach to develop resources (see chapter 6).

7 While based on the same CBT principles, the two approaches have notable differences. For example, while Beck stresses the quality of the therapeutic relationship and places emphasis on the client discovering misconceptions themselves, Ellis sees the therapist more as a directive, persuasive and confrontational teacher.

8 Originally known as rational-emotive therapy (RET), this can be regarded as one of the first systematised integrative models, since Ellis, a psychoanalyst by training, explicitly sought an *existential-humanistic* version of **CBT**.

9 This increased self-awareness, or mindfulness, may be activated in different ways, depending on the approach. In *cognitive-behavioural* work, clients learn to record their thoughts and make connections with their behaviour and feelings. *Person-centred* therapists' use of empathy, congruence and unconditional positive regard within a relationship acts as a catalyst for the client's enhanced self-awareness and self-esteem. *Somatic* trauma therapists teach clients to focus on the present embodied moment as a way of turning down the volume on intrusive images or memories from the past. In the *psychoanalytic* world, the concept of 'mentalisation' is linked to attachment theory. Here, a person's ability to understand their own and others' mental states, and to see themselves as others see them, is nourished by attuned caregiving in early attachments (Fonagy & Bateman, 2006).

10 Arguing against pre-set anger management techniques, therapists from other modalities highlight the need to explore anger's meanings and work through issues, perhaps cathartically. From an *existential* perspective, Deurzen (2014) recommends trying to establish a deep connection with one's angry places. Instead of

166 COGNITIVELY ORIENTATED THERAPY

trying to interpret the anger or prescribe behavioural change, the focus of phenomenological work is on describing the anger. In contrast, Orbach (2014), working *psychoanalytically*, highlights how vulnerability and hard-to-manage feelings tend to lie at the root of anger. Sills (2014), taking a psycho-spiritual perspective involving depth awareness and attunement, regards anger as a protective response which helps maintain spiritual connections. (For more on this, see the special issue (issue 50) of the *Psychotherapist* devoted to different perspectives.)

11 Unlike psychoanalytical approaches, which focus on interpretations about the client's unconscious, CAT places emphasis on the client's cognitive processes. It aims to help the client observe themselves in new ways and adopt an active problem-solving stance.

12 Both DBT and CBT take a psychoeducational approach and focus on changing unhelpful behaviour. DBT differs from CBT in that it places importance on self-acceptance, reality testing and mindfulness and the relationship with the therapist is seen as the key change agent.

13 For instance, the BDI-II (Beck Depression Inventory; Beck, Steer and Brown, 1996) consists of 21 items, each comprising a list of four statements arranged in increasing severity about a particular symptom of depression in clinical and normal patients.

14 The Beck Depression Inventory - II is a widely used tool for diagnosing the intensity of depressive symptoms and measuring change.

12

Existential Phenomenology: Theory and Therapy

[O]ur existential journey requires us to be prepared to be touched and shaken by what we find on the way. ... It is only with such an attitude of openness and wonder that we can encounter the impenetrable mysteries, which take us beyond our own preoccupations and sorrows and which by confronting us with death, make us rediscover life. (Deurzen-Smith, 1997, p. 5)

Take five minutes to reflect on the questions in box 12.1, which go to the heart of an existential-phenomenological approach. Even better, in true existential spirit, discuss these over a drink with friends!

Box 12.1 Case illustration: Reflecting on life	
Question	*Guidelines*
Who are you?	Don't just think about your roles. Who are you as a person? In what ways might others' views differ from how you see yourself?
	(Continued)

Relational Integrative Psychotherapy: Engaging Process and Theory in Practice, First Edition. Linda Finlay.
© 2016 John Wiley & Sons, Ltd. Published 2016 by John Wiley & Sons, Ltd.

Question	Guidelines
How do you experience your body (not your objective, physical body but your subjective sense of it)?	Does it feel big and ungainly? Small and fragile? Does your body feel 'sucked dry'? Do you have a sense of flowing movement or do you feel cumbersome? Are there bits of your body you feel disconnected from?
What makes your life worth living? Are you living your life in a meaningful way?	Friends, family, work? Is there a part of you that struggles to answer? (Perhaps a relationship has just gone sour or you're burnt out at work and not quite convinced life is worth living at the moment.) Are you doing the things that are important to you, in the way you want to do them? What's your work–life balance like?
How are you currently experiencing time (not clock time but your sense of time)?	Do you feel time as a constant pressure and horizon? Is time rushing by or is it going slowly and stretching out?
How are you experiencing the space you are in?	Are you at home, feeling secure, at home? Or are you in a public place that feels less safe and intrusively presses on you? Is there another space you would like to be in, and if so, why?

This chapter starts with a sketch of some of the main **philosophical ideas** – the 'landmarks' – which underpin the practice of existential phenomenology.[1] The second section outlines the nature of *bracketing* and *Being*, which is part of the basic **phenomenological attitude**. The final section describes **existential-phenomenological therapy** as inviting description and focusing on existentials. The commonalities and differences between existential and general humanistic work are highlighted.

Existential-phenomenological philosophy is at times opaque and full of difficult ideas which may challenge taken-for-granted assumptions. But it is worth grappling with the ideas, even briefly; and it can help to focus on their practical application.

Existential Phenomenology: 'Landmarks' in the Philosophical Territory

Existential phenomenology is an umbrella term encompassing two **philosophical movements** (existentialism and phenomenology). It is also an approach to **therapy**, **research** and a **way of being**. The field as a whole is concerned with questions about human experience and existence. It engages human concerns

EXISTENTIAL PHENOMENOLOGY: THEORY AND THERAPY   169

relating to life and death, authentic being and becoming, embodiment and identity, relationships with others, choice and meaningfulness, belonging and needs, freedom versus oppression, the experience of time and space, and spiritual dimensions.

These same philosophical questions can be the focus of therapy. Existential therapy[2] encourages clients to be aware of what it means to be alive, to own choices and potentialities, and to embrace their special capacity as human beings to be reflexive (self-aware) and to reflect on their experiences in everyday life.

In this section I discuss briefly seven interlinked ideas or 'landmarks' which characterise the field and indicate their relevance for practice.

Being-in-the-world

In his early, influential work *Being and Time* (1962), the phenomenological philosopher Heidegger argues that we are *thrown* into a world which is not of our choosing: a pre-existing world of objects, projects, language, people, culture, and history. Rather than seeing humans as self-contained individual subjects in a world of objects, Heidegger describes the human in the world as a *Dasein* ('there-being' or 'being-in-the-world'). For Heidegger, our Being is immersed in the world and inseparable from it.

This concept is relevant to psychotherapy in reminding us always to attend to clients' wider lives. We need to recognise, and remain constantly aware of, their everyday activities and specific socio-cultural context: their particular body–self–world. The following extract from Kemp (2009) shows how a drug addict's existential withdrawal can be explained as a withdrawal from the lived body, from relations with others and from a meaningful world:

> The addict no longer has a lived-body, only a site for instrumental, technological intervention. ... The body cannot be lived any other way. But equally the world is robbed of meaning, now filled with things that are used only to perpetuate the addictive process. ... [T]here is a progressive and painful alienation from self. (2009, p. 130)

Being-with-others

Existentialists argue that the world into which we are thrown is fundamentally relational and social. Even when we are physically alone or when we ignore others, we are still in-relation (with ourselves and with others) through our everyday engagement in our shared social world and culture.

This relational philosophy directs us towards human existence as being grounded in 'caring'. Ineluctably, I find myself in a world that matters to me. Just as our own existence is an issue for us as individuals, we also develop concern for others' welfare by virtue of sharing the world with them.

But while caring for others, we are also at risk of being objectified by them. They may seek to possess us, demand from us, judge us. The gaze of the Other

170   EXISTENTIAL PHENOMENOLOGY: THEORY AND THERAPY

can deprive us of spontaneity and freedom; it can also cause us shame. Hence Sartre's celebrated phrase from his one-act play about life in Hell, *No Exit*:[3] 'Hell is other people.'

Relationally orientated psychotherapists are already well tuned to these *being-with* ideas. All our "knowledge, awareness and experienced understanding of the world, of others and of our selves emerge out of, and through, an irreducible grounding of relatedness" (Spinelli, 2007, p. 12).

Nothingness

For existentialists, the answer to the fundamental existential question 'Who am I?' is nothingness: I am no-thing. Unlike a table, which can be defined as a piece of furniture with a top surface and legs, there are no inherent characteristics to my being.

Despite this, however, we often define ourselves as some-thing: a therapist, say, or a waiter, a depressive, an athlete, a poet .... These objectifying self-definitions only touch our surface activity and roles. I do what I do because of my role: as a commuter, I get up at a set time in the morning in order to go to work; I stand at the same spot on the platform to get the best seat on the train; I make a daily pilgrimage to the local coffee shop for my latte .... My existence is anonymised, routinised and interchangeable with that of other commuters; I simply follow the herd, blandly conforming.

There is safety and comfort in such banal daily life activities and habitual roles. Without them we would have to admit our lack of solidity and selfhood, and there would be no guidelines for living. The thought of this causes us radical anxiety, so we retreat to being an anaesthetised some-thing. We adopt determinant characteristics and fix ourselves (and others) as 'this' or 'that' way. We become a 'They' (*das Man*) in Heidegger's (1962) terminology. In Sartre's (1969) terms, when we objectify ourselves in this way, by identifying with roles and refusing to take responsibility for choice, we are in 'bad faith'.

As psychotherapists, our work is centrally concerned with such questions as 'Who am I?' and 'Who do I want to become?' Existential therapists are concerned to avoid labelling, objectifying and fixing clients as 'things' (e.g., a diagnosis or a personality type) and disavowing an individual's freedom and capacity to change.

Angst (anxiety)

Existentialism calls upon us to reject this objectifying, anonymous, doing-focused 'They' existence by sensing the emptiness of our existence, to feel the core of authentic nothingness, including the non-being that awaits us when we die. As we confront life's meaningless and the abyss of nothingness ahead, we experience 'angst', a pervasive dread that is everywhere and nowhere. Angst stifles our breath and we feel profoundly unsettled, alienated, homeless. We can escape this angst only by fleeing from ourselves and losing ourselves in the 'They'. Animals are guided solely by instinct, says Kierkegaard, while human beings enjoy a freedom of choice that is at once attractive and terrifying.

But humans' awareness of mortality is what also enables us to escape from being lost in the 'They'. Confronting the imminence and inevitability of death, we have the potential to truly live in the here and now. Life now has an intensity and urgency; it is replete with meaning and possibilities. "The sense of void imminent makes my life pulsate for me with anxiety, that is, more palpably, more keenly, more ardently" (Lingis, 1989, p. 113).

Existential therapy taps this energy in its quest to find a more engaged way of living, to avoid or move beyond experiencing life in an automatic, habitual way. Rather than seeking to help people feel better, therapy is geared towards their learning to 'better feel'.[4]

Authenticity and selfhood

Existentialists believe the only way to live fully and authentically is to be present in the moment. Authenticity involves opening up to life as it presents itself to us and owning our part in it.

In this respect, **existentialists** depart from **person-centred** notions that authenticity involves experience of the 'real', fixed, core, essential self (as opposed to 'inauthentic', 'false' selves). For existentialists, the self is fluid, provisional and emergent, arising out of our intersubjective connections and social context. There is no 'Self' as such, but rather a more dynamic process of *self-ing*, which occurs with each choice and relational connection made. We can have a sense of self which comes from our living with ourselves over time and taking responsibility, but this too will change as we open ourselves to further possibilities.

It follows that integrative psychotherapists face a choice about how to perceive Self. Far from being a matter of mere theoretical debate, this choice impacts on our practice.

Freedom

Having the freedom to choose means that we are our own 'authors': we make our own moral code and are responsible for choosing how to be. However, this is not the freedom to do anything. It is a 'situated freedom', since we are thrown into a world not of our choosing (for example, there is no choice about being born into poverty or turmoil). As Sartre[5] (1969) points out, this is freedom we are *condemned* to take up, freedom always found in relation with the world.

Applied to therapy, this concept of freedom prioritises the ideas of choice and responsibility, for example the notion that clients – at some level – choose the lives they lead. Clients who find themselves stuck in a 'drama triangle', for instance, may find it helpful to learn that this is not simply something that *happens* to them, beyond their control; rather, they need to acknowledge some role in co-creating the situation.

Existential feelings

Moods and emotions are not seen as inner subjective colourings or states of mind that somehow react to something outside of Self. Given that Self and world are experientially intertwined, moods exist *in the world*; moods are akin to experiencing an atmosphere. Rather than being an inside force directed at something or someone, existential feelings and moods are woven into our bodily being and our everyday participations.

Ratcliffe (2008) talks about existential feelings as background orientations through which experience is structured and which engage our bodily relationship with the world. For example, we speak of 'feeling trapped in a situation' or 'feeling safe and secure'. Similarly, when describing a mental health disorder, the phenomenological psychiatrist van den Berg talks of how a person's world can 'collapse', or how they can feel 'unbalanced' or 'lose their footing':

> The depressed patient speaks of a world gone gloomy and dark. The flowers have lost their color .... The patient suffering from mania ... finds things full of color and beauty .... The schizophrenic patient sees, hears and smells indications of a world disaster. ... The patient is ill; this means that *his world* is ill. (1972, pp. 45–46)

Existential-phenomenological therapists mostly disagree with those **humanistic** and **psychoanalytic** therapists who view feelings and emotions as being 'inside' the individual. This difference in orientation has profound implications for therapy work and on how we view clients. To understand another person, phenomenologists do not inquire about some *inner* subjective realm. Instead, understanding comes from asking how the person's *world* is lived and experienced: phenomenologists call this the **lifeworld**.

Phenomenology seeks to do justice to everyday experience, to evoke what it is to be human. The aim is to describe embodied experience and the meanings of that experience in the here-and-now (Finlay, 2011). Phenomenological therapists asks clients such questions as 'What is this kind of experience like?', 'How are you experiencing this in your body right now?' The aim is to focus on staying with what is being experienced in the present while drawing out the experiences, meanings, values and perspectives that have shaped the client. Then therapist and client together might explore choices for being and becoming in the future.

The Phenomenological Attitude: 'Bracketing' and 'Being'

The key to practising the phenomenological attitude (in therapy, research or life) is to adopt a particular open, non-judgemental approach – one filled with wonder and curiosity about the world – while simultaneously holding at bay prior assumptions and knowledge. The immediate challenge for a therapist entering a therapeutic encounter is to remain open to new understandings – to be both present and empathically open to the client – in order to go beyond what is already known or assumed (Finlay, 2013).

EXISTENTIAL PHENOMENOLOGY: THEORY AND THERAPY   173

This process taps into the twinned concepts from Buber's phenomenological philosophy of *presence* and *inclusion*. **Presence** is the capacity to be open and both emotionally and bodily present (see chapter 13 where this is discussed further). **Inclusion** is the capacity to put oneself into the experience of the Other (and thereby confirm the Other's existence), simultaneously holding onto oneself. To be present without inclusion is to be cut off or alienated from the other. To be immersed in the other but lose one's sense of self is to be overly merged and confluent with the other. Both presence and inclusion are needed for real contact.

Yontef (1993), writing of relational *gestalt therapy*, considers inclusion in the form of attuned empathy to be the essence of the dialogical relationship. The process of inclusion is seen to provide clients with reparative experiences of a positive relationship in the present. The client gains from being seen and acknowledged – two things that may have been largely absent in their prior experience. Meeting the client in the way they are at the moment – and not making them different – supports the client to feel 'held' and to identify with their own experience.

In my own *existential-phenomenological* practice (Finlay, 2012),[6] my initial concern is simply to invite clients to describe their lived experience and then to dwell with emerging meanings. I try to resist jumping too quickly into making analytical observations and explaining their behaviour as I believe that the process of describing experience is in itself therapeutic. It gives the client a 'voice', and an opportunity to 'make sense of' their lives and to be 'witnessed' (see figure 12.1).

Two key ideas are particularly relevant: being and bracketing.

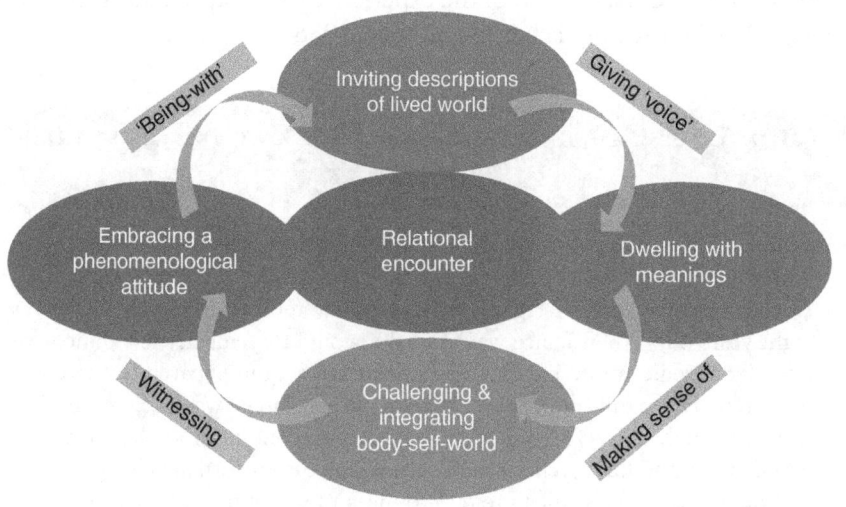

Figure 12.1   Existential-phenomenological approach to Integrative Psychotherapy

Being

I suggest that three specific modes of therapist *Being* are to the fore: being human (being present), being open and being-with (being relational).

1. **Being human** This involves owning one's own challenging existence as a therapist. Often existential dialogues with clients involve sharing experiences of human frailty and vulnerability (a 'we' rather than 'you' approach). The existential therapist allows the 'cloak of professionalism' to fall away, in order to be present as a person who is prepared to be impacted and changed, just as the client is impacted and changed (Barnett & Madison, 2012).

2. **Being open** The existential therapist aims to be open to awe, alive to creative possibilities, ready to explore the unknown, open to the client as a person (disavowing any reductionist gaze and the 'bad faith' of focusing on diagnostic labels), and prepared to open their own self to confrontation with existential givens. Therapists work with clients in their "search for truth with an open mind and an attitude of wonder, rather than fitting the client overtly or covertly into established frameworks of interpretation" (Deurzen & Adams, 2011, p. 11). The *existential-integrative* psychotherapist Schneider (2008) argues that **awe**, in all its humility and wonder in and of life, is a key dimension of human fulfilment, with a crucial role to play in therapy if we can open ourselves first to curiosity and passionate connection and then to that awe (see box 12.2).

3. **'Being-with'** The embodied, intersubjective dialogue between therapist and client becomes the vehicle for exploring the being of the client and how they relate to others. Existential therapists ask, 'What is happening in the mysterious space between myself and the client? What is being revealed? How is the client's relational way of being in the therapy space similar to or different from the way they relate "outside"?' The reality of the *being-with* is greater than the shared sum of the experience of therapist and client (Hycner, 1991/1993). Meeting is healing (Buber, 1958).

Box 12.2 Case illustration: Making 'awe-full' existential connections

Janice was a 45-year-old white working-class female with a history of severe emotional and sexual abuse. Her father was an inveterate alcoholic with an explosive temper, and her grandfather sexually molested her when she was eight years old. When Janice was four, she would be regularly left alone with a 'schizophrenic' aunt. These visits terrified Janice, but apparently, there was no parental recognition of this sentiment. When Janice was five, her mother suddenly died. This left Janice with her volatile alcoholic father, her rapacious grandfather, and her psychotic aunt. How Janice even partially emerged from these circumstances is still a mystery to me, but somehow she managed.

...

[Six months into therapy]

She began by identifying a tension in her neck area, which loosened as she stayed present to it. Then she began perceiving an image of a tiny little girl trapped in a well. She couldn't identify where this well was, or how it got there, but she was clear that it felt fathomless with no end in sight. As I continued to invite her to stay present to this well, she began to feel the girl's terror. 'It's like she's sinking,' Janice told me, 'and she doesn't know where she's going.' Gently I supported her to continue with the experience, while at the same time reassuring her that if she needed to stop, she could do so at any time. She chose to proceed.

At about halfway into our session, Janice noticed that the little girl was fading, while the darkness around her grew. At times, the little girl struggled to unfold herself and peek out of the darkness, but invariably she sank back in. To this point Janice said very little about her relationship to the little girl, but as she 'stayed with' her, her sense of connection grew. Suddenly, Janice panicked. She could no longer find the little girl!

Yet at that very same moment, tears welled up in Janice's eyes. I asked her what brought on the tears and after a long silence she whispered: 'I reached out into the dark to touch her, and she reached out into the dark to touch me.'

With this simple yet profound image, Janice began a remarkable self-transformation. She moved from a position of abject terror to one of wonder to one of love. Through embracing the little girl, Janice at the same time embraced the void in which the little girl (as well as adult Janice) had languished for many years; and now she found solace there, and a chance for self-renewal. (Schneider, 2010)

Bracketing

The field of phenomenology is broad, but one particular idea which therapists of different hues and modalities beyond phenomenology have embraced is 'bracketing'. Sometimes it becomes simplified, misunderstood and misused, having been removed from its philosophical context.[7]

Basically, bracketing means putting previous knowledge into metaphorical brackets – holding them aside but in awareness. This process is not one of being objective and eliminating bias. Rather, it involves a concentrated focus on subjectivity and phenomenon as experienced: a new open, focused and different way of *being* is called for.

In addition to the bracketing of previous knowledge or theory, the very existence (or not) of the phenomenon being considered is put out of question. So, for instance, if a client tells us their dream, we don't say, 'It was only a dream, it wasn't real'. It was *experientially real* for that person. So we attend to dream as we would any recounting of experience in so-called 'real' life.

Engaging the phenomenological attitude, we strive to leave our worlds behind and to enter into our clients' worlds in order to reflect on their meanings and experiential processes. This attitude involves a special attentiveness that savours situations described by the client in a dwelling kind of a way that listens for, and even magnifies, details. This attitude is as free from value judgements and theoretical constructs as is possible. We try instead – at least in the first instance - to focus on the meaning of the situation purely as it is given to our client (Wertz, 2005).

The *psychoanalyst* Bion has argued that therapists should work without desire or memory and with a quiet mind open to making contact with clients' unconscious communications. "'Forget' what you know and 'forget' what you want, get rid of your desires, anticipations and also your memories so that there will be a chance of hearing these very faint sounds that are buried in this mass of noise" (Bion, 2005, p. 17).

What is called for is an especially attentive attitude of receptivity, an emptying of the self in order to be filled by the other and what is occurring *between*. Bracketing is enacted alongside a genuine sense of curiosity, empathy and compassion. Van Manen (2002) describes this process as openness to meeting the utterly strange in the familiar. The aim is "to see through fresh eyes, to understand through embracing new modes of being" (Finlay, 2008, p. 29).

As part of this fresh seeing, phenomenologists believe therapists have an ethical responsibility to respect and be open to the *otherness* of the Other. Thus I strive to maintain a genuinely open and unknowing stance – at least when I am engaging a phenomenological approach (I might take a different stance if I was applying a non-integrative cognitive or psychodynamic approach). While recognising my potential power as a therapist, I also try to hold myself to being humble and modest in any claims, for instance, to understand or 'know'.

Taken as a whole, the phenomenological attitude combines processes of Being and bracketing in terms of non-judgemental receptivity, openness to awe, presence and inclusion.

Existential-phenomenological Therapy

It is probably more accurate to talk about existential and phenomenologically orientated integrative *therapies* than about a singular therapy (Halling & Nill, 1995). The field is diverse and therapists tend to practise in idiosyncratic ways, often shying away from systematised or technical ways of working.[8]

Existential-phenomenological therapies provide a safe time and space to explore those questions asked at the beginning of this chapter. The aim is to encourage clients to see the givens of existence (how we are born into a certain culture, family, time, and so on) through different eyes, to help them achieve a new freedom to change (or accept that which cannot be changed), and to support them in taking responsibility for their future actions.

EXISTENTIAL PHENOMENOLOGY: THEORY AND THERAPY 177

Existential therapy is thus something of a **philosophical approach** which brings clients face to face with life's profound questions: those relating to anxiety, loneliness, alienation, anomie, ageing, despair, grief, guilt, meaninglessness, death .... Out of this dark tapestry emerge the threads for healing: relational connection, creativity, awe, and love.

'Philosophising the nature of self and universe is all well and good,' I hear you say, 'but what does an existential-phenomenological therapist actually *do*?' To which my answer would be, 'Perhaps you're not asking the right question. Instead of asking about a form of activity, think in terms of "How does an existential-phenomenological therapist attempt to be with a client?"'

Two particular processes, discussed below, characterise existential-phenomenological therapy: *inviting description* and *focusing on existentials*.

Inviting description

Box 12.3 shows the kind of use of description (rather than explanation, theorising or interpretation) which distinguishes the phenomenological approach from most other psychotherapeutic ones (except gestalt therapy). The aim is to stay with the manifest material in active, curious ways, not simply through passive reflecting back. It's about opening up a client's accounting so that they can find meaning, not imposing our own meaning, for instance asking, 'What kind of sense do you make of this impossible journey?'.

Box 12.3 Case illustration: Staying with description

CLIENT: When he finally told me that he didn't want to stay in the marriage and that he'd found a new life-partner, I just felt so sick and angry. I hated my self more than I hated him.

THERAPIST: Can you say a bit more about what it was like for you to hear him say these things? How was that sense of feeling sick and angry, for instance?

CLIENT: I can just feel it, you know? It's hard to put words to it.

THERAPIST: [*accessing his own experiences of being rejected and the feelings that arise in him regarding this*] Would it be OK for me to try to speak the words?

CLIENT: Yeah ...

THERAPIST: Now, I'm just guessing here. So anything I say that feels wrong to you, that's fine. You let me know. OK, so what I'm imagining when I put myself in your experience is: I get an overwhelming dizziness; a tightness in my gut; a restriction in my throat so that I can't even reply to him; I see flashes of all sorts of earlier moments in our life together: happy moments, sad ones, silly ones, private ones; and as I see them I hear his voice saying over and over: 'It's finished. This is the end.' I feel a rage that is almost murderous directed toward him,

(*Continued*)

> but oddly it's also directed toward my self. How's that so far? Is it at all close to your experience?
>
> CLIENT: Yes, a lot of it is. But as you were talking, what mainly came up for me was a sense of failure. That was the main thing. 'I've failed and I'm not worthy.'
>
> THERAPIST: OK. So let's stay with that. 'A lot of those statements Ernesto made are correct and they've provoked my overwhelming sense of failure.' Are you feeling it now?
>
> CLIENT: Yes.
>
> THERAPIST: So what's it like to feel it right here with me present?
>
> CLIENT: It's like I felt with Harry when he told me he was leaving me.
>
> THERAPIST: OK. So that feeling with Harry is right here in the room with us. Can you access any words for that feeling?
>
> (Spinelli, 2007, p. 161)

In order to access a person's **lifeworld**, the starting point is usually to ask clients to *describe* their experience, to tell their 'story'. Rather than setting out to analyse or explain, phenomenologists seek down-to-earth description of the lived experience, in as much detail as possible. I might ask, 'Can you describe this experience as it happened?' Some prompts to help return the client to the specific scene may prove helpful: 'Put yourself in that place, and look around. What do you see/hear/smell?'

Often when a person recalls an experience in detail it can be vividly evoked, almost re-experienced. Then it's about staying with this: standing-with the client, encouraging more description and not foreclosing too quickly (for example, avoiding interpretations or assuming a clear understanding). This is an opportunity to go deeper, to ask for more textured description: 'As you're now feeling a little of how it was for you, how are you experiencing it in your body?' 'Stay with that body feeling. What is it saying?' Inviting more metaphorical description is also a possibility: 'What would its colour/sound be if it had one?' (Spinelli, 2015).

In summary, the phenomenological focus is on describing lived experience rather than on dealing with pathological symptoms, analysing unconscious motivations, or attempting to explain and modify behaviour. Rather than seeking to 'educate', 'repair', 'change', 'analyse' or 'explain', phenomenological therapists celebrate the value of *simply describing*.[9] Bringing one's world into focus, and dwelling there, often alters one's being itself. As new awareness arises, subtle shifts occur. Along with other existential phenomenologists, I believe that I just have to be there *with* the client, perhaps in their dark place, and the combined power of both the relational context and the process of description is potentially transformational.

EXISTENTIAL PHENOMENOLOGY: THEORY AND THERAPY   179

Focusing on existentials

The dialogue in box 12.4 illustrates some of the processes and concerns of existential-phenomenological therapy, here in relation to the idea of the client, Darren, making active choices. Note how Darren characterises himself as a 'thing' (a 'commitment-phobe') and how the therapist tries to widen his awareness of his relational 'selves'.

Box 12.4 Case illustration: An existential intervention towards enabling a choice-full commitment to the therapy relationship

Darren had come into therapy to explore commitment issues and his inability to handle long-term relationships. He would fall passionately in love, but the intense relationship would quickly break down (usually because he had an affair), and he would find himself alone and lonely once more. After five sessions, Darren became infatuated with a new woman, declaring her to be 'the One'. He pronounced himself happy and no longer needing therapy. Three months later he was back: yet another relationship had bitten the dust.

THERAPIST: There's part of me that feels a bit used by you, Darren. And I wonder about your commitment to our relationship and therapy. What will stop you ending therapy abruptly next time you fall in love? I wonder if there's some parallel here with what happens to you in relationships outside this room?

DARREN: Yeah, I guess so. I'm a commitment-phobe. And I mess up. I mean, why did I leave that text on my phone for Andrea to see?

THERAPIST: At some level I think you are making choices. Aren't you choosing therapy now, just as you chose to leave before? You chose to have an affair; you chose to keep the text.

DARREN: You mean maybe I set up that break-up 'cos really that's what I wanted?

THERAPIST: I don't know. But I'm interested in what you do want. Might you have chosen to mess up with Andrea because you didn't want that relationship?

DARREN: Yeah. It's always the same. It's like I disappear when I'm in a relationship. I didn't like what my life was turning into when I was with Andrea. When I'm alone, if I wasn't so f***ing lonely, I'd prefer that.

THERAPIST: You disappear? So who and how are you when you're in relationships as opposed to alone?

DARREN: I dunno. I stop doing things I like and want. Instead I'm making her happy doing her hobbies, being with her friends. And then I get bored and turn into this bastard.

THERAPIST: So it's like being different people: your alone self, your wooing-and-pleasing-the-woman self, your bored bastard self?

DARREN: Yeah. I never thought about it in that way.

(Continued)

> THERAPIST: They're all parts of you, I'd say. [*Silence as Darren takes this in.*] So how do you want to *be* when you're in relationship?
>
> DARREN: I don't know. I think I just want to do my hobbies and things and not be the bastard having these affairs, with all the pretence and lies.
>
> THERAPIST: What stops you doing your hobbies and things?
>
> DARREN: She likes to do these other things and I kinda have to go along with it.
>
> THERAPIST: But you're making that choice to go along with it, aren't you?
>
> DARREN: Err, I guess I am.
>
> THERAPIST: And what would it mean to let go of the pretence and lies and show a woman your hobbies and interests and this other side of you?
>
> DARREN: It's hard to imagine.
>
> THERAPIST: What about here? How much are you letting me see these different parts of you?
>
> DARREN: I guess I'm sharing more than I usually do.
>
> THERAPIST: Bringing more of yourself here? [*Darren nods.*] What about the pretence and lies?
>
> DARREN: Err, I guess I haven't been entirely honest. But that was before. I want to make this work this time.
>
> THERAPIST: So you are making a choice and commitment to try to do the therapy differently this time?

Existential versus other humanistic therapies: Commonalities and differences

In some ways, it could be said that all therapy is existential at its root and that phenomenological ways of working can be embraced across all therapeutic modalities. However, the specific practice of *existential therapy* remains a specific field in its own right. Its closest neighbour is probably humanistic, *client-centred therapy*. Existential and humanistic psychotherapy[10] overlap in that they share many of the same values, goals and processes (Rowan, 2001). They are united by their emphasis on understanding human experience and their holistic focus on the client rather than the symptom, the problem, the personality type, etc. Psychological problems are viewed as the result of inhibited ability to make authentic relationships and meaningful, self-directed choices about how to live. A number of client-centred therapists practise in existential ways that seek to increase client self-awareness and self-understanding.

However, existential and humanistic or person-centred therapies also diverge (Spinelli, 2015). Firstly, whereas the latter tend to put much emphasis on the individual and *inner* feelings, existentialists are concerned with *being-in-the-world*. When a client is reeling from having just been rejected by a lover, the issue is not so much her grief but what it says about feeling herself to have been rejected and what that means in terms of how she lives her life. Secondly, humanistic notions of authenticity in terms of being 'real', of being true to an essential core self, contrast with existential notions of owning one's existence in all its darkness and light. While humanistic therapy aims for *self-acceptance* and *growth*, existential therapy favours client *responsibility*, *choice* and *freedom* (Yalom, 2010).

Concluding Reflections

I have tried to show something of the special potential of existential phenomenology for opening up the therapeutic space. While much of the practice discussed could be seen as fitting other ways of engaging relational integrative psychotherapy (particularly those prioritising gestalt, client-centred or relational psychoanalytic approaches), more dialogue to probe and recognise any differences is needed. In my view, we need to apply concepts like existentialism and bracketing thoughtfully with a recognition of those discordant or contradictory spaces between theories.

Not all therapists across the modalities would accept that a deep reflective engagement with existential issues is necessary, however. To what extent do you agree with the existential idea that people's life crises can provide a call of conscience, a jolting reminder to engage life? Would you agree that people's troubles are "not just symptoms of psychopathology but dark nights of the soul, which may lead to enlightenment" (Deurzen, 2012, p. 180)?

For me, these existential messages are profound and apply to both our clients and ourselves. What most excites me is the being-with process and the fleeting moments of awe and wonder which come when we open to another. Such elusive being-with moments can be powerfully transformational. When I'm struck with wonder, the habitual clutter of my mind is suddenly clear (van Manen, 2002). The other's experience – in its uniqueness and otherness – takes me in and I am in awe. And out of muddle, confusion and chaos may emerge a renewed zest for life, a heightened awareness that embraces both client and therapist. The ensuing relational contact (dialogue) forms the ground of self-realisation and transformation.

These themes are continued in the following chapter on gestalt therapy – a field with a focus on individual experience and contact in the present moment which arose, in part, out of this broader phenomenological tradition.

Notes

1 The two philosophical fields of existentialism and phenomenology are separated by a blurred line. They are separate philosophies, but they often overlap. In this chapter I'm concentrating on their convergence, namely the field of *existential phenomenology*. Many of the big names in the existential field, like Sartre and de Beauvoir, were also phenomenologists, while phenomenological philosophers like Heidegger and Merleau-Ponty can be seen as existentialists (though Heidegger never liked that label being attached to him) in that they are interested in the nature of *being*.

2 Spinelli (2015) argues for the use of the term 'existential therapy' to highlight wider counselling

and coaching applications than are implied by the 'psycho-' element in psychotherapy. He also makes a point of distinguishing existential therapy from existentially orientated therapy (which arguably applies to all psychotherapies).

3 The original title in French, *Huis Clos*, means 'behind closed doors', or 'within a confined space'. English versions of the play have been performed under various titles. In the play, three characters are doomed to live in the same space (Hell) without windows or contact with the wider world. The 'hell' is not so much other people as being confronted by one's own self.

4 I am grateful to Ken Evans who first introduced me to this simple but profound insight. I've since shared this with many clients, who have also found it useful.

5 Heidegger (1998) disagreed with Sartre's brand of humanistic existentialism, suggesting that Sartre had misread his work and that he exaggerated the idea of free choice while underestimating the extent of our 'situatedness'.

6 My version of Integrative Psychotherapy is based predominantly on *existential phenomenology*, in association with other relational and developmental models of therapy: *gestalt, transactional analysis* and *intersubjectivity theory/relational psychoanalysis.*

7 The concept of bracketing came initially from Husserl (1970), who suggested it as part of broader processes he called the *reductions*. These involve a radical self-meditative process to temporarily reduce the field which commands one's special focus in order to see the phenomenon in its essence. Psychological bracketing is akin to the use of mathematical brackets (Husserl had a background in mathematics so the metaphor is not surprising).

8 See, for example, the work of psychotherapists who emerged from the *Zeitgeist* of the 1960s: Irvin Yalom (1980), Kirk Schneider (2008) and Rollo May (1995) in the US, and Ernesto Spinelli (2015), Emmy van Deurzen (2012) and Mick Cooper (2003), amongst others, in the UK.

9 This phenomenological way of being contrasts sharply to psychoeducational approaches favoured by cognitive therapists and interpretive styles engaged by psychoanalytically inclined therapists.

10 While existential therapy comes under the rubric 'humanistic', here I am contrasting it with the more general humanistic work embraced by person-centred and other individually orientated approaches. Theoretically speaking, the contrast is between what are called *continental* (arising out of European philosophy) and *analytic* philosophy (stemming from the US and the UK).

13

Gestalt Theory and Therapy

The first reality is contact between. (Yontef, 1993, p. 374)

The dialogue in box 13.1 shows the embodied, experiential, here-and-now focus of gestalt therapy which attempts to enable an integrating awareness. Sills et al. (2012) discuss this passage by noting how Mary starts off relating in *I-It* mode while the therapist tries to stay present in dialogic *I-Thou* mode (see box 9.2). The therapist attempts to empathically understand Mary's experience while authentically sharing her own perception (what Buber would call inclusion and presence respectively). This offers Mary an opportunity for contact, which she accepts.

Box 13.1 Case illustration: A gestalt[1] encounter

(The therapist resonates with Mary's feelings of anxiety and simultaneously is aware of feeling uncomfortable and trapped in the powerful position Mary perceives her to be in.)

THERAPIST: There are two things going on for me now. You fear that I am critical, and I can see how frightening that is for you. But at the same time, while you stay feeling frightened, you break contact with me by looking away, and you won't find out if what you believe is true or not.

(Continued)

Relational Integrative Psychotherapy: Engaging Process and Theory in Practice, First Edition. Linda Finlay.
© 2016 John Wiley & Sons, Ltd. Published 2016 by John Wiley & Sons, Ltd.

MARY:	Find out? . . . Oh yes, I see, I am frightening myself with what I imagine you are looking like and what you are thinking. I could check. [*Looks at therapist*]
THERAPIST:	What are you seeing?
MARY:	Your face. It isn't as I thought [*smiles*] . . . what *are you* thinking of me?
THERAPIST:	At this moment I am thinking how much more confident you look. Your body seemed to relax as you looked at me.
MARY:	I don't feel frightened now. I am pleased that I risked looking at you.

(Sills, Lapworth & Desmond, 2012, p. 106)

The concepts touched on in the first paragraph encapsulate the gestalt approach. They also represent a *phenomenological* approach, which is unsurprising given gestalt's foundations in existential-phenomenological philosophy. Yontef (1979) called gestalt therapy 'clinical phenomenology'. This chapter expands on these ideas in tandem with those of the previous chapter, on phenomenology.

Gestalt embraces a diverse field. I start by outlining the **theoretical foundations** of gestalt, indicating how its ideas are applied in practice. Two noteworthy theoretical concepts – the '**gestalt cycle**' and '**presence**'– are then discussed. In the last section, on **therapeutic methods**, I highlight how gestalt practice straddles relational 'being-with' and 'doing' (via experiments and enactments). Particular attention is paid to the nature of gestalt work in relation to *raising awareness* and in *creative therapies*.

Theoretical Foundations Applied to Therapy

Gestalt, a German term, translates loosely as 'organised wholeness'. The field of gestalt theory and therapy emerges from an integration of many philosophies, theories and approaches (see figure 13.1), notably *phenomenology*. The flexibility of gestalt also allows it to be embraced in diverse fields beyond psychotherapy, including creative therapies, coaching and *systemically* orientated organisational consultancy.

Like phenomenology, gestalt theory offers a 'way of being', a philosophy for living life, as well as a theory and therapy approach. It is based around five significant ideas:

1. immediate **here-and-now** conscious experience (i.e., awareness that is both knowing and being);[2]
2. the existential **embodied dialogical** encounter that is a co-creation between therapist and client;
3. a **holistic** approach, embracing embodied, cognitive-affective, interpersonal, social and spiritual dimensions;

GESTALT THEORY AND THERAPY   185

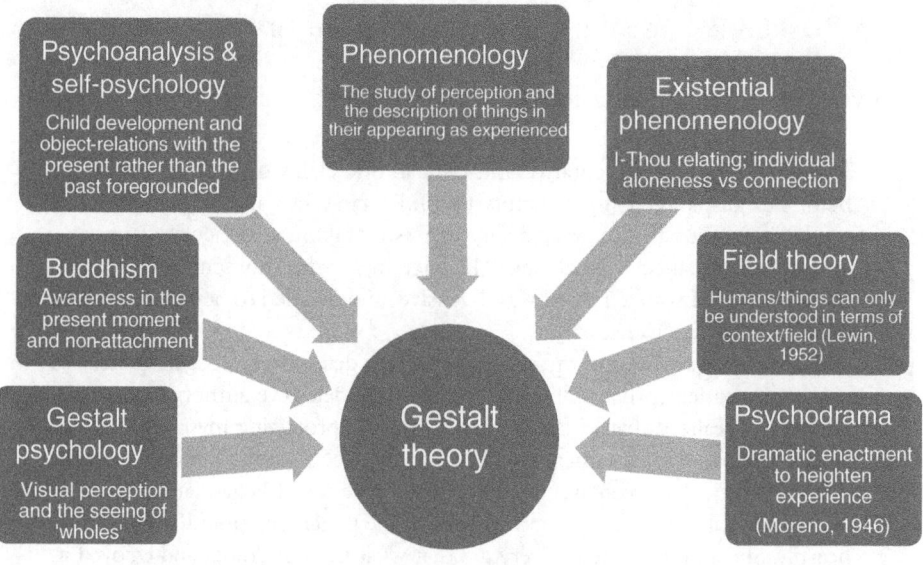

Figure 13.1   The field of gestalt theory.

4. a contextual perspective where the person is seen as being intertwined with their environment/**field**.[3] This field is the web of interconnections between self and others, individual and communal, organism and environment;
5. the view that change and growth take place in the **contact** between organism and environment (Clarkson, 1999).

Gestalt therapy has been described as *psychotherapy of awareness or contact*, a phrase which highlights how interventions are generally geared to increasing clients' awareness, particularly about that which has been out of awareness. Awareness[4] can be defined as being present to the senses involved when we contact our self-environment. The aim of gestalt therapy is to enable awareness and contact (with self and others) so that dispersed, disowned (split-off) parts of self are integrated as far as possible into a whole (Perls, Hefferline & Goodman, 1951).

In practice, there exist variations of 'traditional' and 'relational' versions of gestalt therapy. The iconoclastic, provocative, confrontational style of Fritz Perls and his followers is characteristic of the **traditional** variant, where heavy use is made of the therapist's charismatic presence and lively experiments and enactments.

More recent variants, however, emphasise a phenomenological **dialogical**[5] approach where work is seen to occur at the healing contact boundary *between* (see Jacobs and Hycner, 2009; Yontef, 1993). The aim is relational contact where each impacts on and touches the other (see box 13.2). As Hycner and Jacobs (1995, p. 55) put it, "Any experience of an *I-Thou* moment is a confirmation of the possibility of integration and wholeness, a confirmation of the healing process by which a person can restore his or her relation to the world."

186 GESTALT THEORY AND THERAPY

Box 13.2 Case illustration: A moment of *I-Thou* contact

Lynne Jacobs describes a contactful meeting with a client:

The patient was argumentative and critical. She claimed to be desperate for help, but disparaged my attempts to understand her and to be helpful. I tended to react with unaware defensiveness by taking a particularly superior, authoritative stance toward her. The meeting – the momentary I-Thou – occurred after I realized that I was defensive, and decided to be more attentive to my own defensiveness.

The next hour, I found myself again reacting defensively. I began to disclose this to the patient, while still operating from my defensive authoritative stance. Suddenly I realized that *at that moment* I was still protecting myself by pushing against the patient. I brightened and exclaimed, 'See! Oh my, I'm doing it right now! Damn it, E—, you are just too good. I give up!' I began laughing at my own absurd attempts to coerce the patient. The patient, surprised, also laughed heartily. She admitted she was very good at what she was doing, and enjoyed it, although she [was] always left feeling bitter and dissatisfied. What ensued was our first authentically cooperative exchange of ideas. Both of us had gained a renewed respect for the anxieties that had driven us into defensive styles at the expense of presence with each other. (Hycner & Jacobs, 1995, p. 55)

While space does not permit a fuller discussion of the many ideas revealed here, two planks of gestalt theory – the 'gestalt cycle' and 'presence' – are now explored in some detail.

The Gestalt Cycle

The gestalt cycle of experience[6] is a simplified model of self–environment interaction (see figure 13.2). Life itself is a cycle, and within it there are innumerable cycles in which we engage throughout each day. Gestaltists believe we are programmed to achieve an equilibrium, a sense of internal balance, as we interact with our world. Sometimes life flows smoothly, while at others we get stuck and are not able to complete goals we are striving for.

The model offers a useful tool for understanding the sequences and processes individuals (or groups and organisations) may go through as we develop, expand, act on our environment, and grow. A simple example showing the completion of a gestalt is the experience of being hungry:

Sensation: our stomach growls; we have a physical sensation of hunger
Awareness: we acknowledge we are hungry

GESTALT THEORY AND THERAPY   187

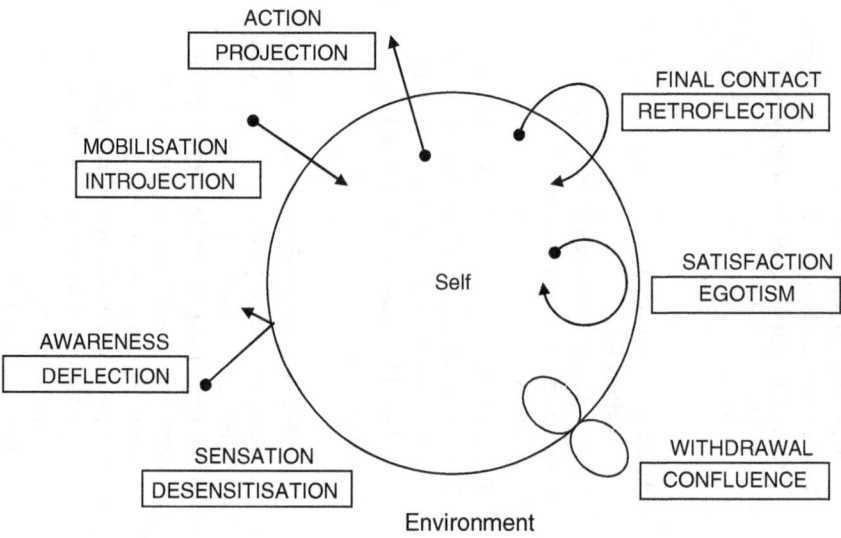

Figure 13.2   The Cycle of Gestalt formation and destruction with diagrammatic examples of typical boundary disturbances at each stage (reproduced from Clarkson, 1999, p. 50)

Mobilisation: we wonder what there is to eat and go searching
Action: we choose the food we want and prepare it
Final contact: we eat
Satisfaction: having enjoyed the meal, we feel replete
Withdrawal: we are content, neither hungry nor uncomfortably full

The cycle also helps to explain such concepts as 'interruptions to contact'. These are also known as modifications to contact or *creative adjustments*, which emphasises their use as survival strategies.

Interruptions occur when the boundary between self and other becomes unclear or blocked, resulting in disturbance of both contact and awareness (Polster & Polster, 1973). In good boundary functioning, people alternate between connecting and separating, between being in contact with the current environment and withdrawing (healthily) from the environment. A healthy individual can complete cycles of experience without getting stuck (see table 13.1, which applies the ideas to therapy).

For example, consider the case of a husband who feels the urge to make love to his wife. If he makes advances and is rebuffed enough times, the cycle gets disrupted and curtailed. He starts to shut down (perhaps through *retroflection*) to protect himself from feeling rejected. He also tends to anticipate rejection from his wife (a *projection* stemming from habitual relational patterns from which he has learned that he is not deserving or worthy) and – out of his awareness – he stops being contactful in his advances (for example, by using

Table 13.1 Applying the gestalt cycle and interruptions to therapy

Healthy cycle phases and contact	Unhealthy contact or blockages (which can occur at any stage but are typically seen at these times)	Related to the therapy process
Sensation Gradually a figure or need emerges which involves a possible future contact with the environment (e.g., a recognition of thirst, or an awareness of feeling in need of a hug). There is a taking in of sensory information about self or environment.	With *desensitisation*, sensations are diluted, deadened or neglected (e.g., there is a disregard of needs or a dissociation from self/body).	Client senses something and becomes aware of a stirring of disturbance. When the client is unhealthily blocked here, they lack (self-)awareness or may be in denial.
Awareness Some understanding of the need for contact with the environment grows.	*Deflection* (e.g. jokiness, intellectualising, avoiding eye contact) involves avoidance, a turning away from others, and a blocking of feedback from the environment.	Awareness of need grows, acting as a spur to seek therapy. When there is an unhealthy blockage, the client avoids or is unable to take in feedback.
Mobilisation Some excitement or energy builds as resources are mobilised: the person is alive and open. This occurs at cognitive (planning) or bodily (energising) levels, or both.	*Introjection* involves swallowing rules or beliefs given by others; there is a lack of self-regulation (shown in the swallowing whole of societal or parental values and prejudices and heard in judgemental 'should' voices).	The client takes action to meet a therapist. With an unhealthy blockage the client may feel overwhelmed by critical introjects and unable to take in the therapist's compassion.
Action In this doing phase, choices are made and the person reaches out to engage and have contact. This is a phase of experimenting and trying things out.	Dysfunction occurs when the action chosen is not appropriate to the need; *projections* (i.e., expectations of others based on ongoing patterns of relating) prevent the person from being with what is needed. This is seen when parts of self are disowned and projected onto others, or compulsions are repeated instead of real needs being dealt with.	The client engages actively with therapy after some initial testing of the therapist to see if they are trustworthy. When there is an unhealthy blockage, the client may continue to be suspicious of the therapist and not see them as a real person. The client may not take responsibility (blames others) or may compulsively repeat unhelpful behaviours without attending to real needs.

Final contact There is a grounded experiential connectedness with the environment and a full-bodied engagement and contact with others: for example, an expression of anger; or feeling in the 'flow'; or feeling able to enjoy a hug and a sense of togetherness. Within the moment of contact all else merges into the background.

Satisfaction In this post-contact phase concerned with completion, the person experiences an afterglow or a sense of achievement, or mourns an ending. This is the quiet after the storm.

Withdrawal There follows a period of rest, sometimes called the 'fertile void': a neutral, transitional time when specific needs are quenched, at least for the present.

Instead of being performed outwards towards the environment, behaviours are turned inwards in the form of *retroflection*, accompanied by 'holding in' self-soothing or self-abusing activities (e.g. holding back tears, hugging oneself, imagining acts of self-harm, or locking emotions within the body as in having tense shoulders).

Satisfaction is interrupted by *egotism* where a focus on self prevents the person fully giving or receiving (e.g. excessive inner commentary, hypersensitivity, or a pattern of grandiosity). Spontaneity is controlled.

Confluence occurs as a blockage where there is a dysfunctional closeness and self–other are insufficiently differentiated (e.g. when members of a couple assume they think alike). There is a loss of self, perhaps as a defence against aloneness (e.g., in a merged partnership there might be a co-dependent carer and a dependant).

The client gets in touch with stuckness and is able to work through conflict, thereby transforming the experience.

Locked-in patterns of retroflection reveal the stuckness when there is an unhealthy blockage to contact.

There is a sense of integration and the client becomes more outward-looking and able to see beyond the therapy room.

An unhealthy blockage is suggested by a client remaining self-absorbed and unaware of the therapist or others outside.

The client prepares for separation and the final goodbye with an openness to possibilities in life outside therapy.

An unhealthy blockage would be revealed if the client seeks to hang on to the therapy or the therapist.

190   GESTALT THEORY AND THERAPY

deflection). Eventually he no longer feels any sexual urges (i.e., *desensitisation* occurs in terms of losing the awareness or sensation related to sexual urges).

Box 13.3 further describes the processes involved.

Box 13.3 Case illustration: Caroline's competent public face and private turmoil

Caroline is a competent, self-controlled woman in senior management who presents a strong 'public face' to the world. Internally, however, she feels a 'mess' and frequently finds herself dissociating or feeling overwhelmed by shame and anxiety. When in relational contact with her therapist, she finds it hard to 'let go' and tends to work at 'head level', almost as if she wants to impress or please the therapist (evidence of *desensitisation*, *retroflection* and *deflection*).

After a few weeks of building their relationship, the therapist gently suggests that Caroline might bypass her usual way of being. She invites Caroline to work imaginally with her eyes closed[7] to see if she can connect internally to those disowned parts of herself. The therapist starts by asking Caroline to connect with what her body might be saying and thereafter encourages Caroline to express in sound and movement whatever comes up.

After some time, Caroline begins to squirm and talks of her sore back (*sensation*, *awareness* and *mobilisation* phases). Eventually she whimpers, 'No, no!' The therapist attunes to this 'protest' without trying to work out what might be going on; the priority is for Caroline to get in contact with herself, not explain things to the therapist. The therapist encourages Caroline to protest some more until eventually Caroline is shouting and pounding the sofa (*action* phase). After some time she starts to sob (*action/satisfaction* phase). The therapist does not move to touch Caroline but stays close, gently reflecting back what Caroline seems to be expressing.

Later, when Caroline feels grounded and calm, they process what happened (*satisfaction* and a new cycle of *awareness* phase). It seems that Caroline may have got in touch with having been anally raped as a child – something of which she didn't have a clear memory but which perhaps had left her with a sense of sick detachment from her body.

Therapists' Being as 'Presence'

The elusive concept of presence relates to the contact-full way therapists strive to be present to their clients in terms of 'energetic availability' and 'fluid responsiveness' (Chidiac & Denham-Vaughan, 2007). Buber (1965, 1958), the phenomenological theologian and philosopher, highlighted how being 'present' and 'presence' are intertwined processes towards *I-Thou* relating.

Humanistic therapists, in particular those with a relational *gestalt-phenom-enological* background, emphasise that the active presence of the therapist is the key tool of practice. A relational therapist with presence is one who is present as a person; they allow their whole being to be felt and are available for contact in a dimensioned, authentic way (i.e., at embodied, cognitive, emotional, social and spiritual levels). The therapist is real (for example, by giving honest, accurate feedback) and open (by self-disclosing sensitively while being prepared to be touched and moved by the client). The therapist gives up any instrumental desire to control and be validated; they seek a more intimate encounter instead based on being-with the client. The hope is that the client will experience this presence as the therapist offering an affirmative solidness where the client can be held and witnessed in a safe, trustworthy way.

Hycner (1991/1993, p. 13) calls upon the therapist to "incessantly struggle to bring his [*sic*] woundedness into play in the therapy", underscoring the fact that they are not alone. Presence, then, is not a technique or tool to be used to manipulate the other. It is not about 'doing to' or being there to 'soothe' the client. Rather it involves being-with the client with humility and a preparedness to face the other without a façade.

Box 13.4 Case illustrations: Therapist presence

A client's experience I remember a particularly powerful moment in my therapy. We were due to finish our session in ten minutes' time when there was a knock at the door. It was the next client who had arrived excessively early. In self-effacing mood, I indicated that we could finish early. My therapist was galvanised into action and became a protective lioness. 'Absolutely not! This is our time and nobody is allowed to intrude! I feel angry and I am very very sorry for the interruption.' She held that safe boundary for me – it was perhaps the most profoundly reparative moment in our whole time together.

A researcher-therapist's experience I interviewed a woman about her experience of a particularly traumatic abortion (Finlay, 2014). As she told her story I found myself crying openly – exhibiting a level of *grief* that was beyond my natural sense of empathy for this woman's horrific experience. The tearing up was probably to be expected but not the sob that escaped me. That she was telling me her story without much emotion, with a deadpan face, made the contrast with my crying more marked. It seemed that I was expressing the grief she had not yet fully explored herself. In the process I was also modelling – and giving permission for – emotional expression.

Being present in engaged, receptive, transparent ways ultimately allows the therapist to *be-with* the client. There is a sharing of joy, sorrow, anger, hopelessness,

192   GESTALT THEORY AND THERAPY

love, humour, sensuality . . . (Yontef, 1993). Through being present, the therapist invites the client also to be as present as possible. Presence allows the possibility of mutuality in the 'between'. Neither person controls the other; they stand
– together and apart - in their difference and vulnerability.

Therapeutic Interventions

Broadly speaking, gestalt therapy tends to involve active experimentation and
enactment, or work through contact in a healing dialogical relationship, or both
(see figure 13.3).

- **Experiments** and **enactments** include such techniques as beating a cushion
  in cathartic work or engaging rituals like creating a memorial service in an
  attempt to shift energies and perhaps complete unfinished business at the level
  of fantasy.
- The **dialogical dimension** involves exploring the *between* and treasuring
  moments of dialogic connectedness. It is a more heartfelt way of being-with
  where persons mutually relate in an *I-Thou* way, valuing and honouring the
  other in a relational context. Healing and integration occur through contact-
  full meeting of another.

In practice, much work involves both experimentation and the maintenance
of a dialogical relationship: As Hycner (Hycner & Jacobs, 1995, p. 5) notes,
"all contact and awareness needs to be understood within this dialogic context".
For instance, when therapists utilise *empty-chair* techniques or invite clients to
re-enact a traumatic experience through *psychodrama*, they remain throughout
sensitively attuned relationally. The resulting work, which aims for lively contact,
is often powerful, playful and paradoxical. Whatever intervention evolves, it
usually emerges in spontaneous, intuitively responsive ways.

Given that its goal is to *raise awareness through contact* and *dialogue*, gestalt
therapy involves more than mere methods and off-the-shelf techniques. There

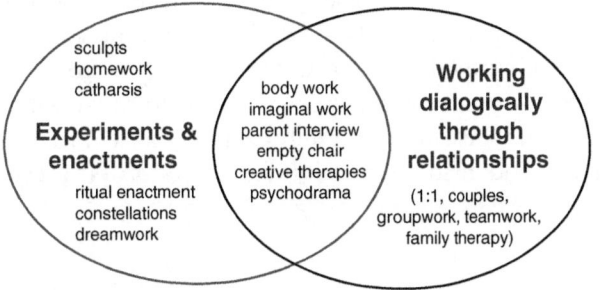

Figure 13.3   Gestalt approaches to 'doing' experiments *and* relational 'being-with'

GESTALT THEORY AND THERAPY   193

is a willingness to be human and let go into the relational process, and there is a loud "permission to be creative" (Zinker, 1978, p. 18), to experiment in spontaneous, lively, creative ways (Yontef, 1993).

The twin processes of awareness-raising and creative exploration merit further discussion and clinical illustration.

Awareness raising

Beyond specific techniques (such as the use of empty chairs), gestalt therapy favours staying with *phenomenological* description (see chapter 12) and tracking awareness through dialogue. 'What is happening for you now?', a gestaltist will ask. 'Stay with that feeling; really go into it.' 'Can you put some words to that sensation?' 'What might your tapping foot be saying?' Such questions invite clients to tune into what is just beyond our everyday consciousness (see box 13.5).

Box 13.5 Case illustrations: Raising awareness through here-and-now dialogue

BEN:	I'm not sure what to talk about this week. [*Looks uneasy*]
THERAPIST:	Take a moment to see what you are aware of as you sit here with me. [*She also brings her attention to her own sensations as she says this.*]
BEN:	I'm not aware of anything.
THERAPIST:	How do you feel right now?
BEN:	Empty. [*Silence*]
THERAPIST:	Can you describe 'empty' to me? What does it feel like?
BEN:	It's like I'm tense and I don't know what to do.
THERAPIST:	How do you know you're tense?
BEN:	I'm tight around my shoulders and I feel embarrassed.
THERAPIST:	Embarrassed?
BEN:	Yes. [*Silence*]
THERAPIST:	I'm interested in how your embarrassment feels to you.
BEN:	I feel sort of shy.
THERAPIST:	And what happens next?
BEN:	I'm afraid that you're criticizing me for how I was at our last session.

(Joyce & Sills, 2014, pp. 32–33)

P[ATIENT]:	I was with my girlfriend last night. I don't know how it happened but I was impotent. [*Patient gives more detail and some history*]
T[HERAPIST]:	Close your eyes. Imagine it is last night and you are with your girlfriend. Say out loud what you experience at each moment.
P:	I am sitting on the couch. My friend sits next to me and I get excited. Then I go soft.

(*Continued*)

194　GESTALT THEORY AND THERAPY

> T:　Let's go through that again in slow motion, in more detail. Be sensitive to every thought or sense impression.
>
> P:　I am sitting on the couch. She comes over and sits next to me. She touches my neck. It feels so warm and soft, I get excited – you know, hard. She strokes my arm, and I love it. [*Pause, looks startled*] Then I thought, I had such a tense day, maybe I won't be able to get it up.
>
> (Yontef, 1993, p. 153)

Therapists raise awareness by encouraging the client to: (1) track their awareness (of both self and environment); (2) clarify or expand that awareness; (3) become aware of preconceptions which could usefully be challenged; and (4) direct their awareness to what may be being avoided or minimised (Joyce & Sills, 2014).

The point is not only to raise awareness; it is to enable the person to be more present and relational. To this end, therapy may focus on what Jacobs (2000) calls *enduring relational themes*, which describes those patterns of relating derived from historical experience.[8] If a child grows up in a household where there is danger, they learn to be watchful. This habitual response may persist in adulthood and show in their expectations and dread that others will probably harm them. If it is enacted in therapy an opportunity is presented to explore, and either embrace or challenge, the pattern. Importantly, as therapists we have a role to play in asking how we might be contributing to the maintenance of any relational pattern which plays into the client's worst ideas of themselves and others.

Creative therapies[9]

Gestalt work is essentially creative in that the therapist responds intuitively to whatever is emerging in the moment. I once invited a client to put her 'mother' on an empty chair and dialogue with her. Unexpectedly the client's 'sister' became figural so she, too, was put on a chair. This time, instead of inviting my client to dialogue with her sister, I suggested she herself sit on that chair and embody her sister's perspective. This led to a new awareness of on the part of the client about how she was carrying something of her sister's issues, which were different from her own.

Gestalt therapists have at their disposal numerous creative activities (involving art, music, drama, poetry) which can be used in a psychotherapeutic way to help individuals gain awareness and work through issues (see box 13.6).

One key example comes from Moreno (1946, 1987), who established the technique of **psychodrama**. This involves a person acting out and working

GESTALT THEORY AND THERAPY   195

> ## Box 13.6 Case illustration: Using a projective art group
>
> **Structure of an ongoing projective art group**
>
> 1. **Check-in** (10 minutes) to enable everyone to arrive, be present and acknowledged.
> 2. **Warm-up** (10 minutes) of painting to music, consisting of different moods and tempos. Aim to have fun and encourage free expression to remind group the aim is not having a 'pretty' picture.
> 3. **Action** Invite group members to divide a large piece of paper into three sections and paint: (1) how I see myself now; (2) how I was 5 years ago; (3) how I would like it to be in five years' time (15 minutes to paint; one hour discussion of group members' paintings with reminders not to interpret the meaning of others' paintings).
> 4. **Wind-down** Paint a large group picture; start by having a 'conversation' via painting with a neighbour and then gradually have contact with all members (10 minutes).
> 5. **Check-out** Brief voicing of anything gained or unfinished business to pick up next time (5 minutes).
>
> **Case illustration: One member's experience**
>
> **Rosa**'s first painting revealed her history of being obese; her second showed she still felt 'fat' in her experienced subjective body, although she had recently lost five stone. In painting 3 she expressed her wish to have a more accurate body image and to feel less crippling shame about her body. She used the group to explore this shame, making links back to critical introjects stemming from her toxic, anorexic mother.

through issues by (re-)creating difficult life events. The components are: 1) the *stage*, where life dramas are re-enacted; 2) the *protagonist*, who is the centre of the drama; 3) the *director* (therapist), who guides the drama; 4) the *auxiliary* egos, who are the group members who act out the protagonist's characters; 5) the *audience*, who take an active part by reacting and giving feedback.

The art therapy example in box 13.6 demonstrates the nature of gestalt work as integrating a phenomenological-dialogical approach with the use of creative media. Gestalt interventions are often combined with other approaches, as seen in numerous prescribed integrative models (e.g. Evans & Gilbert, 2005) and in wider fields such as occupational therapy.

Concluding Reflections

This chapter has highlighted the gestalt project of making contact in the present **dialogic** moment towards encouraging clients to discover themselves more fully. Significantly, the therapist stays in an unknowing place of genuine curiosity in which the client is seen as the 'expert'. What is important is the client's own growing awareness, not the therapist's cleverness or theorising. As in the phenomenological approach discussed in the previous chapter, the therapist resists making analytical interpretations and instead focuses on the relational themes emerging in the moment.

Speaking personally, I enjoy gestalt work (perhaps not surprisingly, given my phenomenological background and original occupational therapy training, where gestalt ideas are common currency). I like its immediacy, its focus on the body and the lively potency of its interventions. When I observe experienced gestalt practitioners at work, I revel in the 'realness' of interactions and the creativity employed to move clients out of habitual stuck places. I also quite enjoy being entertained, and occasionally shocked, by the robust challenges issued!

I especially appreciate the contact-full, relational nature of gestalt work. More than helping an individual become more aware and complete unfinished business, it's about finding a way to help them engage a genuine deeper relationship with their world. I support the call of Hycner and Jacobs (1995, p. 18, emphasis in original), who urge us to place ourselves in the service of the dialogical and ask: "*How can I begin to make contact with this person?*" Then the healing can begin.

Notes

1 In German, the first letter of a noun is capitalised, which is why many writers write 'Gestalt'. Others (myself included) regard the term as in common English usage, so begin the word with the lower case, hence 'gestalt'.

2 Perls's transition away from psychoanalysis involved working actively with *here-and-now* behaviour rather than past history. The focus is on consciousness and awareness and not the unconscious. Gestaltists emphasise how we can only give our full attention to one thing at a time (hence the classic gestalt faces–vase drawing described by Edgar Rubin). The aim is to pay attention to what is figural moment by moment; the ground is the context. A man in conflicted partnership (ground) finds out his partner has maxed out their credit card and is angry with her excessive spending (figure) A woman going into an arranged marriage (figure)

may feel coercively forced (ground) or find it a cause for celebration (ground).

3 Lewin's studies of group dynamics, action research and *field theory* underpin work in management and organisations which takes both a gestalt and a *systemic* perspective.

4 Debate in gestalt circles surrounds the use of terms such as 'awareness', 'mindfulness' and 'consciousness'. I'm taking a simple, pragmatic route by blending the concepts.

5 This relational focus makes contemporary gestalt practice implicitly integrative in the way it draws on ideas from both *phenomenology* and *psychoanalytically* derived self-psychology. See Hycner and Jacobs (1995, 2009) for further discussion on the links between dialogical gestalt and both intersubjectivity and self-psychology theories.

6 This cycle is also called the cycle of contact or awareness. Variations exist, with the 'cycle' sometimes represented as a 'wave'. Here I make use of the cycle as conceptualised by Petruska Clarkson (1989). However conceptualised, the gestalt cycle should be seen as a flowing, iterative process and not a fixed, rigid one.

7 The therapist could equally have chosen another intervention, such as inviting Caroline to do some empty-chair work (perhaps putting her public and 'mess' parts of herself on different chairs). The therapist's choice of asking Caroline to close her eyes was a way of helping her get in contact with her body-self, bypassing her usual interactions with the therapist. Other clients with a high level of dissociation might well benefit from more direct relational contact, involving, say, both chairs and sustained eye contact with the therapist.

8 This contrasts subtly with *psychoanalytic* interpretations that suggest previous relationships are displaced onto the therapist in a kind of distorted perception (such as mistaking a therapist for one's mother). **Gestaltists** focus more on here-and-now intersubjective experience, where relational expectations based on past experience are more straightforwardly seen in present terms.

9 Creative therapies (commonly engaged in groups) are advocated by practitioners across **psychoanalytical**, **humanistic** and **systemic** approaches. My focus here is on the gestalt angle.

14

Relational Psychoanalytic Theory in Practice

'Relational psychoanalysis' now works in subtle, in-depth ways with regression and transference – with powerful, unconscious manifestations of early trauma as they become lived in the therapy relationship. (DeYoung, 2003, p. 29)

Diverse theoretical streams converge in the field of 'relational psychoanalysis' (Aron, 1996; Mitchell & Aron, 1999) constituting an integrative *tradition* rather than a particular school (see figure 14.1).[1] The streams meet in a common focus on relational unconscious process, child development and attachment, and the way that special attention is paid to regression and transference.

Relational psychoanalysis diverges from traditional forms in its *two-person* psychology approach, in which people are seen as always in-relation with others. Rather than an emphasis on the instinctual drives highlighted by traditional theory, interpersonal relationships are seen as the basis of human development. There is an attempt to mediate between the intrapsychic, the intersubjective and the interpersonal, with a focus on the role of relationships in both creating and healing suffering. A person's learned patterns of interactions are seen to be the root of their psychological problems. These patterns are then enacted and re-worked in the therapy situation.

In this chapter, introducing relational psychoanalytic ideas, I selectively focus on two key processes: **transference** and **projective identification**. The last two

---

Relational Integrative Psychotherapy: Engaging Process and Theory in Practice, First Edition. Linda Finlay.
© 2016 John Wiley & Sons, Ltd. Published 2016 by John Wiley & Sons, Ltd.

RELATIONAL PSYCHOANALYTIC THEORY IN PRACTICE   199

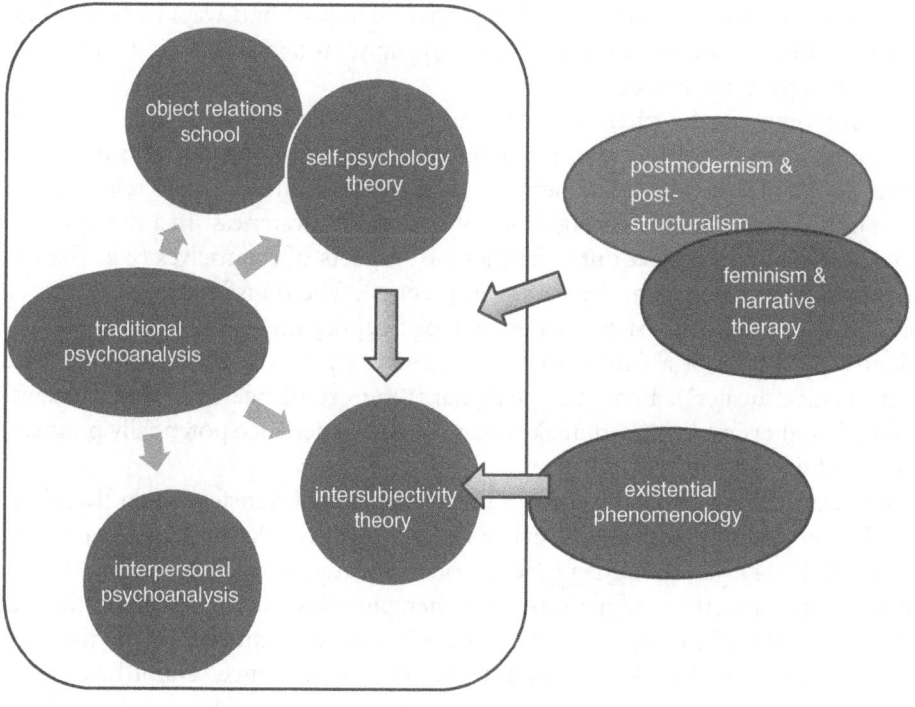

Figure 14.1   The relational psychoanalytic field

sections explore how relational-integrative therapists might **manage** such transferences and deal with **counter-transference**.

What follows is a brief and partial look at transferential processes in relational-centred integrative work (chapters 4 and 5 explore other relevant processes); the psychoanalytic field is too large to do justice to all the ideas. While I indicate some of the theoretical debates at stake – for instance, tensions between *psychoanalytic* and *humanistic* understandings – my focus is on integrative practice as a whole, taking a '*relational-developmental*' perspective. I hope to show something of how transference processes can be tender, powerful and resonant. Experiencing transference can feel both evocative and excruciating; working with transference is always a challenge even as we might be filled with awe at the mysterious process.

Transference

Transference might be the most contested concept in psychotherapy. Not only do therapists from different modalities define transference (and counter-transference) differently, they also debate 'types' of transference and their relative significance. More critically, therapists dispute what to do with transferences once they are recognised. *Psychoanalytic* therapists place the interpretation of transference at the very core of their work while some *humanistic* therapists deny such

200   RELATIONAL PSYCHOANALYTIC THEORY IN PRACTICE

unconscious processes even exist! Integrative therapists find ways to bring these polarised positions into harmony. Unsurprisingly, students grappling with these concepts become confused.

Transference is the phenomenon whereby we (unconsciously) transfer feelings, attitudes or wishes about a past person or situation onto another person or situation in the present. Many argue that it occurs routinely in all relationships (i.e., not just in therapy), though mostly out of our awareness. In a therapy context clients might project onto the therapist aspects of themselves (e.g. shadow self) or relationships from the past (e.g. parents). The transference can be based on a real relationship (such as the therapist representing the 'mother' of the client–'daughter') or a fantasy one (for example where the therapist is idealised as a 'magical healer'). Benign or malignant, the experience of feeling ourselves hooked, and even bewitched, makes transference experience potentially poignant and painful.

All relationships probably contain some elements of transference in that there will be certain similarities to – echoes of – previous relationships in our lives (Spinelli, 1994):[2] a therapist might respond in ways that are experienced by the client as similar to those of her mother; a therapist's presence and manner may remind the client of the mannerisms of a friend; a client might remind the therapist of a sister or a previous lover. The list goes on. Transference cannot be avoided (Clarkson, 2003).

Of particular concern for ***relational-developmental*** therapists is how unresolved child development needs get re-enacted in therapy through the process of *projecting* onto the therapist and the therapeutic relationship. A client who has been habitually disparaged by a parent is likely at some point in the therapy to feel (and fear the possibility that) the therapist is critically judging the client in turn. Thereafter, the process is unpredictable. In a *negative* transference, regardless of the therapist's actual behaviour, the client could regularly need reassurance that the therapist is not thinking about the client harshly. In *positive* transference, an idealising version might appear in which the client feels they've found a more loving, supportive, non-judgemental 'parent' who can be trusted. But even this experience is ambiguously layered in *juxtaposition*, where past deprivations are thrown into painful relief. Here, for instance, a client may resist letting a therapist 'in': it hurts too much because the client then realises what it is they never had.

Different theories lay out types of transference (see Clarkson, 2003). In ***traditional psychoanalysis***, transferences are seen as maternal/paternal, oral, passive, dependent, pre-oedipal, oedipal, archetypal, erotic,[3] and so on, depending on the object transferred and the stage of development being replayed. The transference could be either 'object' or 'narcissistic', depending on whether the analyst is viewed as an external person (who is loved, hated, needed, etc.) or as a disowned part of the client.

In Kohut's (1984) ***self-psychology*** theory, three types of *self-object* transference relate to attempts to complete early developmental needs relating to 'narcissism' (seen as a healthy stage in child development): mirroring, idealization and twinship (see box 4.2).[4] This theory highlights the use of a significant other (as a self-object) to experience oneself in the other's mind as a way of building a sense of self.

In practice, the focus on transference can be a powerful tool in intersubjective relating. Part of our challenge in therapy is to become aware of its presence and to distinguish its different layers, appreciating multiple possible meanings (see box 14.1, which draws on concepts from TA and gestalt alongside relational psychoanalysis). That the process is, more often than not, out of our awareness makes this difficult. It then becomes impossibly complicated if we factor in the metaphorical idea that there are multiple 'selves' in the room, each experiencing various transferences. *Just who is relating to whom?* This question is equally germane when it comes to identifying the communications carried in projective identifications.

Box 14.1 Case illustration: Working intuitively and reflexively with transference

Tina's abusive, withholding, toxic mother frequently seemed to appear in her long-term therapy, both in memory and in the form of Tina's self-disparagement and shame. Mostly the therapist experienced receiving a positive, **idealising transference**; Tina looked forward to her therapy and contact with her warm, supportive, loving therapist. However, as the therapist sought to highlight the way Tina seemed to have introjected (swallowed whole) the mother's disparaging outlook and to challenge Tina's self-damaging scripts, Tina exclaimed, 'I feel so stupid! I should know better! Why do I keep doing this!' Shame once more reared its head.

When the therapist saw that her compassion seemed only to reinforce the disturbance in the room, she followed her intuition to pull back with a view to going more slowly. There would be time later to explore nascent **negative transferences** that the therapist somehow had 'made' Tina feel stupid. Instead, she asked Tina if she would be interested to hear some theory; Tina's response was to soak it up thirstily. The rest of the session was spent discussing basic transactional theory: – in TA terms, the therapist–client interaction moved away from Nurturing Parent to Child, becoming Adult to Adult.

After the session the therapist reflexively explored her intervention. While the rationale of stepping back from the transference seemed effective and intuitively 'right' for that moment, the therapist wondered if she might have unwittingly engaged theory as it felt safer for her. Was she perhaps wanting to avoid the negative transference of being the 'shaming mother'?

Recognising that shame could be disavowed, retroflected anger, it seemed important to encourage Tina to start expressing anger. Yet it also seemed

(Continued)

important to maintain that delicate balance of encouraging Tina's growth while avoiding any implications that something was 'wrong' with her and needing changing (reactivating the shame). Also, what psychological function is being maintained by Tina's 'stupid' script belief, given that it is a part of her sense of continuing self-identity?

The therapist took all these questions to supervision, acknowledging her reluctance to work with negative transferences. When the supervisor asked her, 'Who is it that you don't want to be?', the therapist's aggressive father came to mind. Shame once more came into the frame, with the therapist feeling shame at recognising that she felt a 'failure' for her avoidance: a **parallel process** perhaps, reproducing and re-enacting the client's shame within the supervisory relationship?

Projective Identification

Projective identification (PI) is one of the more fascinating, mysterious, slippery and seductive processes which occur in the 'between' of relationships. It describes a **transference** process in which problematic parts of one's self become re-created and re-enacted in relation with another. We know projective identification has come into the room when we are enlisted to enact something or we experience emotions (rage, shame, anxiety) or bodily sensations (pain, dissociation) which seem strange in that they do not appear to belong to us. It would seem the client has pushed or passed something onto us that they would rather not have or feel; that is, the client projects this unwanted stuff onto the therapist, who then acts or responds impulsively in that manner (i.e. in 'identification').

In turn we have a sense of being carried away, taken over – possessed even – by this projection (see box 14.2). We have the sense of it being both a 'me' and a 'not me' experience. This can result in us somehow experiencing and enacting a psychodrama related to the client's inner world that is subtly directed by them. "The one person does not use the other merely as a hook to hang projections on. He strives to find in the other, or to induce the other to become, the very embodiment of projection" (Laing, 1969, p. 111).

Box 14.2 Case illustrations: PI in practice

In the final year of a degree course, **Natalie** sought support from her college counselling service for exam stress and confusion about her sexuality. During the six contracted sessions, Natalie disclosed that she had been date-raped some years previously. The counsellor supported her to report the incident to the police but the result was unsatisfactory and led to Natalie feeling exposed and publicly humiliated. Compensating for her guilt around encouraging Natalie to report the rape, the therapist offered Natalie extra sessions and their relationship grew. Natalie began to feel much happier with her work, with her college life and in herself. She began to express love and erotic longing for her therapist.

The counsellor herself was struggling with the break-up of a long-term partnership and, after Natalie's graduation, they stopped meeting formally and their relationship became more social and intimate. Later the therapist was shocked and dismayed to be challenged over the gross boundary violation she had committed. She eventually came to recognise the seductive impact of possible erotic or idealising transferences and to understand their potential impact and long-term consequences for both Natalie and her own career.

While engaging **couples work,** the therapist notes the rather needy, dependent, helpless way the wife seems to interact with her husband while in her work-life she is apparently a capable, successful business woman. The husband, for his part, is protective, seemingly 'rescuing' his 'vulnerable' wife, who he sees as being emotionally unstable. In periods when he feels he has to give her extended support, his own needs (for instance, to pursue hobbies and friendships) get sidelined. In this process he becomes controlled by her and by the power of her projective identification. (Intriguingly, the projective identification here may actually work the other way round: the husband could be projecting a fragile part of himself onto his wife who then enacts the role.)

The therapist shared her interpretations and encouraged the partners to experiment with new ways of being. Initially it proved challenging: the husband felt considerable guilt that he was withdrawing his support, while the wife became angry with both the therapist and the husband. (It is not uncommon to experience bitter rage at the thwarting of one's projections!)

After a **supervision** session focused on a trainee's shame about not completing assignments, the supervisor found herself feeling protective of the supervisee and full of unexpected rage against the institution. Somehow it was the inadequate, abusive institution's fault that her supervisee was experiencing such struggle. After reflecting on this process she realised her anger was out of proportion and that she may have been partly carrying the trainee's anger at his trainers (one particularly was a critical authority figure), anger the trainee felt unable to acknowledge at a conscious level.

The concept of projective identification was originally developed in the 1940s by psychoanalyst Melanie Klein, who saw it as an intrapsychic *defence mechanism* that involves getting rid of unwanted 'internal objects' and parts of self in 'phantasy'. Since this original formulation the concept has been extended, and is now associated with a range of unconscious, transferential phenomena and seen more in terms of its relational and **communicative functions**.[5] Here the projector (client) is understood to unconsciously influence the thoughts, feelings and behaviour of the recipient (therapist), making the therapist congruent with what has been ejected. The aim is to create intersubjectively in the recipient (therapist) a state of mind, effectively communicating the projector's (client's) state of mind. Put more simply, the client finds a way to show us their inner world by drawing us in as active participants.

Out of the confusion of entangled intersubjective, transferential boundaries, the self-aware therapist will ask the key question: 'Does this belong to me or has it come from my client?' Then the real work of the therapy can begin ...

Where **empathy** resides, it is not surprising that projective identification finds a home. In empathy, the therapist attunes to the client and sees the world as if through the client's eyes (see chapter 4). Intuitively, the therapist will pick up and mirror certain feelings and sensations. Equally, the therapist is open to receiving and may, in a counter-transferential process, be induced to act out certain projections. In this sense there is a dynamic emergent mutual quality in the process; indeed some commentators talk in terms of twin processes of *projective* identification (originating from the client) and *introjected* identification (originating from the therapist who invites the projection). These relational dynamics lie behind the ambiguous role played by the 'identification' part of projective identification, as it is often not clear whether it is the therapist receiving a projection who is identifying with the client, or vice versa. Davies (2012) beautifully describes the complexity of this process, in which we deal with multiple shifting identifications:

> To dance the dance of then and now, past and present, abuser and victim, doer and done-to, we dance on the head of a pin, spinning dizzily amid these points, changing perspectives, shifting identifications, blurring boundaries, spinning a tapestry of meaning and nuance that has the potential for depth, subtlety, ambiguity, and a multiplicity of rich, self–other experience, but a dance that also holds the forbidding prospect of spinning out of control, of falling over the edge into a miasma of projective-introjective enmeshment, boundarylessness, and deadly negativity. (2012, p. 166)

While letting ourselves go into another's inner world as a therapist, we also must hold on to our own presence and identity. In *traditional* psychoanalysis, therapist self-disclosure would be frowned upon. However, the *relational* psychoanalytic position is more accepting; the norm is to examine co-created patterns and meanings, and therapists' responses are part of the equation.

Ideally – within a *relational psychoanalytic* or *humanistic* integrative frame-work at least – the therapist will share in openness and curiosity, with the client, some of the transferences and projective identifications they recognise. Together, therapist and client might try to understand what these relational processes mean and, in this way, bring any projections more clearly into awareness and work through them. Eventually, they can be gently given back to the client in a safely contained (and thus more manageable) form.

Also, we need to recognise those processes which are part of normal, healthy manifestations and distinguish them from abnormal and unhealthy variants. While projective identification can be seen as an ordinary embedded possibility within all relationships, their mysterious, seductive power always remains thoroughly extra-ordinary.

Managing Transferences

How should we respond to the power and complexity of transferences? We have choices: invite and allow them, avoid and minimise, interrupt and challenge (Clarkson, 2003). Decisions about how to manage them depend in part on the relationship, the context and the therapist's theoretical frame.

In *psychoanalytic* psychotherapy, the aim is to help the client manage the unconscious feelings, needs and expectations they bring into the relationship and resolve the transference. The therapist's role is to mediate, to act as a mirror for the client. In classical psychoanalytic work (Freud, 1958) this meant the analyst needed to be a detached, blank canvas on which clients would externalise and project their inner conflict, which the analyst, in turn, would interpret. In *relational* versions, transference is seen as an opportunity to engage with dissociated parts of self and provide a "relational antidote" (DeYoung, 2003, p. 132). Ideally, the client is moved from behaving in automatic ways to being more self-aware and reflective. En route, the client might resist, might feel silly, misunderstood and puzzled. It can feel shaming to have emotions or behaviour interpreted in terms of archaic patterns. At such times relational therapists may withhold from making explicit transferential interpretations.

Existential-humanistic therapists may not work with transferences at all, considering them pathologising and to be a way to minimise feelings ('It's probably just erotic transference'; 'My anger is not really mine, it's been induced by the client'). They are seen as a deviation from the immediacy of the relational encounter (Spinelli, 2015). If they do acknowledge a transferential energy, emphasis is still placed on being 'present' and meeting the client as a whole person. (The traditional psychoanalytic idea of the therapist as some sort of empty container for the client's bad object is rejected.) Where transferences are worked with relationally, it is with the aim of eventually embracing more authentic, congruent *I-Thou* relating, uncontaminated by strategic impulses and instrumental demands.

Interpretations would be suggested in the spirit of mutual exploration, rather than asserted and imposed.

In the process of being responsive to a client's relational world it is important that *past history is not simply repeated*. It is the therapist's job to spot potential potholes and notice when they themselves have been ensnared. Then the therapist needs to find a different, more creative and corrective, reparative, way forward.

Some good questions to elicit transferential responses are:

- 'As you say that to me, how old are you feeling?'
- 'What are you imagining I might think and say in response to that?'
- 'I'm sensing you're angry with me. I'm wondering if there is an echo here of the way you used to feel angry with your father when …?'
- 'I felt that as a bit of a dig. Instead of discounting me can you ask for what you're really wanting from me?'
- 'You seem to expect me to let you down. Who did that to you in the past?'

If the work is going to have therapeutic value the client needs to be able to begin to disentangle past and present, self and other, recognising the difference between 'here' and 'then' and current resonances of past echoes. The process of managing transferences thus comes down to first spotting the process and then tolerating it. It is not easy to experience transferences (particularly when they are negative). We know they're occurring if we suddenly experience extreme or no feelings; our guts may tell us something is being replayed. Then it's about bringing possible dynamics into awareness. After perhaps making an interpretive link of the significance of past and present relationships (related to both client and therapist), we need to reinforce some clear, reality boundaries.

> The therapist at first allows herself fully to experience her personification in the client's drama. This process may in some sense involve 'losses' of individual self in this process. The therapist then seeks authentically to engage with the client and thus challenges the client's personifications, reasserting his or her own sense of reality[,] and challenges the assigned position as a figure in the client's archaic but ever-present drama. The therapist in effect says 'I respectfully insist on the right to meet you as the person I am, not the person you seek to make me into'. (Paul & Pelham, 2000, p. 119)

There are of course no easy recipes: responses depend on the relationship, the context, and the therapist's way of being and theoretical orientation. Integrative therapists need to make the decision whether to engage transferential interpretation and I-Thou acknowledgement of the depths of the client's feeling and experience (Paul & Pelham, 2000). Whichever path is taken, the therapist needs to be *reflexive* (i.e., critically self-aware) and wonder about what is happening relationally. This is where the relevance of tuning into our counter-transferential experience comes in.

Owning Counter-transferences

When working relationally, it can be useful to ask four particular questions to probe the transferential field:

- Who am I for this client?
- How am I being impacted by this client?
- What part of me comes forth when I am with this client?
- How am I (with my history) contributing to the emerging relationship?

The process of asking and answering these questions ensures we are present *intra*psychically and *inter*personally.

Like transference, counter-transference has been understood in different ways. Basically it is the *response evoked in the therapist by the client*. Racker (1968) distinguishes between 'complementary' and 'concordant' counter-transference to describe the therapist's response to the client's initial transference. Alternatively, the counter-transference may simply be the result the therapist's own projective transference response onto the client ('proactive counter-transference'). In whatever version, counter-transference constitutes a seductive fusion of present and past, reality and fantasy, self and other, conscious and unconscious, and external and internal processes (see box 14.3).

Box 14.3 Theory: Types of counter-transference

Complementary (or **reactive**) **counter-transference** involves powerful responses induced in the therapist which resemble the client's pattern of relating from their historical or fantasised past (which may also hook into the therapist's past). The therapist responds in ways which complete or continue what the client is bringing to the room. When a client projects 'bad' mother onto the therapist and the therapist finds herself responding in an uncharacteristically swipey 'bad' mother way, a complementary reactive counter-transference (some would call this PI) can be said to be operating.

With a **concordant counter-transference**, the therapist experiences an intense empathic attunement, for instance when the therapist feels shame in response to the client's feeling of shame, or has the urge to eat compulsively after seeing a client who has an eating disorder.

With **proactive counter-transferential** responses, therapists' own transferences become figural. Here they must take care to avoid being beguiled into using the client or therapy to work through their own issues.

(Continued)

> Various transferential responses may be in the field and therapists may catch glimpses of how the client reminds the therapist of their own father, mother, sibling, friend, spouse, lover, etc. But the therapist's own agenda should not dictate the work. If issues arise for us in sessions, then the place to take them is to supervision and our own therapy.

Of course, psychotherapists cannot help being affected by private feelings and yearnings (Clarkson, 2003). Therapy – replete with multiple transferential pulls – frequently touches our vulnerable parts. Clarkson offers a heartfelt and passionate acknowledgement of the emotional challenges of our work.

> We have to deal in the fires of love and not get burnt, work in the forge of the irrational and not succumb, toil in the space within hearts and yet remain outside. … We are required to act constantly in the arena of love, yet renounce all personal gratification; … we give solace or wisdom perhaps to those who suffer, knowing full well that we ourselves are wounded healers, scarred by similar terrors, griefs and excesses as those who consult us. Of course, there is joy, satisfaction, awe and wonder as well, but is it any wonder that there is such a high rate of breakdown, loneliness, burnout and cynicism in this profession? (2003, pp. 27–28)

Our clients are often our teachers (Casement, 1985). They bring what we are needing; they challenge and touch just that place where we feel uncomfortable. A therapist struggling with shame, for instance, may well find a client's idealising transference acutely uncomfortable. Or if we find ourselves getting hooked by a transference, is it because our own related issues are involved (for example, when a client asks, 'Are you going to abandon me?', and we immediately jump in to soothe them)?[6] If we find ourselves getting hooked, maybe it's a signal to do something different, challenging both ourselves and our client. The case illustration in box 14.4 demonstrates the value of encouraging a mutual recognition of shame and the modelling of self-acceptance.

Box 14.4 Case illustration: Exploring counter-transferential shame

I tell Karen a little something about the icy, bitchy self I had to struggle with when we fought in our last session, about how painful and shameful it was to feel that part of myself in my work with her. She was amazed that I could feel shame about parts of myself and was uncharacteristically quiet

> .... 'I hate myself most of the time,' she tells me almost in a whisper. ... 'The only time I feel good is when I find the evil parts of other people .... It makes me feel less alone.' Something is clearly happening here to the experience of shame. I can speak with Karen about feeling vulnerable: how it feels for me to be vulnerable with her, how it feels for her to be vulnerable with me .... I like to think that the message here is in the process: that shame is tolerable, that it won't necessarily destroy, that it can be met with love and recognition and self-acceptance even though the aggression and its effect on others must be taken seriously. (Davies, p. 178)

Concluding Reflections

As therapists, we are required to accept, tolerate, manage and boundary various transferences and projections. Ultimately we welcome them in, like a *host with guests*. We welcome them as they give us a kind of **relational compass** to guide the therapy.

I start from a working hypothesis that transference exists and that it is ubiquitous, occurring routinely at different levels and in myriad subtle ways, and that they must be worked through as they interfere with treatment. Unlike some psychoanalysts, however, my personal position is that I deny transferences are a product of an 'unconscious' as such. Rather, I suggest that while transferences may be currently *out of awareness*, they represent relational patterns and can be usefully brought into awareness in tentative, curious, invitational ways (Jacobs, 2000; Spinelli, 1994). Instead of imposing an interpretation, I favour relationally asking the client *if* something *might* have a resonance related to a person or situation in the past.[7]

My preference is to follow the *existential* approach of reflexively exploring *possible* transferential dimensions as part of engaging the fuller relationship (Stolorow and Atwood's intersubjectivity theory particularly appeals in bridging *phenomenology* and *psychoanalysis*). If a client is angry with me, there may be an element of them projecting their mother onto me – a mother they are furious with. But the client might also be angry with *me* for good reason; it might be important for me to accept (and perhaps even celebrate) that protest and take some responsibility. Automatically assuming that only a transferential relationship exists – and that is all – diminishes us both in my mind. It misses an opportunity to relate in an open, here-and-now way.

A key aspect of our work is to try to make sense of what both client and therapist are experiencing, possibly outside our mutual awareness. To this end, it is important for us to keep part of ourselves apart from the entanglements, to be **reflexively aware**, monitoring the multiple relational processes that might be being engaged. Further, we might take responsibility for understanding why this particular projection is managing to 'land', that is, what sensitivity or vulnerability there is in *me* which offers fertile ground for this projective identification. These are the questions we must explore in both therapy and supervision if we are going to avoid being possessed by processes out of our awareness.

And, yes, in that fullest relation, there are likely to be echoes of multiple layers of transference and projections lurking ready to captivate, confuse and beguile us. I end with a heartfelt poem written by a client that speaks to some of those ambiguous, ambivalent layers.

A poem to my therapist

I love you;

I hate you.

I despair that I need you so.

I am a tiny blossom craving the sun;

Pining for your warm gaze; yearning to be held in your loving arms.

At the end of our sessions I feel nourished, ready to grow and flower in abundance.

All too soon that sick, thirsty, parched feeling returns.

You must think me too pathetic, too needy,

A parasitic weed, not a blossom;

Now scorched and burned, I shrivel.

I despair that I need you so.

I hate you;

I love you.

Notes

1 Greenberg and Mitchell (1983) first used the term 'relational psychoanalysis' to bridge the traditions of US-based *interpersonal psychoanalysis* (Sullivan, 1953) and the British *object relations school* (Fairbairn, 1952; Klein, 1952; Winnicott, 1953). (The object relations theorists believe that 'relating' is what drives social life and that a person's internal worlds or selfhood are made up of internalised versions of relationships with others. Introjection and identification are viewed as processes by which the self is created.) Mitchell and Aron (1999) edited what became the first papers on relational psychoanalysis, and this journal became a centrepiece of the movement in the US.

Subsequently the field has grown to encompass the existentially orientated *intersubjectivity* theory of Stolorow and Atwood (1992) (who now talk in terms of 'phenomenological contextualism') and what could be called *feminist-inspired relational* psychotherapy (DeYoung, 2003; Orbach, 2012). Integrative therapists need to decide if and how these various streams might be combined and utilised.

2 Lynne Jacobs (2000) discusses this process in terms of 'enduring relational themes'. These are the patterns of relating that are derived from historical experience which become our embodied-emotional perspective on the world. As a *gestaltist* she maintains a focus on the here-and-now

intersubjective experience rather than assuming past relationships are being displaced onto present ones. Thus, the therapist is seen as co-creating the relationship where a client is expecting, dreading or hoping for certain responses.

3 Rather than pathologising *erotic transference*, relational therapists argue that it needs to be seen broadly in terms of love and longings or attraction and disgust. It's not just about sex (Mann, 1997). Many clients come into therapy feeling unlovable. Faced with a compassionate therapist who is listening so intently, how can they not feel the pull of love? Similarly, the therapist is not immune from the pull of the intimacy inherent in our therapy relationships.

4 After Kohut's death, his loyal colleague Wolf (1988) added further self-object needs which result in **merger transference** (where the client needs the therapist to be so finely attuned to him or her that the therapist doesn't exist as a separate person) and **adversarial transference** (the client takes an oppositional stance attempting to evoke challenging but supportive responses in the therapist).

5 While PI has been theorised in psychoanalytic terms, versions have been acknowledged in the **humanistic** literature. Rogers even acknowledged the way we can become partly possessed by the other: "I may behave in strange and impulsive ways in the relationship, ways which I cannot justify rationally ... but these strange behaviors turn out to be right, in some odd way" (1980, p. 129).

6 In **TA** terms this process might be understood as the therapist having a 'script vulnerability' and being unable to retain enough Adult capacity to think through the process.

7 I would not want to claim authoritatively that I had the 'right' interpretation and to be the arbiter of reality. As a **humanistic-integrative** therapist I want to remain more open and unknowing, and explore processes arising in dialogue. Even psychoanalyst Bion argued that "In every consulting room there ought to be two rather frightened people: the patient and the psychoanalyst. If they are not, one wonders why they are bothering to find out what everyone knows" (1974, p. 13).

15

Systemic Theory and Therapy

You cannot understand a cell, a rat, a brain structure, a family, a culture if you isolate it from its context. Relationship is everything. (Marilyn Ferguson, *The Aquarian Conspiracy*)

Systemic approaches focus on the way different systems interact and how they come together to make a whole greater than the sum of their parts. The central ideas of systemic theory are inherently holistic, relational and integrative and are therefore of special significance for us.

Figure 15.1 identifies the range of **human systems** that interest psychotherapists. Contained as we all are in a web of life (both biological and social[1]), we understand that a problem in one sub-system may create problems for, or disrupt, other sub-systems. For example, dysregulated serotonin levels in a depressed person may lead to instability of affect, disrupting that person's ability to concentrate, problem-solve and interact, all of which impacts on their wider world of family, work and social relationships. Like those from a stone thrown into a pond, the ripples of disturbance (conflict, stress and confusion) roll out across wider relationships, and then back again. At the same time, stabilising community support systems can provide positive feedback into the system.

Therapy engages directly with this wider world of interconnecting systems. It's about calming reverberations within a client's world. Constructive intervention in any part of the whole system may temper, or even halt, a destructive

---

Relational Integrative Psychotherapy: Engaging Process and Theory in Practice, First Edition. Linda Finlay.
© 2016 John Wiley & Sons, Ltd. Published 2016 by John Wiley & Sons, Ltd.

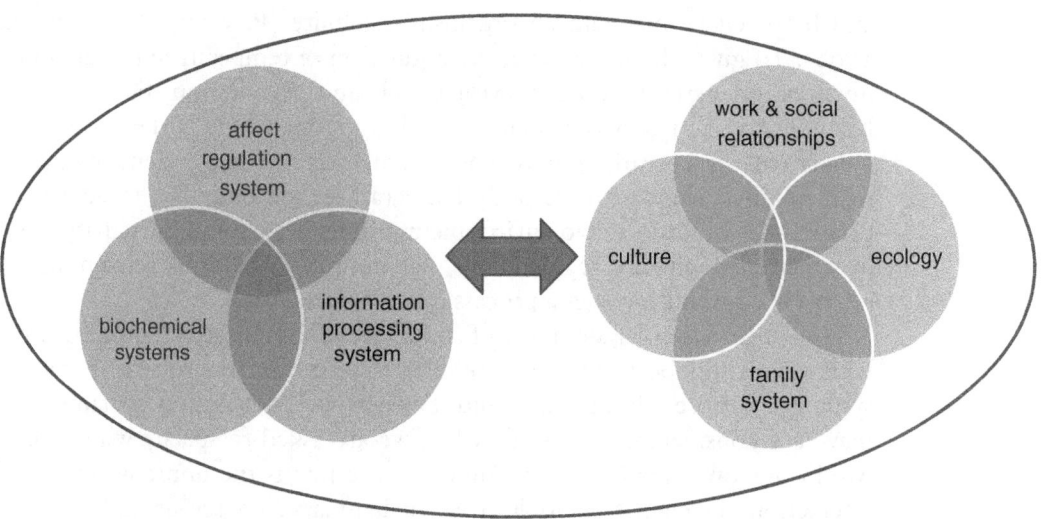

Figure 15.1 An individual's intrapersonal-interpersonal systems

spiral. For example, medication plus cognitive and gestalt approaches may be used to work with the *intra*personal issues, while family therapy is used to address to some of the *inter*personal dimensions.[2] Specifically, systemic therapy tackles problems arising not within the individual as such but rather within their wider life: their family and friends, work, and social (cultural, political, economic) context.

This chapter starts with an introduction to the **systemic perspective**. As systemic therapy is most commonly associated with family therapy, in the next section I examine the values, models and practices of **family therapy**. Finally, I explore some of the extensive **research and evidence** base of systemic family work.

A Systemic Perspective

A phenomenon remains unexplainable as long as the range of observation is not wide enough to include the context in which the phenomenon occurs. (Watzlawick, Beavin & Jackson, 1967, p. 21, cited in Dallos & Draper, 2010, p. 20)

Systems theory is concerned with the web of connections between persons and world, self and others. This focus on wider relationships and **contexts** is mirrored in other theoretical perspectives, notably in the phenomenological concept of 'lifeworld' and the gestalt 'field'. Such a cross-fertilisation of ideas is something we celebrate as relational-integrative therapists.

Systems theory was originally developed within the biological sciences. Here the body is understood to function through interacting systems, coordinated and balanced to maintain an organism's stability (Bateson, 1972; Bertalanffy, 1968). To give a basic example, the regulation of temperature in human bodies involves interactions between sweat glands and perspiration, between skin and hair follicles, and between brain control components and other bodily activity concerned with breathing and blood circulation. All these elements interrelate to maintain a standard core body temperature; the body has to adapt when a person goes out into a cold environment or engages in physical activity. A system in which elements are regulated so that internal conditions remain stable and relatively constant involves a process called *homeostasis.*

Human and social systems are of course more complicated than those involved with regulating body temperature. For a start, the boundaries between our systems are more arbitrary and fluid. For example, our notion of 'family system' may vary considerably, especially when we are asked to specify who is or is not within our own family system. Added to the mix is the unpredictability of our interactions given the symbolic base of language, conscious and unconscious processes, and myriad cultural, political and economic forces.

However, systemic theory offers an interesting way to model some of the regulating and disrupting processes that can be observed in social groupings. Where habitual patterns of behaviour and interacting are maintained out of awareness, and where change is resisted, stability is ensured over time. This is seen, for example, in the way dynamics, whether family ones or those pertaining to work and relationships, may sabotage a client's attempts at change (Dallos, 1991; Jackson, 1957).

Ideally the group or family operates as a dynamic, ever-changing **open system** with a high degree of both contact and differentiation and the capability of being both responsive and open to change. Problematic group or family relationships tend to operate as closed systems with fixed patterns of (for example) blame or manipulation. In closed systems, any change appearing in one person is met with a compensating action by another, and this has the effect of maintaining the status quo. For instance, consider the scene where a mother insists the family starts going out for Sunday drives but the father is silently reluctant. Although the father doesn't vocalise his opposition, his message is effectively broadcast to the rest of the family and it would not be surprising to then find little Johnny becoming 'car-sick', effectively preventing the outings.

Dallos and Draper (2010) acknowledge the evolution of systemic ideas, revealing how they have been applied in therapy from its earliest *modernist* beginnings to *constructivist* approaches and subsequent postmodern, feminist *social constructionist*[3] versions.

Many forms and models of **systemic therapy** are currently practised. These are used in work with individuals, couples and families, groups and communities. While most frequently associated with family therapy, systemic approaches can be found in a range of settings: for instance, a practitioner may work in a residential *group-home* for vulnerable people, or they may undertake organisational or work-based consultancies to evaluate problematic *team* dynamics. Systemic

SYSTEMIC THEORY AND THERAPY   215

practitioners also work with individuals, for instance when engaged in *child-protection* work with social services. Here interventions may be focused on one person but an eye is maintained on the wider family dynamics and community resources. This requires a step back to see the patterns operating at large within wider social systems (see box 15.1).

Box 15.1 Case illustration: Observing a group or family system[4]

1. How does the **family** or **group** communicate as a whole? Is the communication
   - clear or confused?
   - critical or positive?
   - equal or unequal?
   - enmeshed or differentiated?
   - direct or covert?
   - stable or escalating?
   - sensitive or insensitive?
2. What is the sequence of a typical significant **interaction** in subgroups?
3. What **language** is employed by individuals and what impact does that have?
4. Are there **gender** differences in emotional sensitivity, approach and levels of assertion?
5. What is the balance of **power**?
   - How are decisions made and who has the final say?
   - How does each influence the other and what tactics are used?
   - What resources does each have to exert their influence?

(adapted from Dallos & Draper, 2010)

Across all the different contexts of practice, systemic therapists are united by their commitment to a systemic perspective. For example, a systemic therapist working with an individual client who is criticising her husband might ask, 'What would your husband say in response to you saying this?' Clients are encouraged to appreciate different perspectives within their wider system – a key goal for systemic practitioners. Wider social systems are seen to give individuals meaning and identity; systemic therapists (like their gestalt or phenomenological colleagues) never work with individuals without reference to their wider lives.

Applying a Systems View in Family Therapy

A systemic approach views the family as a whole, while also attending to dynamics between members. Minuchin (1974) used the term *family dance* in an attempt to capture the way family members move in tandem with each other. Therapy interventions are designed to help clients become aware of their specific family dance and how they might change their steps.

This section explores how systemic ideas are applied in family work by considering key *processes*, *models* and the debates concerning decisions to engage *family versus individual* work.

Key processes

The primary focus of a family systems perspective is on **function** and the **process** of interactions, rather than content: in other words, *how* people interact rather than what they are saying. A family therapist might ask, 'What unwritten rules guide this family?' A loving family that does not tolerate the open expression of anger, for example, needs both individual and collective 'creative adjustments' to deal with anger. The therapist examines what each of the members is doing while at the same time exploring the overall gestalt; the family is viewed as a 'self' with its own agency and wisdom.

Box 15.2 Case illustration: Functions for a family of a child who self-harms

Following the acrimonious separation and divorce of her parents, 14-year-old **Iphgenia** (who lived with her mother on weekdays and spent weekends with her father and his new partner) began to self-harm by cutting herself. Iphgenia's therapist could have chosen to work at an individual level, exploring tensions about adolescent stresses which were clearly in the mix. However, she chose instead to work with the family. The key question she posed was 'What function does the self-harm have in the family?'

Iphgenia and her parents (and the new partner) were concerned to help in any way they could to sort out the problem. All four agreed to family therapy. The therapist pointed out that the only time Iphgenia's parents cooperated and worked together as a team was when they were dealing with their daughter's problems. The parents soon realised how severely their own conflictual behaviour had impacted on Iphgenia, and that she had found a way to stop her parents arguing. They had come together to support her.

Therapy also revealed two further impactful systems. Firstly, two of Iphgenia's close friends had also engaged in self-cutting, perhaps romanticising the act of self-harm. Iphgenia was encouraged to re-evaluate their behaviour while also recognising how important a supportive, constant peer group was to her. Secondly, the father's new partner, who had something invested in stoking the acrimony between her partner and his ex-wife, realised that she too had a role to play. This enabled her to hold out an olive branch to the ex-wife so they could work together regarding Iphgenia's care, rather than being split.

Each member of the family, including Iphgenia, could see the part they played in maintaining self-destructive behaviours and high levels of conflict. Through discussion and homework exercises, all four family members were guided to find new, more nourishing ways of being together.

Box 15.2 offers a somewhat idealised illustration of the nature of family work. It emphasises how family therapy perspectives locate the problem in the workings of the system rather than at the level of the individual. It is the system that requires adjustment, rather than individuals' difficulties.

Three other concepts in frequent use in family therapy are:

- **Identified patient** In family therapy terms, there is often an *identified patient* (IP), who is the family member with a 'problem' and has brought the family into treatment. Children are frequently the IP in family therapy – this was the case with Iphgenia in box 15.2. Family therapists focus on keeping the family from scapegoating the IP or using them as a way of avoiding problems in the rest of the system.
- **Diads and triads** Family systems theory argues that the emotional relationships in families are often triangular: they tend to involve, say, two parents and a child, or one parent and two children, or a parent, a child and a grandparent, or three siblings, or an ex-husband, a wife and a step-parent, and so on. The coalitions and alliances of interest to therapists concern the way members interrelate to maintain family homeostasis. In a problematic marital triangle, for instance, a wife who is upset with her husband might turn to her child for comfort. While this can result in a temporary reduction of marital tension, the essential problem remains unresolved. The third party (child, friend) who is sensitive to one spouse's emotions or situation may then be pulled into a drama triangle by being cast as a 'rescuer'.
- **Conflict detouring** Detouring occurs when a conflict between two people is transferred or projected onto others as a way of coping with conflict and stabilising their own relationship. For instance, instead of directing anger towards each other, parents may 'triangle in' their child and focus their negativity on the child. Similarly, a parent–child conflict may distract from marital tensions, maintaining the illusion of a harmonious relationship

218   SYSTEMIC THEORY AND THERAPY

between the parents, even at the expense of their child (Minuchin, 1974). Other versions of this dynamic can be seen in cross-generational coalitions, for example when a parent tries to enlist the support of the child against the other parent, or when a grandparent responds to the child's needs with excessive devotion (enmeshment) while the parent is left less responsive (detachment).

Models of family therapy

To give some idea of the range and complexity of the field, consider the different (though sometimes overlapping) categories of family therapy practised: structural, psychodynamic, strategic, humanistic-experiential, intergenerational and more.

All these models are **integrative** in the way they draw on a range of cognitive, psychodynamic and humanistic practice and principles. The integration can also be seen where different family therapy models are combined to increase the breadth and possibilities of the therapy. In practice, most family therapists pragmatically blend models rather than maintain theoretical purism.[5]

- **Structural family therapy**, created by Minuchin, is a short-term therapy that examines family relationships, behaviours, and patterns (as they are exhibited within the therapy session) in order to evaluate the structure of the family. Therapists are alert to problematic subsystems, such as destructive alliances and triadic subsystems. A visual depiction of the family will be attempted through the use of *genograms* (family trees), *family sculpts* (involving the use of group members or objects such as assorted stones), or artwork (paintings or drawings) in order to represent and recognise current and past relationships as well as events and their impact. Typical goals include strengthening parental leadership, clarifying boundaries and developing coping skills. Role-play activities in therapy sessions are used to bring about changes in entrenched interaction patterns, such as extremely enmeshed or disengaged interactional styles.[6] (See box 15.3.)
- **Psychodynamic family therapy**[7] This therapy focuses on unconscious processes such as unresolved conflicts and the projection of unacceptable feelings onto others. It also seeks to counteract the lasting effects of traumatic experiences of abuse and family breakdown. Couples' or family members' defences and anxieties are accessed in part through transference or counter-transference and are then interpreted to foster change. Throughout, the therapist remains mostly neutral rather than directive, and provides emotional holding and containing. As the focus is on a family's intergenerational history rather than specific symptoms or behaviour, this tends to be a longer-term approach.
- **Strategic family therapy**, created by Jay Haley and others, looks at family processes and functions, such as communication and problem-solving patterns. The aim of this brief, *solution-focused* approach is to identify symptoms (concrete problems) and find solutions by modifying dysfunctional

communication patterns. The therapist directively teaches members how to listen, ask questions and respond non-defensively instead of reacting negatively and impulsively. Therapeutic techniques include reframing a problem scenario and using paradoxical interventions (that is, suggesting the family take action that appears to be in opposition to their therapeutic goals in order to create the desired change). Strategic family therapists believe that change can occur rapidly, without intensive analysis of the source of the problem; their focus is on family behaviour outside the therapy session.

- **Humanistic-experiential family therapy** involves a range of approaches,[8] drawing on gestalt, TA, psychodrama, attachment theory and ego-psychology. For instance, gestalt two-chair and encounter work may be used to raise awareness and experiment with new ways of connecting. Virgina Satir, a key name in this field, sees problems in families arising when emotions (anger and concern, for example) are not communicated in clear, direct ways, and when members' self-esteem is not mutually enhanced. Satir highlights the role played by love, compassion and nurturing in helping families heal.

- **Intergenerational family therapy** focuses on the generational legacy and its influence on family and individual behaviour. Identifying multigenerational behavioural patterns (for example, how shame, anger and anxiety are managed) is seen as helping people understand how their current struggles may be rooted in previous generations: for example, an adolescent's rebellious behaviour may mask unresolved grief passed down generations. Murray Bowen, a pioneer of this approach, used techniques such as normalising a family's problems, encouraging communication by, for example, getting members to describe their reactions rather than act them out; and inviting clients to respond with 'I' statements rather than ones which place the blame on others.

Box 15.3 Case illustration: Minuchin's family therapy approach

Excerpt from a family therapy session

MOTHER: No not today, sweetheart. No, put that back, we don't have any paper to draw on. Put them back, Patti. Patti, do what you were told. Put them back. Her belligerence is so – ...

MINUCHIN: Is that how Patti and you spend your time together?

MOTHER: Yes – yes ...

  [During this period, the mother makes seven ineffective controlling statements to Patti, whose amount of hyperactivity is matched by the mother's intensity of ineffective control. To the family's definition of the problem – that Patti is uncontrollable – can now be added another

(Continued)

> definition, that the mother is hyper-responsive in her controlling requests, that her control is ineffective, and that she feels helpless.] ...
>
> MINUCHIN: Do you find this present arrangement a difficult one? For example, the two girls going around while we talk? How do you respond to that?
>
> MOTHER: How do I respond to it? I get tense ...
>
> MINUCHIN: So, you would prefer that she stay in one place?
>
> MOTHER: No, I can see them walking around when there are toys for them to play with.
>
> MINUCHIN: What would you like?
>
> MOTHER: Right now?
>
> MINUCHIN: Yes, what would make it more comfortable for you?
>
> MOTHER: For them to sit over there and play with the puppets.
>
> MINUCHIN: Okay. Do that. Make it happen [...]
>
> [The stage is now set for a changed sequence of interaction. Rather than Patti and her mother playing their accustomed parts, in this scenario the script has been changed. The therapist–director has given the mother a new part: she will act to get her four-year-old daughter to behave in such a way that the mother is more 'comfortable'. By saying to the mother, 'Make it happen', Minuchin has also conveyed an important message to her: that is, she is in fact capable of controlling her child.]
>
> (Minuchin & Fishman, 1961, p. 83)

Family versus individual approaches

Many family therapists assert the value of family work over one-to-one therapy. They argue, firstly, that 'problems' are located **in the system** rather than the individual, so it makes sense to intervene at a broader level. Working with the family or the wider system allows all the members involved to take responsibility for their common problems. The more experience family members have of working through difficulties together and becoming more aware of the impact of their behaviours on each other, the more empowered, resourced and hopeful they will feel.

Secondly, family therapists point out that while the benefits of individual therapy can often **transfer** to the rest of a client's life, sometimes they do not; when individuals return home from their therapy they can fall back into the same old patterns of dysfunctional relating. If change is to occur within the family then all members need to be involved in the move towards a new equilibrium.

Working with the family or group directly, rather than through a hearsay account, can allow the therapist to see problematic interactional patterns being enacted in **immediate**, vivid ways (see box 15.4).

SYSTEMIC THEORY AND THERAPY   221

> ## Box 15.4 Case illustration: Finding a positive connection
>
> Barrett describes some couples therapy with Steve and Carol.
>
> > I watched Steve shut down, roll his eyes, avoid topics, change subjects, and basically block Carol out as she tried with increasing desperation to get and keep his attention. After a minute or two of this, her face began to contort with bitterness as her voice grew shrill. 'I know why you won't talk to me,' she hissed[.] 'You can't talk to *anybody*. You don't trust anybody because you're a narcissist. All you think about is yourself.'
> >   … There it all was, in living color: she tries to connect, he turns away. She feels rejected, tries harder, and he grows even stonier. She blasts him with cruel, sarcastic jabs, and he withdraws completely. In one session – actually, in one five-minute segment of one session – I was able to glean more valuable information about Steve's life at home than I was after months of working with him individually. (2014, p. 23)
>
> Barrett goes on to describe the subsequent work, which focused on enabling Steve and Carol to shift each others' moods through light-hearted **humour** and gentle connection, the repetition of positive experience being the engine of change. "Helping family members rediscover some of what they like and love about each other", Barrett says,
>
> > is a necessary preliminary to their being able to share their underlying pain and deeply troubled history with each other. To create the safety that will allow clients to be more vulnerable and less defensive, family members need to develop some of the qualities that we therapists try to cultivate in ourselves. (2014, p. 24)

When the relationships of our clients are enacted right in front of us, we have a much more realistic view of what's happening at home, what's triggering their traumatic symptoms, and what's helping or hurting their ability to function. With a systems approach, we're not just hearing stories about people, but actually experiencing them ourselves, feeling in our own bodies what happens between people and seeing the patterns acted out. (Barrett, 2014, p. 23)

Further, as individuals share their deepest traumas and stories, they can be emotionally held and supported not simply by their therapist but also by the important people in their lives. Once change begins, members can **support each other** to engage the change process; the burden is thus spread beyond client and therapist.

Instead of separating clients from their families, our task is to encourage healing partnerships within families, allowing them to support each other in the process of healing, rather than relying exclusively on the therapist as the primary agent of change. (Barrett, 2014, p. 24)

Finally, systemic practitioners argue that there are certain circumstances in which individual work can be **contra-indicated**, for example when the client's relationship with the therapist may be perceived by a spouse or other family member as a form of infidelity, thereby triggering insecurities.

Individual therapists, in turn, argue for in-depth, intrapsychic exploration. They also point out that psychological and systemic thinking are *not* mutually exclusive. The two paradigms have the potential to complement each other in a way that suits an integrative way of working. For instance, the emphasis in therapy may well shift from individual to system (or vice versa) as it progresses.

Even if we do not practise systemically, our interventions could still be geared to engaging wider systems: for instance, we can do 'family sculpts' in dramatherapy, or intergenerational constellations work, or we can engage two-chair work to help a client dialogue imaginally with a family member. In all these examples, we can expect a direct, two-way impact on family systems as the client becomes more aware of their 'family dance' and the relational context.

Research on Family Therapy

The field of family therapy has been researched extensively via a variety of quantitative and qualitative methods, with the focus on both outcomes and process.

Numerous **systematic reviews** of research demonstrate a strong evidence base for both the effectiveness and the cost-effectiveness of systemic family and couples therapy (SFCT); see Stratton (2011) and Heatherington, Friedlander, Diamond, Escudero and Pinsof (2015) for comprehensive reviews.

Four specific research studies are introduced below in order to give a sense of this wider range of research. The first two examples relate to *outcomes*, while the other two explore *process*. Their findings provide further evidence of the value and benefits of a systemic approach.

1. **A randomised controlled trial** Leff et al. (2000) compared three distinct approaches to the treatment of severe depression: CBT, systemic couples therapy and drug treatment. In each couple, one member was identified as suffering from severe and chronic depression, as measured by the Beck Depression Inventory and other indicators. Participants were randomly allocated one of the three approaches (which were manualised to ensure results were consistently comparable).

   One key finding was that there was a high dropout rate (over 70%) from the CBT part of the study. However, systemic couples therapy was found to produce more favourable outcomes on a range of measures, when compared with the drug group. Significantly, independent observers could not reliably identify the partner who had been initially diagnosed in the systemic group, affirming systemic analysis of depression as residing in the relationship rather than the individual.

2. **An observational outcomes study** Vostanis, Burnham and Harris (1992) explored changes in *expressed emotion* as a result of systemic family therapy. Videotapes of the first, second and final sessions of therapy for 12 families were rated by an independent assessor. Emotional over-involvement and criticism were found to decrease significantly right from the early stages of therapy, and warmth between members increased in later sessions.

   The relatively simple design of this study shows how a data set (videos) can be used in different ways to monitor changes in behaviour.

3. **An experimental study** Minuchin (1974) offered a now classic demonstration of the interconnection of family members in a family where both daughters (Dede, aged 17, and Violet, aged 12) suffered from diabetes. He showed how changes in the relationships were experienced at a bio-chemical level and how these could be stabilised by family dynamics.

   Minuchin employed a physiological measure of emotional arousal: the free fatty acid (FFA) level in the bloodstream. He interviewed the parents for one hour while the girls watched from behind a one-way mirror; then they joined the parents. In the interview the parents were encouraged to discuss an issue of conflict which led to some experience of stress by all parties. Significantly, the parents' level of stress reduced once the children joined them.

   At this point it became apparent that the parents performed different roles and that Dede became trapped between the two of them as each tried to get her support. The impact of the parents' conflicting roles became apparent in the FFA results: both children showed increased FFA during the interview and even higher levels when they joined their parents. While Violet's FFA had returned to normal by the end, it took much longer for Dede's to recover.

4. **A qualitative phenomenological study** Wong (2008) studied intergenerational differences in worldviews and their impacts on first-, second- and third-generation Chinese-American family relations, opening a window into the context of their conflicts. The use of phenomenological methodology elicited deep experiential accounts of the nature of family life.

   The findings showed that stressors were related to acculturation and that the generation gap was further widened by different degrees of assimilation into American society, with its associated cultural values. For example, parents saw 'playing before homework' as tantamount to destroying their children's future, whereas the teenagers placed a high premium on leisure.

Although this broad range of research testifies to the value of family work, this is not to say that individual work is any less efficacious. More comparative research, geared to establishing the circumstances in which family approaches might be more beneficial than individual ones, or where an integrated approach might be advised, appears in order. Current practice suggests that in respect of dual diagnosis or substance misuse and in situations where children or young people are involved, keeping an eye on wider family dynamics is essential (Stratton, 2011).

Concluding Reflections

I last worked in an explicitly systemic way back in the 1970s when I was a co-therapist in family therapy work, observing from behind one-way glass. Since then, I have applied systemic ideas routinely in my practice, for instance when considering the functions of particular behaviours. As a phenomenologist who views the individual as intertwined with their wider lifeworld, I recognise that systems thinking remains an implicit element of my practice framework.

Beyond alerting us to the wider context, systems theory highlights how we are all caught up in a relational web, one spun with threads that become characteristic interactional patterns that hold us in and are not readily broken. Individuals are best understood "not in isolation, but in the context of their relations with others, past and present, internal and external, actual and fantasised" (Mitchell, 2000, p. 107). This idea is echoed in Nichols's (1987, p. 85) comment that "attempting to do therapy without transforming the context may at best be slow, at worst futile". The client's relationships and wider context must always remain figural.

Therapists are also a part of the web. I suggest that it would be remiss, if not unethical, for any of us to be unaware of the impact of our therapeutic interventions on a client's family, work relationships or broader social activities. Our own family, work and social relationships similarly impact on therapy. More than this, surely all therapists need to have awareness of the significance of cultural contexts – our own and our clients'. I also would like to think our values require us to stand up for social justice against oppression and inequality.

Just as distinctive 'dances' take shape within families, patterns form and reproduce themselves both within therapy and within wider institutional and cultural contexts. Reflexive awareness of them can help distinguish dances that are helpful from those that are obstructive, distorting or damaging.

Notes

1 An *ecological* perspective goes further, encompassing environmental, spiritual and transpersonal dimensions.

2 Such multi-level interventions may involve a pragmatic, *eclectic* approach, as often found in multi-disciplinary teamwork, where different professionals intervene with their particular interests to the fore. A deliberately merged and managed approach is favoured by systemic integrative therapists.

3 **Constructivism**, more cognitive in focus, examines how humans actively construct meanings, which influences their actions. **Social constructionism** places language at the centre, highlighting the

significant role played by discourse and culture. Language here is seen not as the expression of inner feelings or beliefs but as action; humans are seen to be constructed by language.

4 These questions can equally be applied to work in organisations (e.g. consultancy work and executive coaching). Additional questions might include: What is the staff turnover like? Are staff members able to criticise and express frustration? What do individuals need in order to function better in a team?

5 Dallos and Draper (2010) acknowledge the growing tendency (and relational-integrative impulse) to move away from the competitive

enshrining of particular schools of thought. (Tongue in cheek, they express sympathy for students suffering migraines as a result of having to sort through the perplexing field of claim and critique.)

6   The concept of *differentiation* is relevant here. Differentiation is the ability of each family member to maintain their own sense of self while remaining emotionally connected to the family (i.e., neither enmeshed nor disengaged). A mark of a healthy family is its capacity to allow members to be different, and be respected for that difference, while enabling all members to experience a sense of belonging to the whole.

7   Other integrative psychodynamic approaches include the **Milan School** (Palazzoli is a key name), where systems are seen to operate in relation to cognitive errors and fixed, unhelpful beliefs (e.g., 'I am correct and she is wrong'). As work is mostly done out of sessions, family therapy may only occur once a month.

8   Two particular relational approaches of note are ***emotionally focused*** couples therapy (EFT) (see, for instance, the demonstration on https://www.youtube.com/watch?v=xaHms5z-yuM) and ***imago therapy*** (see https://www.youtube.com/watch?v=HUSKejGLZe8). Note that emotionally focused therapy (EFT) (also called emotion-focused therapy) is different from the tapping approach used in 'emotional freedom technique' (also called EFT).

16
Transactional Analysis

It always crept onto my lap again, clutched at my clothes. ... I bent to its broken face, and it was horrible but I kissed it. I think one must finally take one's life in one's arms. Arthur Miller, *After the Fall*

A family discussion:

FATHER: Tone-deaf people shouldn't do karaoke. Couldn't you have sung with a friend who can sing?

JASON: I really suck at singing. I made a fool of myself didn't I? I'll not do that again.

MOTHER: Nonsense, you sang it fine and it was lovely seeing you enjoy yourself.

FRIEND: You showed guts in getting up on stage; it wasn't that bad and everyone had fun.

This dialogue could have occurred in the pub ... It could equally have occurred internally, in the head of the singer. It illustrates the kind of relational dynamics transactional analysts engage.

Transactional Analysis (TA) offers a theory of personality and an approach to psychotherapy, making it too big a topic to do justice to here. However, I think an introduction to the TA idea that people can be understood to be structured psychologically as ego states (different subjectivities) is helpful. TA presents complex relational dynamics in elegantly simple, appealing ways. I frequently introduce it to clients: it helps them make sense of their own mixed responses and messy relational dynamics.

Relational Integrative Psychotherapy: Engaging Process and Theory in Practice, First Edition. Linda Finlay.
© 2016 John Wiley & Sons, Ltd. Published 2016 by John Wiley & Sons, Ltd.

Initially developed by Berne (1961), who was originally a psychoanalyst, as a kind of *cognitive-behavioural* therapy, the field has evolved through different manifestations such as *psychoanalytic* versions, the Cathexis school and Redecision therapy.[1] Modern TA tends to be more theoretical, relational and integrative. Its particular strength is the way it can be used flexibly like an adaptable tool-kit and can be integrated into many ways of working, both theoretically and in other fields (e.g. therapy, coaching, education and management) (Stewart & Joines, 1987).

In this chapter I start by outlining the traditional **PAC model** (Berne, 1961), comprising three ego states. Some **developmental-relational** elaborations are then touched upon to show the wider potential of the approach. The third section discusses the specific concept of the **drama triangle**. In the final section I discuss the **application** of these ideas in therapy, using a 'Parent Interview' example.

The Three Ego States: PAC

Presented as three stacked circles (see figure 16.1), the three *ego states* of Parent, Adult, Child symbolise parts of ourselves. (The capital letter distinguishes the ego state from the usual use of these terms.) Ordinarily, we move rapidly between these: for instance, I might be functioning in Adult at a formal work meeting when I have a brief argument with a colleague, which puts me into Parent but ends me in Child.

The **Parent ego state** is made up of behaviour and responses copied from parents and other authority figures. It is the repository of personal values and social rules about how we 'should' behave (this includes internalised cultural norms passed down through generations). 'Tone-deaf people shouldn't do karaoke.'

In experiential terms, this ego state manifests as either a Nurturing or a Critical Parent. The *Nurturing Parent* is loving, caring and compassionate, replaying the

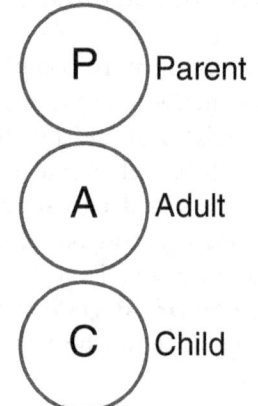

Figure 16.1 Three ego states

behaviours we experienced when we were being taken care of as a child, with comfort and cuddles (assuming we had internalised a nurturing parent). A person who tries to help or 'rescue' in a patronising or overwhelming way (a 'smother mother') is a negative version, taking the behaviour to extremes. The *Critical Parent* is the internalised parent part who judges, criticises and controls. 'You are being silly; boys don't cry'; 'Never take drugs, it is bad for you'. The positive impulse here is one of trying to protect others but applied negatively the person becomes punitive, punishing and persecutory.

The **Adult ego state** involves our grown-up resources: we can think, analyse, evaluate, be rational, make decisions and systematically work through problems. At best our Adult strikes a balance between working out how our Child can get what it needs and acknowledging that our Parent says what 'should' be done. 'You showed guts in getting up on stage; it wasn't that bad and everyone had fun.'

The **Child ego state** is the part of us preserved from our childhood and it represents our potential to play, have fun, and to express ourselves, be it in delight, anger, rage, terror, sadness or joy. It is the source of our creativity, curiosity and spontaneity as well as of confusion and unknowingness. When we are in this mode we behave, think and feel as we did when we were children.

This ego state also has two manifestations: Free and Adapted Child. Our *Free Child* is most clearly seen when we are watching a sporting event and we jump with untrammelled joy when our team wins; or when in our new car we deliberately speed down the motorway; or in response to music at a party we dance without inhibition. It's that free expression that comes spontaneously without reference to Parental rules or societal control that characterises Free Child. Our *Adapted Child* is the part of us which learned to get by and fit in with parents' and teachers' expectations and rules. It's that part that wants to please the 'grown-ups' and obey authority (shown in our being compliant, submissive or precocious) or to rebel against them (being naughty, resistant or withdrawing in a sulk).

Developmental-relational Elaborations

The basic PAC model becomes a lot more complicated and sophisticated once developmental and relational dimensions are taken into account.

Contemporary TA is more relational and integrative and there are different versions: Hargaden and Sills (2002) elaborate the theory with **psychoanalytic** focus on transference and the Child ego state; Lapworth and Sills (2010) integrate TA with cognitive and psychodynamic theories in an intersubjective relational **humanistic** way; Summers and Tudor's (2000) *Cocreative TA* similarly presents a here-and-now **constructivist–gestalt** narrative approach; Erskine's (2011) relational integrative work draws heavily on TA alongside **gestalt** and developmental understandings.

A **developmental** perspective considers the evolution of the ego states and focuses on early deficits and Child confusion. When we are children our Adult

TRANSACTIONAL ANALYSIS   229

and Parent parts are simplified childlike versions, still in the process of being elaborated (these parts are sometimes referred to as $P_1A_1C_1$).[2] Consider the client who has been referred to counselling to develop her mothering skills. At times this client shows her baby love and care similar to those a child displays when playing with a doll; at other times she gets frustrated and is at risk of damaging the child. This mother could be said to be 'parenting' from the (Nurturing and Critical) **Parent in her Child** (P_1 in C_2).

Beyond the use of these ego states to describe parts of our subjective experience, the theory is most usefully applied *inter*subjectively, i.e. interactionally (see figure 16.2). Here, transactions between people can be complementary, crossed and ulterior. Explicit and implicit meanings can get entangled, and there is room for much confusion when messages are not received in the way they are intended!

In a **complementary transaction**, there is a reciprocal dialogue which occurs between Adult and Adult; or Parent and Child; or Child and Child. In a **crossed transaction**, the ego state spoken to is not the one that responds; for example, an Adult to Adult transaction is intended but is responded to from a Child or Parent position. In an **ulterior transaction**, there is an overt social message (Adult–Adult) and an implicit psychological one (Child–Parent; Parent–Child).

As an example, consider the situation in a relatively new supervision group where the supervisees chattered outside, making them late for the group.

SUPERVISOR: Can I remind you all about the importance of starting on time to ensure everyone gets their full half hour? It's a question of respecting each other. (Adult to Adult)

SUPERVISEE A: Thank you for reminding us. Sorry, we had got rather carried away with our chatting. (Complementary Adult to Adult)

SUPERVISEE B: (Is clearly upset. She has a family history of being brought up with the injunction 'never be late'. She feels dreadful and fears the supervisor is angry.) I am really really sorry. I didn't mean to be disrespectful. It won't happen again. (Adapted Child to Critical Parent.)

While in this example we might see Supervisee B's response as coming from her Child, it's also possible she was sensitive to a lurking ulterior Parent to Child

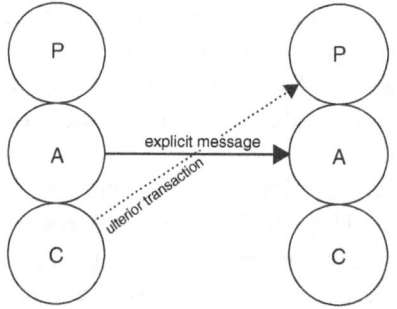

Figure 16.2 Transactions

message, and the supervisor was actually telling the group members off in Critical Parent for their lack of respect.

A different example highlighting crossed transactions is seen in the following dialogue from a marital therapy session where the husband expresses concern about his wife's alcohol use and they are invited to share their points of view.

HUSBAND: Last night is a good example when we got into an argument about whether or not you should drive. I thought you had had too much to drink. (Adult to Adult; possible ulterior Parent to Child message)

WIFE: It's my business! (Child to Child)

HUSBAND: I'm worried about you. (Parent to Child)

WIFE: Ha! How about all those nights I've waited worrying for you to come home from the club? (Parent to Child)

HUSBAND: If you think I'm giving you the keys to the car when you're drunk, you're crazy! (Parent to Child)

WIFE: You're always trying to control me! (Child to Parent)
[Silence]

WIFE: (in a different tone) I wasn't drunk last night you know. I had been crying. I hardly had – (Adult to Adult)

HUSBAND: (interrupting) Sure and pigs fly. (Child to Child)

THERAPIST: Can I ask how much you had had to drink? (Adult to Adult)

WIFE: Two glasses of wine. He's right though, I will often have more. (Adult to Adult)

'Drama Triangle' Dynamics

The drama triangle was originally created by Steve Karpman (1968; see also 2014).[3] The triangle[4] plots behavioural (transactional) moves between people, where the roles of Persecutor, Victim and Rescuer are played out as familiar, favoured positions (see figure 16.3; the capital letters denote the roles played rather than the persons being persecutors, victims or rescuers in real life). These roles are usually played out of awareness and are a psychological attempt to meet unmet needs. Often they replicate childhood dynamics and early beliefs, so have a familiar 'feel' experientially.

Persecutor: Persecutors use their power against others to blame, punish, abuse, insult, neglect and attempt to control others. They turn their anger on others, taking an 'I can make you feel bad' position, discounting the Victim's value and rights. People tend to take up the Persecutor role in order to feel strong and avoid being the Victim themselves.

Victim: Victims are needy and feel hurt, misunderstood, inadequate, powerless, hopeless and helpless. They both discount themselves and are victimised by the Persecutor's abuse and control (including manipulations, broken promises, and ultimatums). This is the 'You can make me feel bad or good' position. Sometimes Victims will seek out Persecutors to confirm their belief that they are helpless. They also call out seductively to Rescuers with messages like 'I need help; only you can make me feel better'.

Rescuers: Rescuers are driven to try to fix, care for and bail out victims. While they appear caring and supportive, their 'I can make you feel good' message also contains the less helpful, discounting message 'You're unable to help yourself; only I can help you'. A person is likely to be rescuing when they are working too hard to do something they don't want to do and not asking for what they themselves want or need. Often the Rescuer can be found rescuing to bolster their own self-importance or to give to others what they are needing themselves.

Each 'player' attempts (usually out of awareness) to get their unspoken psychological needs met without recognising the potential damage to others and the broader dysfunctions at stake. As an example of how the drama triangle is played out, consider what is sometimes called the 'Addiction Game' (see Steiner, 1971). Here, the addict plays the role of the Victim of addiction: they are dependent, sick, needy and at risk. The Rescuer plays their role by generously and selflessly trying to help the addict; however, this is probably being done without first establishing that the addict is invested in the process of giving up substance abuse. After a certain amount of frustrating failure the Rescuer can get angry and in danger of switching into Persecuting the addict. The addict can equally jump from Victim to Persecutor by counter-attacking (for example, by becoming aggressively drunk and violent or by creating midnight emergencies). The Rescuer thus becomes Victim. This process of switching is repeated again and again, with all parties being caught in the web of the Drama Triangle (see box 16.1).

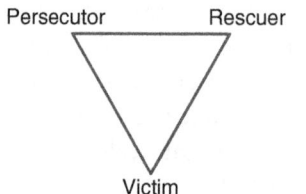

Figure 16.3 The drama triangle

Box 16.1 Case illustration: Getting hooked into a drama triangle

A trainee therapist found herself being regularly mocked and disparaged by her boyfriend. At weekends, fuelled by excessive alcohol use, he would beat her up, once landing her in hospital with a broken nose and severe facial contusions.

(*Continued*)

The trainee, on her part, saw her boyfriend as needing support as he was 'depressed'. What kind of therapist was she if she turned her back on him?

Therapy focused initially on trying to understand why she was so driven to Rescue her abuser despite often ending up severely damaged in Victim. Links were made to the trainee's own childhood struggle of trying (unsuccessfully) to Rescue her father, who had been diagnosed with bipolar disorder. Her relationship with her boyfriend was seen as a way of replaying those dynamics in a futile attempt to heal her 'father' and herself. The therapist tried to strengthen the trainee's Adult by discussing the theory underlying the drama triangle. When the trainee understood her own part in the triangle, she turned to disparaging herself for being so weak and gullible, inviting the therapist to concur with this self-criticism. Challenging this shift into Victim once more, the therapist gently encouraged her to find ways of stepping out of the triangle and to engage more self-compassionate, healthy patterns.

Eventually, the trainee had the resolve to break up with her boyfriend without feeling caught by his desperate pleas to return. She learned to protect and care for herself in relationships. She also forgave herself for her tendency to get hooked into unhealthy drama triangle dynamics. It helped to recognise that all therapists have the potential to be a Rescuer!

The basic emotions that commonly drive the drama triangle are feelings of rage or envy, terror, shame and helplessness, and these are the underlying emotions that might be usefully explored in therapy. Therapeutic interventions aim to raise the client's awareness of both the origins of their roles (for instance, having been a child who suffered from abuse, neglect or other trauma) *and* the part they are playing in keeping the drama going. It can help to teach the theory to clients as it gives an easy shorthand to highlight healthy versus destructive ways of relating both with others and with oneself.

It can also help to recognise that the triangle positions are not fixed but are comparable to dance patterns, albeit a somewhat macabre dance without real contact or intimacy. More specifically, it is useful to explicitly discuss ways of **stepping out of the triangle** and turning unhealthy dynamics into healthy ones. One nice way of conceptualising the shift is to retain the P–V–R letters but transform them. The Persecutor is encouraged to hold their Power and be Potent and compassionate. The Victim is invited just to be Vulnerable (for example, feeling sick, sad or scared), owning their vulnerability without being helpless. The Rescuer is encouraged instead to be Responsive and to Reach Out. Choy (1990) and others offer the concept of the 'Winner's triangle', which highlights the choice of being Assertive, Vulnerable and Caring (see figure 16.4 and the therapy examples in box 16.2).

TRANSACTIONAL ANALYSIS   233

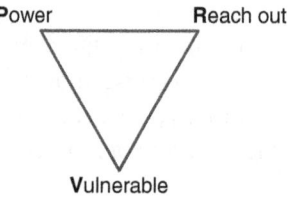

Figure 16.4 The 'healthy' triangle

> ## Box 16.2 Case illustration: Creative interventions
>
> ### A role-play
>
> **Niamh**, a client in her mid-twenties, recognised that her unhealthy relationship with food and her bingeing–purging behaviour increased markedly after contact with her persecutory (belittling, blaming and invasive) mother. Over time Niamh began to realise her mother probably suffered from anorexia nervosa, and she could see that her mother was obsessively attempting to control both her weight and the environment.
>
> In therapy, Niamh practised positive responses to her mother's critical, controlling comments, which enabled her to avoid going into Victim or counter-attacking in Persecutor. For instance, when visiting Niamh, the mother would often bring a present of a large box of bran cereal. Feeling 'forced' to eat this, Niamh would find herself over-eating and then purging. In therapy, Niamh practised refusing to take the cereal in a kind but assertive manner: 'Thank you mum, I know you are trying to make sure I eat good food but I prefer my fruit breakfast. I know you like bran so why don't you keep it?' Niamh particularly dreaded public scenes in restaurants. For instance, in response to her mother's comments like 'You don't want any dessert, you'll just get even fatter' (Critical Parent-to-Child transaction), she practised an Adult-to-Adult response of saying, 'I'm okay with my weight mum; I think the odd treat is actually good for me'.
>
> ### A psychodrama
>
> **Adebayo** used psychodrama to explore his ambivalent feelings about becoming a father. He was frightened that he was going to damage his baby. He acted out his worst nightmare in a dramatic construction where he bashed in the baby's face. The 'Director' guided him to become the 'baby' and another group member played the 'father'. He was then invited into dialogue with 'father'. The role reversal allowed him to express his feelings towards his own abusive father (owning his Child
>
> *(Continued)*

fear and anxiety about what he may have internalised in this Critical Parent part). He was able to recognise that it was not inevitable that he would succumb to being similarly abusive and persecutory. The session ended with the group holding and rocking Adebayo.

Applying TA in Relational-integrative Ways

Relationally orientated TA prioritises the "co-created, authentic relationship as the central vehicle for change" (Lapworth & Sills, 2010, p. 4). Working developmentally, therapy would focus on naming and working through archaic needs and wants. We also have a role in helping individuals avoid simply repeating less effective self-management dynamics towards finding new relational ways of being (Hargaden & Sills, 2002).

TA therapy might attempt to help the **Child find a voice**, to **turn down the volume of the Critical Parent**, or to **strengthen the Adult**. Any or all of these might be the focus, but impact can be felt at different levels. For instance, helping the Child express their inner longings will deepen the Adult's understanding; hearing the Child's vulnerability may enable the Nurturing Parent to step in as a 'self-management strategy' rather than allowing full reign to the Critical Parent.

To show these relational-integrative layers of TA at work, consider the dialogue in box 16.3 between Danny and his therapist. Danny, a grown man, is exploring his (Child) need to take care of his alcoholic mother; the therapist attempts a conversation with Danny's Adult which challenges his *rescuing script*.[5] Over time he begins to see that he has some choice and that his urge to be a carer may in part come from a need for his father's approval. Eventually Danny recognised the power of his (societal? parental?) *introjects* about what it means to be a 'man'.

Box 16.3 Case illustration: A therapist attempts to engage a client's Adult

DANNY: I *have* to take care of her.
THERAPIST: You feel it is your job to care for your mother?
DANNY: Yes. Now that my father has left, it falls on me.
THERAPIST: You have to step into your father's shoes?
DANNY: Yes ... No ... [*pause, looking confused*] He's done it for 20 years but couldn't do it any more.

TRANSACTIONAL ANALYSIS   235

> THERAPIST: So if he failed, how are you going to manage?
> DANNY: [*looks uncertain*] I don't know. But I *have* to keep trying. She needs me.
> THERAPIST: What does your father say about this?
> DANNY: He wants me to live my own life.
> THERAPIST: What do you *think* about that?
> DANNY: [*after a pause*] I'm, er, I'm not … living my life; I'm her carer.
> THERAPIST: So at the moment, are you making the *choice* to be her carer instead of living your life?
> DANNY: [*looks a bit confused then nods slowly*]
> [*In a subsequent session, Danny and his therapist talk again about how he feels so responsible for taking care of his mother.*]
> THERAPIST: It seems like it is really important to your sense of yourself to see yourself as taking on that responsibility.
> DANNY: Yeah, it's really important. I need to be responsible.
> THERAPIST: Can you say more about what's important to you?
> DANNY: It's like what you do when you're a man. You take care of the family.
> THERAPIST: And what would happen if you didn't take care of your mother?
> DANNY: Someone has to look out for her.
> THERAPIST: First it was your dad's role and now it's yours? [*Danny nods*] What would your dad think if you stopped caring for your mother?
> DANNY: [*long pause; looking confused*] It's really weird 'cos he wants me to stop. So why am I worried he won't respect me any more?
> THERAPIST: Is it like you're kinda showing him that you're a grown-up man who can take responsibility and you get his approval for that? It's like you're following in his footsteps?

As well as working in this more classical **cognitive** way, some integrative therapists employ dramatherapy-type **gestalt** techniques:

- *Role-plays* focused on finding constructive ways to respond to invitations to play destructive games in the triangle can be helpful. Therapist and client might work together to come up with some creative phrases or ways of being that can be used in life (see the Niamh example, box 16.2).
- In a *psychodrama* the ego states can be brought alive as 'characters' who can be worked with in dialogue or cathartically (see the Abedayo example, box 16.2)
- Using *chair work*, a client engaged in their own persecutory inner dialogues can place Critical Parent, Adult and Child (or Persecutor–Victim–Rescuer) voices on different chairs in order to begin to distinguish their source and power. As each speaks, links might be made, for instance, between the inner-Persecutor voice and highly critical parent voices from childhood, while the inner-Victim is the confused, hurt but passive child.

236   TRANSACTIONAL ANALYSIS

In my own practice I use TA concepts (often explicitly) in five main ways to guide treatment.

1. **Strengthening or growing the Adult** Given that the Adult mediates between Child needs and Parent demands, strengthening the client's Adult is often a central strategy. If we want to nurture a client's Adult then we need to invite that Adult to be present by being in Adult ourselves. If we talk to a hurt, helpless child from a Nurturing Parent position, then we shouldn't be surprised if their Child gets hooked and comes forward. A good question to ask in relational-centred therapy is 'What part of you is talking now?' Such an intervention helps the client recognise the feelings, thoughts, and behavioural impulses arising from different subjectivities and ego positions. Then they can begin to make sense of their needs and relational patterns towards empowering more choice-full ways of being.

2. **Decontaminating the Adult** An early aim of a lot of TA-orientated therapy is to 'decontaminate' the Adult from the intrusion of archaic messages (Hargaden & Sills, 2002).

   Sometimes this information-processing part can be subject to the control of Parent or Child. Parental judgements or Child needs might creep into Adult out of our awareness (a process called 'contamination'). For instance, statements like 'Too much masturbation is unhealthy' or 'Immigrants can't be trusted' are often presented as rational fact, yet they contain some Parent prejudice or Child fear; 'Alcohol helps me have confidence' or 'We'll be happy once we have a baby' is spoken from Child neediness and reveals *magical thinking*. Growing up, having little experience to go by, we might have believed the social message and now see it as fact. Work on decontamination involves probing and challenging the client's beliefs, helping them recognise the nature of any distorted or magical thinking. For instance, a valuable opportunity to do some decontaminating arises when a client expresses the view that therapy is self-indulgent. In response, the therapist could explore where these views come from, or ask what meanings are carried in the idea of being self-indulgent. (See box 16.1 where the client showed some distorted thinking in seeing her depressed boyfriend as her responsibility simply because she was training to be a therapist.)

3. **Working with the internalised Parent** Commonly, therapists highlight those Critical Parent messages apparent in clients who habitually put themselves down in shame and self-loathing. I explicitly talk with clients about turning down the volume of those critical voices. Ultimately the goal is to enhance the client's Nurturing Parent so they can give their own Child the care and compassion it yearns for (enabling a self-parenting process so critical for the long term). A less common approach to working with the internalised Parent is the *Parent Interview* to help decommission toxic components of either the 'Child in the Parent' or the 'Parent in the Child'.

TRANSACTIONAL ANALYSIS   237

4. **De-confusion of the Child** Whereas work with the Adult can be largely cognitive, work on Child de-confusion is fundamentally relational and developmental. It involves clarifying and exploring the unmet needs and longings of the Child. Over time, healing comes when the client internalises the therapist's empathy and compassion. (Hargaden and Sills (2002) call this process of internalising the healing relationship 'introjective transference').

5. **Practising new alternatives** Therapists often have a significant role in giving clients permission to behave, think and feel in ways that run counter to critical injunctions and restraining *scripts*: 'It's okay to cry; it's not a sign of weakness' or 'Does that mean you must never make a mistake? Whose voice is that?' Sometimes the therapist might even model the process; for instance, when we tear up or let out a deep belly laugh we model letting go and presence. As part of encouraging spontaneity and playfulness, we might invite the client's Free Child to come forward by suggesting the client joins us on the floor to play in a sand tray.

An extended illustration: A Parent interview[6]

Beth was engaged in doctoral research exploring her personal experience of motherhood (in the double sense of being a mother and being mothered) by using a reflexive, hermeneutic autobiographical *phenomenological* methodology.

Beth's mother, Joyce, had mental health problems, and in the face of her toxic, irrational behaviour, Beth grew up feeling drained of life when around her.

I was Beth's mentor and together we decided she might benefit from some therapeutic work to explore issues around mothering that were potentially out of Beth's awareness. Together, we joined a five-day personal and professional development group for psychotherapists run by Ken Evans and Joanna Hewitt-Evans. Ken did a **Parent interview** with 'Joyce' while I took part in the group as a support for Beth.

Beth reflects retrospectively on her research journey:

I noticed a shift of significance that occurred in my relationship with my mother after … the internalized Parent interview. On my return, I heard a new voice inside me, perhaps the internal Child that was demanding protection, demanding life, demanding I create boundaries with my mother that would keep 'us' safe.

For the first time ever I expressed to my mother, 'I no longer want to be called names, hung up on, or yelled at.' I used to make excuses for her and accept her quick apologies after these episodes. For some reason after the internalized Parent interview … I felt it was okay, and even necessary for me to create some space for myself with her; that I could take care of her without accepting her bad behavior. I reflect now that maybe this new preparedness to respond to my 'Child' has come from my having my internalized 'Mother's Child' seen and soothed by Ken. Perhaps too, the interview has allowed my mother and I to separate that much more – to individuate – allowing me to establish and maintain healthier boundaries with my mother.

Before [the interview] ... I was aware of the internal chaos and confusion around my mother. It was something I tried not to think about too much aside from fulfilling my responsibility to her and trying to love and take care of her as best I could. (Haggett, 2012, pp. 98–99)

In her dissertation, Beth touched upon her feeling of being cared for (by Ken and myself as well as the group). In turn, the protective paternal/maternal counter-transferential feelings evoked in both of us (Ken and myself) in relation to the different 'subjectivities' of Beth need acknowledging. But the picture is also more complicated. While Ken experienced compassion in relation with 'Joyce', I was more wary. I experienced some confluence with Beth as an abused daughter, prompting me to want Beth to distance herself from the 'craziness' of 'Joyce'.

These various transferences can be understood as simply another way of meeting and remain fundamentally relational. They also call attention to something deeper, something that may continue to diminish the potential for intimacy unless we probe the multiple intersubjective processes at work. Rather than being obstacles to meeting they summon us to deeper levels of meeting, to new possibilities (Finlay & Evans, forthcoming).

Concluding Reflections

In summary, transactional analysis offers a thoroughly relational-integrative model to understand relationships, both internally with oneself and externally, involving interactions with others. The concept of ego states offers a shorthand way of talking which is simultaneously simple and profound.

A particular value of TA is the fact that the model can be presented in a relatively simple catchy way which clients can readily understand. The theory can be shared openly in the service of *psycho-educational* and *cognitive* (e.g. decontamination of Adult), or *developmental* (e.g. de-confusion of Child) processes. It can also be fun to spot the 'games' we play in our interactions. In particular, the drama triangle is a particularly powerful concept or image which can be usefully shared with clients to help them understand and handle situations where they have been pulled into unhealthy relationship dynamics. The ensuing *systemic* insight can be transformative, as the client is then in the position of being able to make an active decision to engage in another less destructive way of being.

With our project of integration through relationship, a key goal must surely be awareness and acceptance of *all* those different parts of us which emerge in our intersubjective relating. Then we are able to be more fully present when interacting with others. As we engage these fuller relationships with self and other, we are *en route* to some healing.

Notes

1 Goulding and Goulding's (1979) Redecision Therapy, for instance, is a short-term version of **TA** which combines *gestalt* techniques towards positively reframing and re-evaluating early childhood injunctions and decisions which are causing problems today.

2 Our adult PAC versions – sometimes called second- order ego states or $P_2A_2C_2$ – are an *evolved* version of the childhood $P_1A_1C_1$. This theory is then further developed:, for instance, A_1 in C_2 is sometimes referred to as 'Little Professor'. Children who care for parents often have a well-developed Little Professor.

3 Karpman's 1968 paper made links with classic fairy tales, for instance the Pied Piper. First the Pied Piper is the Rescuer who saves the city from the rat infestation; then he becomes the Victim, betrayed by the townspeople; eventually he is the Persecutor, bewitching all the children with his musical pipe and luring them away. Karpman's 2014 book offers a systemic view of a 'three-sides-at-once Compassion Triangle', and of personal inner levels of the triangle, tracing the development over time of 12 levels, including family, scripting, biological, genetic, particle physics, and archaeological equivalents of the three-sided dynamic. See Karpman's website: www.KarpmanDramaTriangle.com.

4 Also called 'racquet' or 'game' in TA.

5 The therapist followed her intuition to work in this TA way as they had only contracted for eight sessions. Had the therapy involved longer-term work, it is possible the focus might have shifted onto psychoanalytically oriented **relational-developmental** work related to Danny's attachment to his mother and the need to separate and individuate. The therapist was aware that issues of abandonment lurked and he speculated that when Danny was a child his alcoholic mother might well have been absent for significant chunks of time.

6 The *Parent interview* originally evolved as a *gestalt* projective two-chair technique embraced by transactional analysts (Erskine, Moursund & Trautmann, 1999; McNeel, 1976). In this 'interview', the therapist talks with one of the internalised parents in the Client's Parent ego state. The aim is to help the client externalise their internal family and experience this part as separate from themselves. For example, here Beth's mother's shame is owned by (a version of) the 'mother', relieving Beth of having to carry it as well. In turn, as the 'mother' feels respected and witnessed, there is an opportunity for healing: in essence, the 'parent' (the Parent in the Child) gets therapy. In practice, Parent interview encounters are often powerfully intense and stirring (for both participants and observers). The client's way of being can change dramatically as they work their way into their parent's shoes and approximate the parent's being. Sometimes the client will surprise themselves by revealing information that had been outside their conscious awareness.

Postscript

We hear some music playing: a song whose lyrics speak of needs, damage and dreams, whose melody expresses longing, loss and love. The rhythm is that of life. I hold out my hand and invite you to dance. You accept, a little uncertain. Stiff and awkward at first, we stumble and collide. I accidentally step on your toes. It takes time to move in step with grace, but eventually we find the shared rhythm. We improvise and try out different interpretive dance steps. At times we break apart, and when the dizzying spins threaten to overwhelm I bring you back into hold. Together again, we sway and twirl, revelling in our new freedom of expression. Our movements are synchronised and it's hard to say who leads, who follows. The embodied intersubjective space between us no longer involves division but connection.

As the music ends, we bow in celebration of our new dance. And with some reluctance we go our separate ways.

References

Adams, M. (2014). *The Myth of the Untroubled Therapist: Private Life, Professional Practice*. Hove, Sussex: Routledge.

Ainsworth, M., Blehar, M.C., Waters, E. and Wall, S. (1978). *Patterns of Attachment: A Psychological Study of the Strange Situation*. Hillsdale, NJ: Erlbaum.

American Psychiatric Association (2010). *American Psychiatric Association Practice Guidelines for the Treatment of Patients with Major Depressive Disorder*, 3rd edn. Arlington, VA: American Psychiatric Publishing.

Anderson, R. (2006). Body Intelligence Scale: Defining and measuring the intelligence of the body. *Humanistic Psychologist*, 34(4), 357–367.

Anderson, R. (2007). Intuitive Inquiry: Five Cycles of Interpretation. Accessed October 2014 from www.wellknowingconsulting.org/inquiry.html.

Aron, L. (1996). *A Meeting of Minds: Mutuality in Psychoanalysis*. Hillsdale, NJ: The Analytic Press.

Ashworth et al. (2004). *PSYCHLOPS*. Accessed June 2014 from www.psychlops.org.uk/.

Atwood, G.E. and Stolorow, R.D. (2014). *Structures of Subjectivity: Explorations in Psychoanalytic Phenomenology and Contextualism*, 2nd edn. London: Routledge.

Axline, V. (1989). *Play Therapy*. Edinburgh: Churchill Livingstone.

Barnett, L. and Madison, G. (eds) (2012). *Existential Therapy: Legacy, Vibrancy and Dialogue*. London: Routledge.

Barrett, J.-J. (2014). Outside the box: Bringing families into trauma treatment. *Psychotherapy Networker*, May/June, 21–25.

Bateson, G. (1972). *Steps to an Ecology of Mind*. New York: Ballantine Books.

Baumeister, R. (1991). *Meanings of Life*. New York: Guilford Press.

Beck, A.T. (1967). *Depression: Causes and Treatment*. Philadelphia: University of Pennsylvania Press.

Beck, A.T. (1976). *Cognitive Therapy and Emotional Disorders*. New York: International Universities Press.

Beck, A.T., Steer, R.A. and Brown, G.K. (1996). *Manual for the Beck Depression Inventory-II*. San Antonio, TX: Psychological Corporation.

Berne, E. (1961). *Transactional Analysis in Psychotherapy: A Systematic Individual and Social Psychiatry*. New York: Grove Press.

Berne, E. (1972). *What do You Say after You Say Hello?* London: Corgi.

Bertalanffy, L. van (1968). *General System Theory: Foundations, Development, Applications*. New York: Braziller.

Bion, W.R. (1961). *Experiences in Groups and Other Papers*. London: Tavistock Publications.

Bion, W.R. (1962). *Learning from Experience*. London: Heinemann.

Bion, W.R. (1967). *Second Thoughts: Selected Papers on Psycho-Analysis*. London: William Heinemann Medical Books.

Bion, W. R. (1974). *Bion's Brazilian Lectures 2*. Rio de Janeiro: Imago Editora. (Reprinted in one volume with *Bion's Brazilian Lectures 1* London: Karnac Books 1990.)

Bion, W.R. (2005). *The Tavistock Seminars 1976–1979*. London: Karnac.

Bohart, A.C. and Tallman, K. (1999). *How Clients Make Therapy Work: The Process of Active Self-healing*. Washington, DC : American Psychological Association.

Bordin, E.S. (1979). The generalizability of the psychoanalytic concept of the working alliance. *Psychotherapy: Theory, Research, Practice, Training*, 16(3), 207–221.

Bowlby, J. (1969). *Attachment and Loss. Volume 1: Attachment*. New York: Basic Books.

Bowlby, J. (1988). *A Secure Base*. New York: Basic Books.

British Psychological Society (2011). Response to the American Psychiatric Association: DSM-5 development. Accessed June 2014 from http://apps.bps.org.uk/_publicationfiles/consultationresponses/DSM-5%202011%20-%20BPS%20response.pdf.

Brogan, M.M., Prochaska, J.O. and Prochaska, J.M. (1999). Predicting termination and continuation status in psychotherapy using the transtheoretical model. *Psychotherapy: Theory, Research, Practice, Training*, 36(2), 105–113.

Brown, J., Dreis, S. and Nace, D. (1999). What really makes a difference in psychotherapy outcome? Why does managed care want to know? In M.Hubble, B.Duncan and S.Miller (eds), *The Heart and Soul of Change*. Washington, DC: APA Press, pp. 389–406.

Brown, R. and Stobart, K. (2008). *Understanding Boundaries and Containment in Clinical Practice*. London: Karnac Books.

Brownell, P. (2010). *Gestalt Therapy: A Guide to Contemporary Practice*. New York: Springer.

Buber, M. (1958). *I and Thou* (trans. R.G. Smith). New York: Charles Scribner's Sons. (Original work published 1923.)

Buber, M. (1965). *The Knowledge of Man: A Philosophy of the Interhuman* (Introduction M.S. Friedman, trans. M.S. Friedman & R.G. Smith). New York: Harper & Row. (Original work published in 1951.)

Burns, G.W. (ed.) (2007). *Healing Stories: Your Casebook Collection for Using Therapeutic Metaphors*. Hoboken, NJ: Wiley.

Cannon, B. (2012). Applied existential psychotherapy. Accessed August 2014 from http://vimeo.com/46856569.

Casement, P. (1985). *On Learning from the Patient*. London: Routledge.

Casement, P. (1990). *Further Learning from the Patient*. London: Routledge.

Chidiac, M.-A. and Denham-Vaughan, S. (2007). The process of presence: Energetic availability and fluid responsiveness. *British Gestalt Journal*, 16(1), 9–19.

Choy, A. (1990). The Winner's Triangle. *Transactional Analysis Journal*, 20(1), pp. 40–46.

Clark, D.M., Salkovskis, P.M., Hackmann, A., Middleton, H., Anastasaides, P. and Gelder, M. (1994). A comparison of cognitive therapy, applied relaxation, and imipramine in panic disorder. *British Journal of Psychiatry*, 164, 759–769.

Clarkson, P. (1999). *Gestalt Counselling in Action*, 2nd edn. London: Sage.

Clarkson, P. (2003). *The Therapeutic Relationship*, 2nd edn. London: Whurr.

Cooper, M. (2001). Embodied empathy. In S. Haugh and T. Merry (eds), *Empathy*. Ross-on-Wye: PCCS Books, pp. 218–229.

Cooper, M. (2003). *Existential Therapies*. London: Sage.

Cooper, M. (2008). *Essential Research Findings in Counselling and Psychotherapy: The Facts are Friendly*. Los Angeles, CA: Sage.

Cooper, M. and McLeod, J. (2011). *Pluralistic Counselling and Psychotherapy*. Los Angeles, CA: Sage.

Crossley, D. and Stowell-Smith, M. (2000). Cognitive analytic therapy. In S.Palmer and R.Woolfe (eds), *Integrative and Eclectic Counselling and Psychotherapy*. London: Sage, pp. 202–217.

Crossman, P. (1966). Permission and protection, *Transactional Analysis Bulletin*, 5(19), 152–154.

Dallos, R. (1991). *Family Belief Systems, Therapy and Change*. Buckingham: Open University Press.

Dallos, R. and Draper, R. (2010). *An Introduction to Family Therapy: Systemic Theory and Practice*, 3rd edn. Maidenhead, Berks: Open University Press.

Damasio, A. (1999). *The Feeling of What Happens: Body and Emotion in the Making of Consciousness*. San Diego, CA: Harcourt.

Davidson, R.J., Kabat-Zinn, J., Schumacher, J., Rosenkranz, M., Muller, D., Santorelli, S.F., ... Sheridan, J.F. (2003). Alterations in brain and immune function produced by mindfulness meditation, *Psychosomatic Medicine*, 65(4), 564–570.

Davies, J.M. (2012). Whose bad objects are we anyway? Repetition and our elusive love affair with evil. In L.Aron and A.Harris (eds), *Relational Psychoanalysis. Volume 5: Evolution of Process*. New York: Routledge, pp. 163–181.

Department of Health (2009). New Horizons: Towards a shared vision for mental health – consultation. Accessed May 2015 from http://webarchive.nationalarchives.gov.uk/+/www.dh.gov.uk/en/consultations/liveconsultations/dh_103144.

Department of Health (2013). 2010 to 2015 government policy: mental health service reform. Accessed May 2015 from https://www.gov.uk/government/publications/2010-to-2015-government-policy-mental-health-service-reform.

Deurzen-Smith, E. van (1997). *Everyday Mysteries: Existential Dimensions of Psychotherapy*. London: Routledge.

Deurzen, E. van (2012). *Existential Psychotherapy and Counselling in Practice*, 3rd edn. London: Sage.

Deurzen, E. van (2014). Existential perspectives on anger. *The Psychotherapist*, 58, 13–14.

Deurzen, E. van and Adams, M. (2011). *Skills in Existential Counselling and Psychotherapy*. Los Angeles, CA: Sage.

DeYoung, P.A. (2003). *Relational Psychotherapy: A Primer*. New York: Brunner-Routledge.

du Plock, S. (2006). Bibliotherapy and Beyond. An Existential-Phenomenological Approach to Therapeutic Use of Narrative. Unpublished PhD thesis, University of Middlesex.

Egan, G. (2010). *The Skilled Helper: A Problem Management and Opportunity Development Approach to Helping*, 9th edn. Belmont, CA: Brooks/Cole.

Elliot, R., Mack, C. and Shapiro, D. (1999). Simplified Personal Questionnaire Procedure. Accessed June 2014 from www.experiential-researchers.org/instruments/elliott/pqprocedure.html.

Ellis, A. (1973). *Humanistic Psychotherapy: The Rational-Emotive Approach*. New York: Julian Press.

Ellis, A. (2000). Rational emotive behavior therapy. In R.J.Corsini and D.Wedding (eds.), *Current Psychotherapies*, 6th edn. Itasca, IL: F.E. Peacock, pp. 168–204.

Ellis, C. (2007). Telling secrets, revealing lives: Relational ethics in research with intimate others. *Qualitative Inquiry*, 13, 3–29.

Erskine, R.G. (2011). Attachment, relational-needs, and psychotherapeutic presence. Accessed September 2014 from http://www.integrative-therapy.com/en/articles.php?id=73.

Erskine, R.G. (2014). Nonverbal stories: The body in psychotherapy. *International Journal of Integrative Psychotherapy*, 5(1), 21–33.

Erskine, R.G. (2015). *Relational Patterns, Therapeutic Presence: Concepts and Practice of Integrative Psychotherapy*. London: Karnac.

Erskine, R.G. and Moursund, J.P. (1988). *Integrative Psychotherapy in Action*. London: Sage/Karnac.

Erskine, R.G., Moursund, J.P. and Trautmann, R.L. (1999). *Beyond Empathy: A Therapy of Contact-in-Relationship*. London: Taylor & Francis.

Evans, K.R. and Gilbert, M.C. (2005). *An Introduction to Integrative Psychotherapy*. Basingstoke: Palgrave Macmillan.

Fairbairn, W.R.D. (1952). *Psychoanalytical Studies of Personality*. London: Routledge.

Faranda, F. (2014). Working with images in psychotherapy: An embodied experience of play and metaphor. *Journal of Psychotherapy Integration*, 24(1), 65–77.

Faris, A. and van Ooijen, E. (2012). *Integrative Counselling and Psychotherapy: A Relational Approach*. London: Sage.

Finlay, L. (2004). *The Practice of Psychosocial Occupational Therapy*, 3rd edn. Cheltenham, Glos.: Nelson Thornes.

Finlay, L. (2005). Reflexive embodied empathy: A phenomenology of participant–researcher intersubjectivity. *Humanistic Psychologist*, 33, 271–292.

Finlay, L. (2008). A dance between the reduction and reflexivity: Explicating the 'phenomenological psychological attitude'. *Journal of Phenomenological Psychology*, 39, 1–32.

Finlay, L. (2011). *Phenomenology for Therapists: Researching the Lived World*. Chichester, Sussex: Wiley-Blackwell.

Finlay, L. (2012). An existential-phenomenological approach to integrative psychotherapy, *British Journal of Psychotherapy Integration*, 9(2), 17–32.

Finlay, L. (2013). Unfolding the phenomenological research process: Iterative stages of 'seeing afresh'. *Journal of Humanistic Psychology*, 53(2), 172–201.

Finlay, L. (2014). Embodying research. *Person-Centered & Experiential Psychotherapies*, 13(1), 4–18.

Finlay, L. (forthcoming). Sensing and making sense: Embodying metaphor in relational-centred psychotherapy. *The Humanistic Psychologist*.

Finlay, L. and Evans, K. (2009). *Relational-centred Research for Psychotherapists: Exploring Meanings and Experience*. Chichester, Sussex: Wiley-Blackwell.

Finlay, L. and Evans, K. (forthcoming). Sensing and making sense: Embodying metaphor in relational-centred psychotherapy. In J.Roubal, P.Brownell, G.Francesetti, J.Melnick and J.Zeleskov-Djoric (eds), *Towards a Research Tradition in Gestalt Therapy*. Gestalt Research Press.

Finlay, L. and Gough, B. (eds) (2003). *Reflexivity: A Practical Guide for Researchers in Health and Social Sciences*. Oxford: Blackwell.

Fonagy, P. and Bateman, A. (2006). Mechanism of change in mentalization-based treatment of borderline personality disorder. *Journal of Clinical Psychology*, 62, 411–430.

Freud, S. (1953). The interpretation of dreams. In J.Strachey (ed. and trans.), *The Standard Edition of the Complete Psychological Works of Sigmund Freud*, vols 4–5. London: Hogarth Press. (Original work published 1900.)

Freud, S. (1958). The dynamics of transference. In J.Strachey (ed. and trans.), *The Standard Edition of the Complete Psychological Works of Sigmund Freud*, vol. 12. London: Hogarth Press, pp. 97–108. (Original work published 1912.)

Friedman, M. (1985). Healing through meeting and the problematic of mutuality. *Journal of Humanistic Psychology*, 25(1), 7-40.

Gebler, F.A. and Maercker, A. (2014). Effects of including an existential perspective in a cognitive-behavioral program for chronic pain: A clinical trial with 6 months follow-up. *The Humanistic Psychologist*, 42, 155–171.

Gelso, C.J. (2011). *The Real Relationship in Psychotherapy: The Hidden Foundation of Change*. Washington, DC: American Psychological Association.

Gendlin, E.T. (1996). *Focusing-oriented Psychotherapy: A Manual of the Experiential Method*. New York: Guilford Press.

Gendlin, E.T. (2000). Eugene Gendlin introduces Focusing (International Conference). Accessed May 2015 from https://vimeo.com/2299660.

Gibertoni, C. de Sena (2013). An occupational therapy perspective on Freud, Klein and Bion. In L.Nicholls, J.C.Piergrossi, C.deS.Gibertoni and M.A.Daniel (eds), *Psychoanalytic Thinking in Occupational Therapy: Symbolic, Relational and Transformative*. Chichester, Sussex: Wiley, pp. 32–56.

Gilbert, M. and Evans, K. (2000). *Psychotherapy Supervision: An Integrative Relational Approach*. Buckingham: Open University Press.

Gilbert, M. and Orlans, V. (2011). *Integrative Therapy: 100 Key Points and Techniques*. London: Routledge.

Goulding, M.M. and Goulding, R.L. (1979). *Changing Lives through Redecision Therapy*. New York: Grove Press.

Gravell, L. (2010). The counselling psychologist as therapeutic 'container'. *Counselling Psychology Review*, 25(2), 28–33.

Greenberg, E. (1999). Love, admiration, or safety: A system of gestalt diagnosis of borderline, narcissistic, and schizoid adaptations that focuses on what is figure for the client. In M. Spagnuolo Lobb (ed.), *Studies in Gestalt Therapy*, No. 8, Ragusa-Siracusa-Italy. Accessed June 2014 from http://gestaltnyc.org/uploads/LoveAdmiration-andSafety-Sicily_fromElinor-imac-LBK_.pdf.

Greenberg, J. and Mitchell, S. (1983). *Object Relations in Psychoanalytic Theory*. Cambridge, MA: Harvard University Press.

Greenberg, L. (2014). The therapeutic relationship in emotion-focused therapy. *Psychotherapy*, 51(3), 350–357.

Greenberg, L.S., Rice, L.N. and Elliott, R. (1993). *Facilitating Emotional Change: The Moment-by-Moment Process*. New York: Guilford Press.

Gutheil, T.G. and Gabbard, G.O. (1993). The concept of boundaries in clinical practice: Theoretical and risk-management dimensions. *American Journal of Psychiatry*, 150, 188–196.

Hackmann, A., Bennett-Levy, J. and Holmes, E.A. (2011). *Oxford Guide to Imagery in Cognitive Therapy*. Oxford: Oxford University Press.

Haggett, B.A. (2012). The Lived Experience of Motherhood: A Personal Exploration. PhD dissertation, Saybrook University, CA.

Halling, S. and Nill, J.D. (1995). A brief history of existential-phenomenological psychiatry and psychotherapy. *Journal of Phenomenological Psychology*, 26(1), 1–45.

Hargaden, H. (2013). Building resilience: The role of firm boundaries and the third in relational group therapy. *Transactional Analysis Journal*, 43(4), 284–290.

Hargaden, H. and Sills, C. (2002). *Transactional Analysis: A Relational Perspective*. London: Routledge.

Hargaden, H. and Sills, C. (2002). *Transactional Analysis: A Relational Perspective*. London: Routledge.

Hart, T. (1999). The refinement of empathy. *Journal of Humanistic Psychology*, 39(4), 111–125.

Heatherington, L., Friedlander, M.L., Diamond, G.M., Escudero, V. and Pinsof, W.M. (2015). 25 years of systemic therapies research: Progress and promise. *Psychotherapy Research*, 25(3), 348–364.

Heidegger, M. (1962). *Being and Time* (trans. J.Macquarrie and E.Robinson). Oxford: Blackwell. (Original work published in 1927.)

Heidegger, M. (1998). Letter on 'Humanism'. In W.McNeill (ed.), *Pathmarks*. Cambridge: Cambridge University Press. (Original version published 1946.)

Heron, J. (2001). *Helping the Client: A Creative Practical Guide*, 5th edn. London: Sage.

Hinshelwood, R.D. (1987). *What Happens in Groups*. London: Free Association Books.

Hoffman, I.Z. (1998). *Ritual and Spontaneity in the Psychoanalytic Process: A Dialectical Constructivist View*. Hillsdale, NJ: Analytic Press.

Homeyer, L.E. and Sweeney, D.S. (2010). *Sandtray Therapy: A Practical Manual*, 2nd edn. New York: Routledge.

Horvath, A. and Bedi, R.P. (2002). The alliance. In J.C.Norcross (ed.), *Psychotherapy Relationships that Work: Therapist Contributions and Responsiveness to Patients*. New York: Oxford University Press, pp. 37–69.

Horvath, A.O., Delre, A.C., Flückinger, C. and Symonds, D. (2011). Alliance in individual psychotherapy. *Psychotherapy*, 48, 9–16.

Horvath, A. and Symonds, B. (1991). Relation between working alliance and outcome in psychotherapy: A meta-analysis. *Journal of Counseling Psychology*, 38, 139–149.

Hubble, M.A., Duncan, B.L. and Miller, S.D. (1999) (eds). *The Heart and Soul of Change: What Works in Therapy*. Washington, DC: American Psychological Association.

Husserl, E. (1970). *The Crisis of European Sciences and Transcendental Philosophy* (trans. D.Carr). Evanston, IL: Northwestern University Press. Originally published 1936.

Hycner, R. (1991/1993). *Between Person and Person: Toward a Dialogical Psychotherapy*. Highland, NY: Gestalt Journal Press.

Hycner, R. and Jacobs, L. (1995). *The Healing Relationship in Gestalt Therapy: A Dialogic/Self Psychology Approach*. Highland, NY: Gestalt Journal Press.

Institute for Integrative Psychotherapy (n.d.). What is Integrative Psychology? Accessed November 2014 from www.integrativetherapy.com/en/integrative-psychotherapy.php.

Jackson, D. (1957). The question of family homeostasis. *Psychiatric Quarterly Supplement*, 31, 79–90.

Jacobs, L. (1991). The therapist as 'other': The patient's search for relatedness. Presented at the conference 'Martin Buber's contribution to the humanities', October. Accessed September 2014 from www.gestalttherapy.org/_publications/therapist_asothers.pdf.

Jacobs, L. (2000). Interviewed by Jenny Mackewn: Respectful dialogues. *British Gestalt Journal* 9(2), 105–116.

Jacobs, L. and Hycner, R. (eds.) (2009). *Relational Approaches in Gestalt Therapy*. New York: Gestalt Press/Routledge.

Johnson, S.M. (2009). Attachment theory and emotionally focused therapy for individuals and couples: Perfect partners. In J.H.Obegi and E.Berant (eds), *Attachment Theory and Research in Clinical Work*. New York: Guilford Press, pp. 410–433.

Jorm, A.F., Medway, J., Christensen, H., Korten, A.E., Jacomb, P.A. and Rodgers, B. (2000). Public beliefs about the helpfulness of interventions for depression: Effects on actions taken when experiencing anxiety and depression symptoms. *Australian and New Zealand Journal of Psychiatry*, 34, 619–626.

Joyce, A.S., Piper, W.E., Ogrodniczuk, J.S. and Klein, R.H. (2007). *Termination in Psychotherapy: A Psychodynamic Model of Processes and Outcomes*. Washington, DC: American Psychological Association.

Joyce, P. and Sills, C. (2014). *Skills in Gestalt Counselling and Psychotherapy*, 3rd edn. London: Sage.

Jung, C.G. (1966). The aims of psychotherapy. In *Collected Works of C.G. Jung. Volume 16: The Practice of Psychotherapy*, 2nd edn. Princeton, NJ: Princeton University Press, pp. 36–52. (Original work published 1931.)

Jung C.G. (1953). *Psychological Reflections; An Anthology of the Writings of C.G. Jung* (ed. J. Jacobi). New York: Pantheon Books.

Jung, C.G. (1970). The meaning of psychology for modern man. In *Collected Works of C.G. Jung. Volume 10: Civilization in Transition*. Princeton, NJ: Princeton University Press.

Jung, C.G. (1968). *Collected Works of C.G. Jung. Volume 12: Psychology and Alchemy*. Princeton, NJ: Princeton University Press.

Kabat-Zinn, J. (1990). *Full Catastrophe Living: Using the Wisdom of your Body and Mind to Face Stress, Pain, and Illness*. New York: Delacorte.

Karpman, S. (1968). Fairy tales and script drama analysis. *Transactional Analysis Bulletin*, 7(26), 39–43.

Karpman, S.B (2014). *A Game Free Life*. San Francisco, CA: Drama Triangle Publications.

Kazantzis, N., Whittington, C., and Dattilio, F. (2010). Meta-analysis of homework effects in cognitive and behavioral therapy: A replication and extension. *Clinical Psychology Science and Practice*, 17, 144–156.

Kelly, J.R. (2007). Mindfulness-based and cognitive-behavior therapy for anger-management: An integrated approach. *PCOM Psychology Dissertations*, Paper 68.

Kemp, R. (2009). The lived-body of drug addiction. *Existential Analysis*, 20(1), 120–130.

Kepner, J. (2003). The embodied field. *British Gestalt Journal*, 12(1), 6–14.

King, N., Finlay, L., Ashworth, P., Smith, J.A., Langdridge, D. and Butt, T. (2008). 'Can't really trust that, so what can I trust?' A polyvocal, qualitative analysis of the psychology of mistrust. *Qualitative Research in Psychology*, 5, 80–102.

Klein, M. (1952). The origins of transference. *International Journal of Psychoanalysis*, 33, 433–438.

Kohut, H. (1984). *How Does Analysis Cure?* Chicago, IL: University of Chicago Press.

Krüger, A. (2007). An introduction to the ethics of gestalt research with informants. *European Journal for Qualitative Research in Psychotherapy*, 2, 17–22.

Lacey, H. (1983). An outpatient treatment program for bulimia nervosa. *International Journal of Eating Disorders*, 2(4), 209–214.

Laing, R.D. (1969). *Self and Others*, 2nd edn. New York: Pantheon Books.

Lakoff, G. and Johnson, M. (1980). *Metaphors We Live By*. Chicago, IL: University of Chicago Press.

Lambert, M.J. (1992). Implications of outcome research for psychotherapy integration. In J.C.Norcross and M.R.Goldfried (eds), *Handbook of Psychotherapy Integration*. New York: Basic Books, pp. 94–129.

Lamprecht, L. (2013). Therapeutic letter writing as relationally responsive practice: Experiences of clients receiving letters during therapy. Presented at the conference The Challenge of Establishing a Research Tradition for Gestalt Therapy, Cape Cod, MA, 17–20 April.

Lapworth, P. and Sills, C. (2010). *Integration in Counselling & Psychotherapy: Developing a Personal Approach*, 2nd edn. Los Angeles, CA: Sage.

Leff, J., Vearnals, S., Brevin, C.R., Wolff, G., Alexander, B., Asen, K., … Everitt, B. (2000). The London Depression Intervention Trial. Randomised control trial of antidepressants v. couple therapy in the treatment and maintenance of people with depression living with a critical partner: Clinical outcome and costs. *British Journal of Psychiatry*, 177, 95–100.

Lewin, K. (1952). *Field Theory in Social Science: Selected Theoretical Papers by Kurt Lewin* (ed. D. Cartwright). London: Tavistock. (Original work published 1947.)

Linehan, M.M. (1993). *Cognitive-Behavioral Treatment of Borderline Personality Disorder*. New York: Guilford Press.

Lingis, A. (1989). *Deathbound Subjectivity*. Studies in Phenomenological and Existential Philosophy. Bloomington, IN: Indiana University Press.

Lopes, R.T., Goncalves, M.M., Machado, P.P.P., Sinai, D., Bento, T. and Salgado, J. (2014). Narrative therapy vs. cognitive-behavioral therapy for moderate depression: Empirical evidence from a controlled clinical trial. *Psychotherapy Research*, 24(6), 662–674.

Luborsky, L. Singer, B. and Luborsky, L. (1975). Comparative studies of psychotherapies: Is it true that 'everybody has won and all must have prizes'? *Archives of General Psychiatry*, 32, 995–1008.

Main, M. and Solomon, J. (1990). Procedures for identifying infants as disorganized/disoriented during the Ainsworth strange situation. In M.T.Greenberg, D.Cicchetti and M.Cummings (eds), *Attachment in the Preschool Years: Theory, Research, and Intervention*. Chicago, IL: University of Chicago Press, pp. 121–160.

Mann, D. (1997). *Psychotherapy: An Erotic Relationship*. London: Routledge.

Markin, R.D. (2014). Toward a common identity for relationally oriented clinicians: A place to hang one's hat. *Psychotherapy*, 51(3), 327–333.

Marx, J.A. and Gelso, C.J. (1987). Termination of individual counseling in a university counseling center. *Journal of Counseling Psychology*, 34, 3–9.

Maslow, A. (1954). *Motivation and Personality*. New York: Harper & Row.

Masterson, J. (1976). *Psychotherapy of the Borderline Adult: A Developmental Approach*. New York: Brunner/Mazel.

May, R. (1983). *The Discovery of Being: Writings in Existential Psychology*. New York: Norton.

McCann, L. and Pearlman, L.A. (1992) Constructivist self-development theory: A theoretical framework for assessing and treating traumatized college students. *Journal of American College Health*, 40(4), 189–196.

McCullough, J.P. (2005). Cognitive behavioral analysis system of psychotherapy (CBASP) for chronic depression. In J.C.Norcross and M.R.Goldfried (eds), *Handbook of Psychotherapy Integration*, 2nd edn. Oxford: Oxford University Press, pp. 281–298.

McGown, L. (2013). Reaching into the relational unconscious: Integrating spontaneous mental imagery into clinical practice. *British Journal of Psychotherapy Integration*, 10(2), 21–32.

McGuire-Bouwman, K. (2006). 'Caring confrontation' in experiential psychotherapy. Accessed July 2014 from www.cefocusing.com/pdf/2F2cCarin gConfrontationinExperientialTherapy.pdf.

McNeel, J.R. (1976). The parent interview. *Transactional Analysis Journal*, 6(1), 61–68.

Mearns, D. and Cooper, M. (2005). *Working at Relational Depth in Counselling and Psychotherapy*. London: Sage.

Merleau-Ponty, M. (1964). *Signs* (trans. R.C.McCleary). Evanston, IL: Northwestern University Press. (Original work published 1960.)

Merleau-Ponty, M. (1968). *The Visible and the Invisible* (trans. A.Lingis). Evanston, IL: Northwestern University Press. (Original work published 1964.)

Messer, S. and McWilliams, N. (2007). Insight in psychodynamic therapy: Theory and assessment. In L.G.Castonguay and C.E.Hill (eds), *Insight in Psychotherapy*. Washington, DC: American Psychological Association, pp. 9–29.

Miller, S.D. and Duncan, B.L. (2000). *The Outcome Rating Scale*. Chicago, IL: Authors.

Miller, S.D., Duncan, B.L., Brown, R., Sorrel, G.S. and Chalk, M.B. (2006). Using outcome to inform therapy practice. *Journal of Brief Therapy*, 5(1), 5–22.

Miller, S.D., Duncan, B.L. and Hubble, M.A. (2005). Outcome-informed clinical work. In J.C.Norcross and M.R.Goldfried (eds), *Handbook of Psychotherapy Integration*, 2nd edn. Oxford: Oxford University Press, pp. 84–102.

Miller, S.D., Duncan, B.L. and Johnson, L. (2000). *The Session Rating Scale*. Chicago, IL: Authors.

Miller, S.D., Duncan, B.L., Johnson, L.D. and Hubble, M.A. (2002). Why the field of therapy is on the verge of extinction and what we can do to save it. In J.K.Zeig (ed.), *Brief Therapy: Lasting*

Impressions. Phoenix, AZ: Milton H. Erickson Foundation Press, pp. 208–230.

Minuchin, K.S. and Fishman, H.C. (1961). *Family Therapy Techniques.* Boston: Harvard University Press.

Minuchin, S. (1974). *Families and Family Therapy.* Boston: Harvard University Press.

Mitchell, S.A. (2000). *Relationality: From Attachment to Intersubjectivity.* Hillsdale, NJ: Analytic Press.

Mitchell, S.A. and Aron, L. (1999). *Relational Psychoanalysis: The Emergence of a Tradition.* Hillsdale, NJ: Analytic Press.

Moreno, J.L. (1946). *Psychodrama.* New York: Beacon House.

Moreno, J.L. (with Fox, J.) (1987). *The Essential Moreno: Writings on Psychodrama, Group Method and Spontaneity.* New York: Springer.

Moursund, J.P. and Erskine, R.G. (2004). *Integrative Psychotherapy: The Art and Science of Relationship.* Southbank, Victoria, Australia: Thomson/ Brooks Cole.

Murdin, L. (2000). *How Much is Enough? Endings in Psychotherapy and Counselling.* London: Routledge.

Murphy, B. C. and Dillon, C. (1998). *Interviewing in Action: Process and Practice.* Pacific Grove, CA: Brooks/Cole.

Nevis, E.C. (1983). Evocative and provocative modes of influence in the implementation of change. *Gestalt Journal,* 6(2), 5–12.

Ng, Chi Ting Connie and James, S. (2013). Counselor empathy or 'having a heart to help'? An ethnographic investigation of Chinese clients' experience of counseling. *The Humanistic Psychologist,* 41(4), 333–349.

NICE (National Institute for Health and Clinical Excellence) (2009). *Depression: Management of Depression in Primary and Secondary Care.* London: Author.

Nichols, M. (1987). *The Self in the System.* New York: Brunner/Mazel.

Nolan, P. (2012). *Therapist and Client: A Relational Approach to Psychotherapy.* Chichester, Sussex: Wiley-Blackwell.

Norcross, J.C. (2005). A primer on psychotherapy integration. In J.C.Norcross and M.R.Goldfried (eds), *Handbook of Psychotherapy Integration,* 2nd edn. New York: Oxford University Press, pp. 3–23.

Norcross, J.C. (2006). Integrating self-help into psychotherapy: 16 practical suggestions, *Professional Psychology: Research and Practice.* 37(6), 683–693.

Norcross, J.C. (2011). *Psychotherapy Relationships that Work: Evidence-based Responsiveness,* 2nd edn. New York: Oxford University Press.

Norcross, J.C. and Goldfried, M.R. (eds) (2005). *Handbook of Psychotherapy Integration,* 2nd edn. New York: Oxford University Press.

Norcross, J.C., Santrock, J.W., Campbell, L.F., Smith, T.S., Sommer, R. and Zuckerman, E.L. (2003). *Authoritative Guide to Self-Help Resources in Mental Health,* 2nd edn. New York: Guilford Press.

O'Brien, M. and Houston, G. (2007). *Integrative Therapy: A Practitioner's Guide,* 2nd edn. Los Angeles, CA: Sage.

Ogden, P. (with Fisher, J.) (2015). *Sensorimotor Psychotherapy: Interventions for Trauma and Attachment.* New York: Norton.

Ogden, T.H. (1997). Reverie and metaphor: Some thoughts on how I work as a psychoanalyst. *International Journal of Psychoanalysis,* 78, 719–732.

Ogden, T.H. (2004). On holding and containing, being and dreaming. *International Journal of Psychoanalysis,* 85, 1349–1364.

Omylinska-Thurston, J. and Cooper, M. (2014). Helpful processes in psychological therapy for patients with primary cancers: A qualitative study. *Counselling and Psychotherapy Research: Linking Research with Practice,* 14(2), 84–92.

Orbach, S. (2012). Dr Susie Orbach on psychoanalysis. www.psychotherapyexcellence.com/watch/ watch-listing/2012/november/susie-orbach-on-relational-psychoanalysis.

Orbach, S. (interviewed by S.Serning) (2014). Psychoanalytic perspectives on anger. *The Psychotherapist,* 58, 17–18.

Orlinksy, D.E., Grawe, K. and Parks, B.K. (1994). Process and outcome in psychotherapy: Noch einmal. In A.E.Bergin and S.L.Garfield (eds), *Handbook of Psychotherapy and Behavior Change,* 4th edn). New York: Wiley, pp. 270–378.

Palmer, S. and Woolfe, R. (2000). *Integrative and Eclectic Counselling and Psychotherapy.* London: Sage.

Paul, S. and Charura, D. (2015). *An Introduction to the Therapeutic Relationship in Counselling and Psychotherapy.* Los Angeles, CA: Sage.

Paul, S. and Pelham, G. (2000). A relational approach to therapy. In S.Palmer and R.Woolfe (eds), *Integrative and Eclectic Counselling and Psychotherapy*. London: Sage, pp. 110–126.

Pearmain, R. (2001). *The Heart of Listening: Attentional Qualities in Psychotherapy*. London: Continuum.

Pekarik, G. (1992). Relationship of clients' reasons for dropping out of treatment to outcome and satisfaction, *Journal of Clinical Psychology*, 48(1), 91–98.

Perls, F.S. (1969). *Ego, Hunger and Aggression: A Revision of Freud's Theory and Method*. Highland, NY: Gestalt Journal Press. (Originally published 1947.)

Perls, F.S., Hefferline, R. and Goodman, P. (1951). *Gestalt Therapy: Excitement and Growth in the Human Personality*. New York: Julian Press.

Philippson, P. (2012). *Gestalt Therapy: Roots and Branches – Collected Papers*. Karnac.

Piper, W.E., Ogrodniczuk, J.S., Joyce, A.S., McCallum, M., Rosie, J.S., O'Kelly, J.G. and Steinberg, P.I. (1999). Prediction of dropping out in time-limited, interpretive individual psychotherapy. *Psychotherapy: Theory, Research, Practice, Training*, 36(2): 114–122.

Pollio, H.R., Barlow, J.M., Fine, H.J. and Pollio, M.R. (1977). *Psychology and the Poetics of Growth: Figurative Language in Psychology, Psychotherapy, and Education*. Hillsdale, NJ: Lawrence Erlbaum.

Polster, E. and Polster, M. (1973). *Gestalt Therapy Integrated: Contours of Theory and Practice*. New York: Random House.

Prochaska, J.O. and DiClemente C.C. (1982). Trans-theoretical therapy: Toward a more integrative model of change. *Psychotherapy: Theory, Research and Practice*, 19(3), 276–288.

Prochaska, J.O. and DiClemente, C.C. (2005). The transtheoretical approach. In J.C.Norcross and M.R.Goldfried (eds), *Handbook of Psychotherapy Integration*, 2nd edn. New York: Oxford University Press, pp. 147–171.

Puddicombe, A. (2011). *Get Some Headspace: 10 Minutes Can Make All the Difference*. London: Hodder.

Quintana, S.M. and Holahan, W. (1992). Termination in short-term counseling: Comparison of successful and unsuccessful cases. *Journal of Counseling Psychology*, 39, 299–305.

Rabu, M., Haavind, H. and Binder, P.-E. (2013). We have travelled a long distance and sorted out the mess in the drawers: Metaphors for moving towards the end in psychotherapy, *Counselling and Psychotherapy Research*, 13(1), 71–80.

Racker, H. (1968). *Transference and Countertransference*. New York: International Universities Press.

Ratcliffe, M. (2008). *Feelings of Being: Phenomenology, Psychiatry and the Sense of Reality*. Oxford: Oxford University Press.

Reider, N. (1972). Metaphor as interpretation. *International Journal of Psychoanalysis*, 53, 463–469.

Robbins, B. (2011). Open Letter to the DSM-5. Accessed June 2014 from www.ipetitions.com/petition/dsm5/.

Roe, D., Dekel, R., Harel, G. and Fennig, S. (2006). Clients' reasons for terminating psychotherapy: A quantitative and qualitative inquiry. *Psychology and Psychotherapy: Theory, Research, and Practice*, 29, 529–538.

Rogers, C.R. (1951). *Client-Centered Therapy: Its Current Practice, Implications and Theory*. Boston: Houghton Mifflin.

Rogers, C.R. (1975). Empathic: An unappreciated way of being. *Counseling Psychologist* 5(2), 2–10.

Rogers, C.R. (1980). *A Way of Being*. Boston: Houghton Mifflin.

Romanyshyn, R.D. (2001). *Mirror and Metaphor: Images and Stories of Psychological Life*. Pittsburgh, PA: Trivium. (Originally published in 1982 as *Psychological Life: From Science to Metaphor*.)

Romanyshyn, R.D. (2006). Therapy and the Theater of Soul: The Drama of Performance. Keynote Address: New Zealand Association of Psychotherapy, 23–26 February. Accessed July 2014 from www.robertromanyshyn.com/Therapy%20and%20the%20Theater.pdf.

Romanyshyn, R. (2007). *The Wounded Researcher: Research with Soul in Mind*. New Orleans, LA: Spring Journal.

Rothschild, B. (2003a). *The Body Remembers Casebook: Unifying Methods and Models in the*

Treatment of Trauma and PTSD. New York: W.W. Norton & Co.

Rothschild, B. (2003b). *The Body Remembers: The Psychophysiology of Trauma and Trauma Treatment*. New York: W.W. Norton & Co.

Roubal, J., Gecele, M. and Francesetti, G. (2013). Gestalt therapy approach to diagnosis. In G.Francesetti, M.Gecele and J.Roubal (eds), *Gestalt Therapy in Clinical Practice: From Psychopathology to the Aesthetics of Contact*. Siracusa, Italy: Istituto di Gestalt.

Rowan, J. (1990). *Subpersonalities: The People Inside Us*. London: Routledge.

Rowan, J. (1993). The transpersonal in psychotherapy and counselling. *Inside Out*, 13. Accessed July 2014 from http://iahip.org/inside-out/issue-13-summer-1993/the-transpersonal-in-psychotherapy-and-counselling.

Rowan, J. (2001). Existential analysis and humanistic psychotherapy. In K.J.Schneider, J.F.T.Bugental and J.F.Pierson (eds), *The Handbook of Humanistic Psychology: Leading Edges in Theory, Research, and Practice*. Thousand Oaks, CA: Sage, pp. 447–464.

Rowan, J. (2002). Three levels of empathy. *Self & Society*, 30(4), 20–27.

Rowan, J. and Jacobs, M. (2002). *The Therapist's Use of Self*. Buckingham: Open University Press.

Ruppert, F. (2008). *Trauma, Bonding & Family Constellations: Understanding and Healing Injuries of the Soul*. Frome, Somerset: Green Balloon Publishing.

Ryle, A. (1990). *Cognitive Analytic Therapy: Active Participation in Change*. Chichester, Sussex: John Wiley.

Sabel, V. (2012). *The Blossom Method*. London: Vermilion.

Samuels, A. (1989). Analysis and pluralism: The politics of psyche. *Journal of Analytical Psychology* 34(1), 33–51.

Sartre, J.-P. (1969). *Being and Nothingness* (trans. H.Barnes). London: Routledge. (Original work published in 1943.)

Schneider, K.J. (2008). *Existential-Integrative Psychotherapy: Guideposts to the Core of Practice*. New York: Routledge.

Schneider, K. (2010). The case for existential psychotherapy. *Psychology Today*, 29 September. Accessed December 2014 from www.psychologytoday.com/blog/awakening-awe/201009/the-case-existential-psychotherapy.

Schneider, K.J. and May, R. (1995). *The Psychology of Existence: An Integrative, Clinical Perspective*. New York: McGraw-Hill.

Schore, A.N. (1994). *Affect Regulation and the of the Self: The Neurobiology of Emotional Development*. Mahwah, NJ: Erlbaum.

Schore, A.N. (2012). *The Science of the Art of Psychotherapy*. New York: Norton.

Seligman, M.E.P., Park, N., Peterson, C. and Steen, T.A. (2005). Positive psychology progress: Empirical validation of interventions. *American Psychologist*, 60(5), 410–421.

Shapiro, F. (2001). *Eye Movement Desensitization and Reprocessing: Basic Principles, Protocols and Procedures*, 2nd edn. New York: Guilford Press.

Shonin, E., Van Gordon, W. and Griffiths, M.D. (2014). Mindfulness in psychology: A breath of fresh air? *The Psychologist*, 28(1), 28–31.

Siegel, D.J. (2010). *Mindsight: The New Science of Personal Transformation*. New York: Bantam. (Reprint edn.)

Sills, C., Lapworth, P. and Desmond, B. (2012). *An Introduction to Gestalt*. Los Angeles, CA: Sage.

Sills, M. (2014). Toward a compassionate understanding of anger in our human condition. *The Psychotherapist*, 58, 15–16.

Simms, E.M. (2008). *The Child in the World: Embodiment, Time and Language in Early Childhood*. Detroit, MI: Wayne State University Press.

Skårderud, F. (2007). Eating one's words, part II: the embodied mind and reflective function in anorexia nervosa – theory. *European Eating Disorders Review*, 15, 243–252.

Smith, E.W.L., Clance, P.R. and Imes, S. (eds) (1996). *Touch in Psychotherapy: Theory, Research, and Practice*. New York: Guilford Press.

Spinelli, E. (1994). *Demystifying Therapy*. London: Constable.

Spinelli, E. (2007). *Practising Existential Therapy: The Relational World*. Los Angeles, CA: Sage.

Spinelli, E. (2015). *Practising Existential Therapy: The Relational World*, 2nd edn. London: Sage.

Steiner, C. (1971). *Games Alcoholics Play*. New York: Grove Press.

Stern, D.N. (1985). *The Interpersonal World of the Infant*. New York: Basic Books.

Stern, D.N. (2003). *The Interpersonal World of the Human Infant: A View from Psychoanalysis and Developmental Psychology*, 2nd edn. London: Karnac.

Stern, D.N. (2004). *The Present Moment in Psychotherapy and Everyday Life*. New York: Norton.

Stern, P. (1972). *In Praise of Madness*. New York: Norton.

Stewart, I. (2014). *Transactional Analysis Counselling in Action*, 4th edn. Los Angeles, CA: Sage.

Stewart, I. and Joines, V. (1987). *TA Today: A New Introduction to Transactional Analysis*, 2nd edn. Nottingham: LifeSpace Publishing.

Stolorow, R.D. (2011). *World, Affectivity, Trauma: Heidegger and Post-Cartesian Psychoanalysis*. New York: Routledge.

Stolorow, R.D. and Atwood, G.E. (1992). *Contexts of Being*. Hillsdale, NJ: Analytic Press.

Stolorow, R., Atwood, G.E. and Branchaft, B. (eds) (1997). *The Intersubjective Perspective*. Northvale, NJ: Jason Aronson.

Stratton, P. (2011). The evidence base of systemic family and couples therapies. Association for Family Therapy. Accessed December 2014 from www.aft.org.uk/SpringboardWebApp/userfiles/aft/file/Training/EvidenceBaseofSystemicFamilyandCouplesTherapies(Jan2011).pdf.

Stricker, G. and Gold, J. (2003/2005). Assimilative psychodynamic psychotherapy. In J.C.Norcross and M.R.Goldfried (eds), *Handbook of Psychotherapy Integration*, 2nd edn, pp. 221–240). New York: Oxford University Press.

Sullivan, H. S. (1953). *The Interpersonal Theory of Psychiatry*. New York: Norton.

Summers, G. and Tudor, K. (2000). Cocreative transactional analysis. *Transactional Analysis Journal*, 30(1), 23–40. Accessed December 2014 from https://www.academia.edu/1824513/Cocreative_transactional_analysis.

Todres, L.A. (1990). The rhythm of psychotherapeutic attention: A training model. *Journal of Phenomenological Psychology*, 21(1), 32–45.

Todres, L. (2007). *Embodied Enquiry: Phenomenological Touchstones for Research, Psychotherapy and Spirituality*. Basingstoke: Palgrave Macmillan.

Todres, L. and Galvin, K. (2010). 'Dwelling-mobility': An existential theory of well-being. *International Journal of Qualitative Studies of Health and Well-being*, 5(3). Accessed June 2014 from www.ijqhw.net/index.php/qhw/article/view/5444.

Totton, N. (2010). Boundaries and boundlessness. *Therapy Today* 21(8). Accessed September 2014 from www.therapytoday.net/article/show/2101/print/.

Tronick, E. (2009). Still face experiment. Accessed August 2014 from www.youtube.com/watch?v=apzXGEbZht0.

Tudor, K. (1995). What do you say about saying good-bye? Ending psychotherapy. *Transactional Analysis Journal*, 25, 228–233.

van den Berg, J.H. (1972). *A Different Existence: Principles of Phenomenological Psychopathology*. Pittsburgh, PA: Duquesne University Press.

Van Gennep, A. (1960). *The Rites of Passage*. Chicago, IL: University of Chicago Press.

van Manen, M. (2002). The heuristic reduction: Wonder. *Phenomenology Online*. Accessed November 2007 from www.phenomenologyonline.com/inquiry/11.html.

Vedder, B. (2002). On the meaning of metaphor in Gadamer's hermeneutics. *Research in Phenomenology*, 32, 196–209.

Vostanis, P., Burnham, J. and Harris, Q. (1992). Changes of expressed emotion in systemic family therapy. *Journal of Family Therapy*, 14(1), 15–27.

Wachtel, P. (2014). An integrative relational point of view. *Psychotherapy*, 51(3), 342–349.

Wallin, D.J. (2007). *Attachment in Psychotherapy*. New York: Guilford Press.

Wampold, B.E., Mondin, G.W., Moody, M., Stich, F., Benson, K. and Ahn, H. (1997). A meta-analysis of outcome studies comparing bona fide psychotherapies: Empirically, 'all must have prizes'. *Psychological Bulletin*, 122, 203–215.

Watzlawick, P., Beavin, J. and Jackson, D. (1967). *Pragmatics of Human Communication*. New York: Norton.

Wertz, F. (2005). Phenomenological research methods for counseling psychology. *Journal of Counseling Psychology*, 52(2), 167–177.

Whitaker, D.S. (1985). *Using Groups to Help People*. London: Tavistock/Routledge.

Wierzbicki, M. and Pekarik, G. (1993). A meta-analysis of psychotherapy dropout, *Professional Psychology: Research and Practice*, 24(2), 190–195.

Wiggins, S. (2013). Assessing relational depth: Developing the Relational Depth Inventory. In R.Knox, D.Murphy, S.Wiggins and M.Cooper (eds), *Relational Depth: New Perspectives and Developments*. Basingstoke: Palgrave Macmillan.

Winnicott, D.W. (1953). Transitional objects and transitional phenomena; A study of the first not-me possession. *International Journal of Psycho-Analysis*, 34(2): 89–97.

Winnicott, D.W. (1971). *Playing and Reality*. New York: Basic Books.

Wolf, E. (1988). *Treating the Self: Elements of Clinical Self Psychology*. New York: Guilford Press.

Wong, M. (2008). Impact of intergenerational differences on Chinese Americans in family therapy: A qualitative study. PhD dissertation, Texas Woman's University.

Yalom, I.D. (1980). *Existential Psychotherapy*. New York: Basic Books.

Yalom, I.D. (1985). *The Theory and Practice of Group Psychotherapy*. New York: Basic Books.

Yalom, I.D. (1989). *Love's Executioner*. London: Penguin.

Yalom, I.D. (2010). *The Gift of Therapy: An Open Letter to a New Generation of Therapists and their Patients*, rev. and updated edn. London: Piatkus.

Yontef, G.M. (1979). Gestalt therapy: Clinical phenomenology. *Gestalt Journal*, 2(1), 27–45.

Yontef, G.M. (1988). Assimilating diagnostic and psychoanalytic perspectives into Gestalt therapy. *Gestalt Journal*, 11(1), 5–32.

Yontef, G.M. (1993). *Awareness, Dialogue, and Process: Essays in Gestalt Therapy*. Highland, NY: Gestalt Journal Press.

Zinker, J. (1978). *Creative Process in Gestalt Therapy*. New York: Vintage Books.

Index

abandonment issues, 39, 104, 108, 126, 137, 143, 160

abuse, 18, 42, 43, 61, 96, 113, 131, 174

affect regulation, 54, 213

aims of therapy, 24, 25, 31, 37, 130, 174, 181

alliance, therapeutic, 15, 30–34, 44, 144
    See also therapeutic relationship

anchoring, 78

anger management, 35, 42, 43, 68, 110, 158, 165–166, 201

anxiety, approach to, 19, 33, 35–36, 78, 83–85, 139, 153, 162, 170, 183–184
    See also diagnosis, categories

art therapy, 195, 218

attachment theory
    humanistic version, 28
    research, 22–23, 100
    theory, 18, 22, 53, 64, 124, 165, 210

attunement, 38, 42, 47, 52–56, 78
    See also empathy

authenticity, 127, 171, 180–181, 191, 127

awareness, 52, 89, 94, 102, 107, 111, 123, 128, 130, 156, 183, 185–186, 188, 190, 193–194

Beck, Aaron, 154–155, 165, 222, 243

behaviour therapy. *See* cognitive behavioural therapy, approach

being
    existential, 7, 168–172, 174–175
    therapist's being, 49, 58, 174
    versus doing, 3, 13, 73, 192

being-with, 3, 56–57, 70, 87, 101, 108, 169–170, 174, 191
    See also intersubjectivity

bereavement, 17, 165

Berne, Eric, 37, 118, 227, 243
    between, the, 4, 48, 74, 185, 192
    See also intersubjectivity

Bion, Wilfred, 42, 176, 211, 243–244

bodily sensing, therapist, 16, 38, 39, 48, 55, 88, 94–96, 100–102, 125

body language. *See* non-verbal responses

body work, 78, 102, 106–107, 128–130, 158, 165

borderline personality adaptations
    description, 18, 20, 108
    working with, 62, 106, 107

boundaries
    boundarying to hold and contain, 60–64
    ethical, 62–64, 70–71
    healthy, 60–61, 187
    nature of, 26, 28, 34, 59
    time, 61–62
    types of, 60, 74
    violation, 75, 203

Bowlby, John, 22, 23, 244
bracketing, 7, 71, 168, 175–176, 182
brief therapy, 6, 25, 147, 154, 162, 165
Buber, Martin, 4, 50, 51, 58, 127–128, 136, 173, 174, 183, 190, 244

Casement, Patrick, 52–53, 64, 66–67, 71, 75, 82, 208, 244
catharsis 35, 64, 70, 98, 165, 192
chair work, 55, 103, 122–123, 192, 194, 197, 222, 235
challenging
    case illustrations, 35–36, 104, 106–107, 109, 111–113
    effective, 114–117
    process, 33, 104–119
    types of, 105
change
    cycle of, 6, 40–41, 45, 143
    enabling, 19, 24, 38–41, 100, 156, 160–161
child development theory, 50, 53–54, 200
Clarkson, Petruska, 68, 185, 197, 208, 244
client-centred approach. *See* person-centred approach
Clinical Outcomes for Routine Evaluation (CORE-OM), 17, 144
    See also outcomes, measurement tools
co-creation, 3, 38, 133, 184, 204, 234
cognitive behavioural therapy
    approach, 24, 39, 84–86, 153–165
    case illustration, 9, 33, 84–85, 153–154
    concepts, 152
    language, 28, 81
    models, 152, 154, 165
    theory, 152–155, 159–161
cognitive orientation, 151, 154–155, 157, 225, 238
    See also mindfulness
cognitive therapy, 8, 84, 108, 154–155
cognitive-analytic therapy (CAT), 6, 152, 159–160, 165
collaboration, between therapist and client, 3, 17, 86
compassion, 7, 33, 35, 39, 42, 52, 57, 94, 112–113, 124, 126, 133, 156
confidentiality, 60–61
    See also ethics
confluence, 141, 143, 187, 189
    See also empathy
congruence, 3, 11, 32, 165, 204, 205

constellations, 131–132, 135, 192
contact, 25, 26–27, 181, 183, 185, 189
contact boundary, 21, 111
containing
    against, 70–71
    and holding, 59–75
    humanistic version, 68
    process, 40, 64, 65–66, 70, 218
context, 15, 164, 213
continuing professional development (CPD), 72, 74, 123
    See also supervision
contracting, 25–27, 74, 137, 146
coping mechanisms, 64, 76, 106, 158
    See also creative adjustment
corrective emotional experience, 23, 50
counter-transference
    process, 16, 114, 207–209
    somatic, 95, 130
    See also bodily sensing
couples work, 24, 61, 203, 217, 221, 230
creative adjustment, 21, 28, 38, 45, 119, 187, 216
creativity, 28, 42, 74, 100, 197
Critical Parent, 10, 16, 111, 126, 228–229, 233–236
culture, 7, 18, 44, 57, 102, 116–117, 176, 214, 224
curiosity, 42, 56, 121, 172, 176, 196, 228

defence mechanisms, 4, 21
    See also creative adjustment
defensive practice, 26, 71, 74
deflection, 33, 44, 59, 69, 188, 190
denial, 140, 188
dependency, 70, 73, 78, 141–142
depression, 79, 100, 111, 140, 142, 153–154, 156, 163, 222
    See also diagnosis, categories
Deurzen, Emmy van, 18, 19, 63, 79, 86, 165–166, 167, 174, 181, 245–246
desensitisation
    gestalt cycle, 39, 45, 187–188, 190
    systematic desensitisation, 85, 165
developmental approach, 8–9, 18, 159, 200, 228, 234, 237, 238
DeYoung, Patricia, xiii, 3, 59, 62, 120, 130, 147, 198, 246

diagnosis
  categories, 18–23, 81
  critique of, 19–20
dialectical behavior therapy (DBT), 6, 152, 160–161
dialogical approach, 10, 19, 59, 173, 183–185, 192, 196
diaries, use of, 154, 159
directive approach, 24, 83, 154–155, 165, 219
dissociation, 7, 38, 72, 113, 119, 129–130, 162, 188, 197
  See also diagnosis, categories; dissociative identity disorder
dissociative identity disorder 21, 79, 125
drama therapy. *See* psychodrama
drama triangle, 43, 82, 142, 171, 217, 230–234, 238–239
dreamwork, 96–99, 175, 192
DSM-5, 19–21

eating disorders, 153–154, 159, 165, 207, 233
  See also diagnosis, categories
eclecticism, 5, 11, 159
ecology, 44, 213
ego states, 227–230
  See also Critical Parent; Nurturing Parent; transactional analysis
egotism, 187, 189
embodiment, 16, 48–49, 58, 88, 94–96, 100, 102, 168,
EMDR, 165
emotion-focused therapy; emotionally-focused therapy (EFT), 54, 225
empathic attunement, 54–56
  See also empathy; attunement
empathy
  definition, 47–48
  levels of, 49–52
  process, 46–58, 115, 204
  See also attunement; bodily sensing
empty chair technique. *See* chair work
ending therapy
  deciding to end, 137–139, 142
  process, 136–148, 189
  research, 145
  stock-taking, 143–146
  working through loss, 139–141

Erskine, Richard, xiii, 5, 28–29, 38, 45, 55, 99, 102, 103, 110, 111, 120, 134, 239
ethics, 25, 61–64, 70–71, 224
Evans, Ken, iv–v, x, xiii, 5, 8–10, 21, 27, 36, 44, 57, 182, 237–238, 246
evidence-based practice, 6, 161–163
  See also research
existential phenomenological
  approach, 8, 10, 18, 56, 74, 148, 165–166, 172–173, 176–181
  case illustration, 33, 125–126, 174–175, 179–180
  research, 163
existentialism
  philosophy, 168–172, 181
  reflecting on life, 167–168
  versus humanistic approach, 180–181, 182

family therapy
  approach, 159, 213–214, 216, 220
  research, 222–223
  versus individual approach, 220, 222
fantasy, 89–90, 99, 102, 140, 200
  See also dreamwork; imaginal work
feedback, giving to clients, 62, 81, 108–109, 115
field theory, 8, 185, 196, 213
Finlay, Linda, 10, 42, 48, 57, 90, 135, 154, 172–173, 176, 237–238, 245–246
first meeting, with client, 15, 16–17, 28
Focusing, 94
Freud, Sigmund, 7, 97, 205, 246

gestalt cycle, 45, 143, 186–190, 197
gestalt therapy
  approach, 39, 62, 74, 119, 165
  case illustration, 8–9, 33, 89–90, 111, 131–132, 183–184, 186, 190–191, 193–195
  language, 9, 81
  theory, 184–192
  therapeutic interventions, 192–195
  tradition, 21, 106
gift-giving, 61, 146, 148
Gilbert, Maria, 3, 5, 8–9, 20, 22, 27, 36, 44, 136, 246
goals, therapy. *See* aims of therapy
grief, 17, 55, 69, 80, 97, 113, 140–141, 191
group therapy, 66, 68, 112, 138, 159
guided fantasy. *See* imaginal work

happiness. *See* positive psychology

healing, 2, 3, 177, 185, 196, 238

here and now relationship, 17, 72, 183–184, 197, 210

holding
  against, 70–71
  and containing, 59–75
  definition, 64

holistic
  practice, 1, 4, 7, 10, 184
  versus reductionism, 162, 164

homework, 84, 87, 143, 148, 158

hope, 18, 28, 35, 77, 191

humanistic approach, 5, 7, 10, 18, 28, 68, 74, 85–86, 98–99, 111–112, 151, 205, 219

humour, use of, 44, 77, 85, 92, 116, 186, 221

Hycner, Richard, xi, 34, 44, 127, 185–186, 191–192, 196, 247

ideology, 6, 20, 117, 164

imagery, use of. *See* imaginal work; metaphors

imaginal work, 89–90, 99–100, 102, 143, 193

Improving Access to Psychological Therapies (IAPT), 6

inclusion, 51, 58, 173, 183

insight, 24, 28, 39, 77, 81–82, 91, 94, 120–121, 131, 135, 212

integration
  challenges of theoretical integration, 6–10
  client integration, 4, 10, 56, 122, 124, 125–133, 189
  levels of, 121–125
  models of, 5–6, 157, 218–219
  process of, 120–135
  theoretical, 1, 4–11, 224

intergenerational. *See* transgenerational

interpretation, 82, 96–97, 102, 117, 197, 199, 203, 205–206, 209, 211

intersubjectivity, 4, 10, 16, 50, 67, 92, 99, 210

intrapsychic, 3, 44, 67–69, 74, 121–122, 124, 204

introjection, 9, 43, 187, 188, 204, 210

intuition, 18, 25, 32, 42, 57, 63, 74, 88, 93, 101

I-Thou, I-IT (Buber), 58, 127–128, 185, 190, 192

Jacobs, Lynne, xiii, 3, 34, 185, 186, 192, 194, 196, 210

Jung, Carl, 1, 4, 98, 102, 248

juxtaposition, 113, 118–119, 200

Kohut, Heinz, 50–51, 57, 135, 200, 248

letter writing
  to clients, 62, 160
  to therapist, 124, 132–133, 146

life script. *See* script

lifeworld, 172, 178, 213, 224,

listening, 36–37, 49, 57, 101, 211

love, 88, 113, 132, 177

marital therapy. *See* couples work

meaning, search for, 87, 130, 152, 157, 168, 171, 177

mentalisation, 53, 165

metaphors, 90–93, 102, 127

mindfulness, 7, 74, 77, 84, 89, 152, 156–158, 165, 196

mirroring, 32, 50, 52, 64, 200

motivation, clients', 23, 26, 40, 87, 138

multi-disciplinary teamwork, 159, 224

narcissistic personality adaptation, 18, 64, 107–108

narrative, 17–18, 63, 101

neuroscience, 45, 54, 58, 74, 135

NICE guidelines, 6, 157

non-directive approach, 8, 69, 74
  See also person-centred approach

non-judgmental, therapist being, 45, 58, 85, 115, 172,

non-verbal responses, 8–9, 16, 37, 47, 53, 78, 94, 183–184
  See also embodiment; bodily sensings

normalisation, 33, 81–82, 85

Nurturing Parent, 70, 74, 122, 201, 227, 234, 236

object relations theory, 5, 185, 199, 210

outcome studies. *See* research

outcomes
  measurement tools, 24, 162, 163, 165
  measuring, 17, 24, 31, 145, 162, 222–223

pain, 16, 163, 202

parallel process, 202

Parent Interview, 68–69, 111, 118, 237–238, 239

personality, adaptations, 7, 18, 62, 107–108, 118
personality disorders, 18, 20, 62, 81, 160
    See also diagnosis, categories
person-centred approach, 32, 44–47, 69, 119, 158, 165
phenomenological description, 98, 168, 173, 177–178, 193
    See also existential phenomenology
play therapy, sand-tray, 69
polarities, 4, 10, 123, 126, 134
positive psychology, 152, 165
potency, 34, 35, 196
power issues, 35, 42, 60, 70, 115, 176, 205, 215, 232
    See also potency
presence, 3, 34, 41–43, 48, 148, 156, 173, 183, 190–192
private practice, 6, 15, 26, 29, 137, 146
problem formulation, 17–18
process, in therapy, 40–43
professional guidelines, 61, 71, 74
projection, 9, 35, 48, 64, 66, 68–69, 187–188
    See also projective identification
projective identification, 202–205, 210
    See also transference
psychoanalytic
    approach, 8 , 39, 64, 67, 74, 151, 166, 205
    case illustration, 52–53
    language, 9, 28, 119
    relational psychoanalysis, 22, 46, 53, 97, 135, 198, 205
    theory, 65–66, 199–209, 211
psychodrama, 131, 185, 192, 194–195, 233–234
psychodynamic. *See* psychoanalytic approach
psychoeducational
    approach, 81–86, 154, 159, 165
    case illustration, 33, 158

questions, therapist interventions, 18, 23, 24, 28, 110, 145, 206, 207

Rational Emotive Behavior Therapy (REBT), 152, 155–156, 165
reflexivity, 32, 44, 48, 72, 96, 100, 206, 209
regression, 7, 55, 63, 89–90, 107, 140, 198
Relational integrative model (RIM), 6, 16, 157
relational

approach, 2–4, 48, 62, 71, 99–100, 204–205
    case illustration, 8–9, 16, 55, 92–93, 94–96, 109, 112–113, 201–203, 208–209
    therapist way of being, 41–43, 57, 114
relational psychoanalysis. *See* psychoanalytic, approach
relational themes, enduring, 196, 207–208, 210, 222
relaxation, technique, 33, 79, 84–85, 89, 163,
research
    abortion, traumatic, 191
    attachment, 22, 100
    cognitive approach, 162
    effectiveness of psychotherapy, 31, 84, 86, 163, 222
    empathy, 57
    endings, 144–145
    family therapy, 222–223
    happiness, 152
    metaphors, 91
    mindfulness, 156–157
    neuroscience, 54, 58, 135
    outcomes research, 87, 144, 161–163, 222–223
    therapeutic relationship, 31–32, 145, 162
resistance, 22, 36, 40, 106, 111, 115, 123, 139
resources
    identifying and mobilising, 25, 77–80, 82, 84, 143
    self-help, 78–80
    therapist's, 74
    trauma work, 78, 165
    types, 76–77
    See also resourcing
resourcing, 76–87
retroflection, 38, 165, 187, 189
risk and safety issues, 17, 26, 30, 35, 42, 118, 144, 229, 231
Rogers, Carl, 32, 44, 47, 58, 118, 211, 251
role-play exercises, 99, 123, 131, 143, 218, 233
Rothschild, Babette, 76, 77, 121, 128, 131, 251–252
rupture and repair, 43, 45, 53, 56, 63–64

safety, ensuring, 34–36, 59, 61, 62, 64, 68, 71, 72, 99
    See also risk and safety issues
schizoid personality adaptations, 18, 107
Schore, Allan, 45, 54, 58, 252

script, 16, 43, 83, 87, 201–202, 211, 220, 234, 237
self
  core self, 7, 107, 135, 181
  multiple relational selves, 125–126, 135, 179, 201
  parts of, 7, 94, 98, 135, 159, 179–180, 197, 237–238
self-disclosure, therapist, 107, 130, 204
self-psychology theory, 32, 44, 50–51, 148, 196, 200–201
shame, 17, 38–39, 63, 73, 96, 104, 106, 108, 110, 112–113, 130, 139, 170, 195, 201–203, 208–209
Spinelli, Ernesto, xiii, 3, 8, 15, 79, 114, 142, 146, 148, 170, 178, 181, 252
spiritual aspects, 87, 99, 132, 135, 163, 184, 224
  See also transpersonal
Stern, Daniel, 16, 53, 58, 99, 119, 252–253
story, client's, 17–18, 38, 92–93, 95, 102, 125, 128, 131–132, 178
  See also narrative
suicidal client, 17, 26, 70, 125, 161
supervision, 14, 58, 72–74, 75, 116–117, 202–203, 208, 210, 229
systemic
  approach, 6, 8, 39, 151, 196, 216
  case illustration, 216–217
  family therapy models, 218–220
  systemic therapy, 214–215
  systems theory, 212–222

temporality (time), past present, future, 2, 7, 22, 131, 168, 206
termination of therapy. *See* ending therapy
therapeutic alliance. *See* alliance, therapeutic
therapeutic relationship, 3, 11, 27, 28, 34, 38, 41, 46, 59, 60, 112, 114, 120, 124, 127
  See also alliance, therapeutic
therapy,
  as dance, 47, 241

as journey, 27, 38
as microcosm, 3, 17
touch, 34, 42, 63–64, 190
transactional analysis
  approach, 8–9, 34, 37, 110, 119, 151, 211, 234–238
  case illustration, 43–44, 201–203, 231–235
  concepts, 74, 226–228
  developmental-relational elaborations, 228–233, 239
  language, 81
transference
  about, 9, 16, 50–51, 198, 199–202, 218, 238
  managing, 205–209
  types, 201, 207–208, 210
  See also projective identification
transgenerational, 92, 121, 131–132, 135, 142, 218, 219, 222, 223
transitional object, 74, 77
transpersonal, 50, 99, 102, 121, 131–132
  See also spiritual aspects
transtheoretical model, 40, 143
trauma, 78, 128–132, 174–175, 198
  See also diagnosis, categories
trust, 10, 28, 73, 99, 101, 114, 132

unconscious, 32, 35, 39, 66, 91, 96–98, 102, 117, 135, 176, 178, 196

validation, 18, 82, 102, 110, 146, 161
values, 6, 10, 45, 60, 86–87, 119, 223–224
visualisation, 89–90, 103, 135

working alliance. *See* therapeutic alliance

Yalom, Irvin, xiii, 3, 19, 42, 44, 79, 81, 83, 99, 114–115, 136, 181, 254
Yontef, Gary, 21, 34, 83–84, 104, 108, 118, 184, 192–194, 254